I found this book a
introduction to life
and to the results of
and bureaucratic Government in any
country.
I am sure you will find it
interesting, and I give it to you
with fond wishes and memories.

Barbara Friedlander
May, 1973.

ROLAND HUNTFORD The New
Totalitarians

ALLEN LANE
THE PENGUIN PRESS

First published in 1971
Reprinted 1972 (twice)

Allen Lane The Penguin Press
74 Grosvenor Street, London W1

ISBN 0 7139 0260 4

Printed in Great Britain by
Hazell, Watson & Viney Ltd,
Aylesbury, Bucks

Set in Monotype Bembo

Contents

1. The New
Totalitarians

The vindication of prophets of doom is perversely fascinating, for men love scourging themselves with proof that they really are as ridiculous as they have always been telling each other. It is therefore scarcely surprising that, in all the literature of prediction that has flourished in the wake of science, the lamentations have achieved the greater fame. Two pessimistic visions of the future have already passed into folklore; two classic nightmares of what very likely awaits us; two sketches of the prison that we appear bent on erecting around ourselves with the most disastrous ingenuity. They are, of course, George Orwell's *Nineteen Eighty-Four* and Aldous Huxley's *Brave New World*.

Brave New World was first published in 1932; *Nineteen Eighty-Four* in 1949. Time has already shown how far both were written with the gift of prophecy. Both divined something that is now becoming uncomfortably apparent: that the advance of science is producing a new kind of ruling class with powers unknown before. Both foretold the final subservience of human beings to a revolutionary hybrid of technological manipulator and political manager.

But, although the end in both cases is roughly the same, *Brave New World* seems more applicable to the West at this time. Where *Nineteen Eighty-Four* describes the logical conclusion of a Communist dictatorship, the climax of the Bolshevik Revolution, as it were, *Brave New World* presents the final corruption of a Western style of life. The crux of the difference is this. Orwell postulates a reign of terror to secure the position of the new ruling class, but Huxley supposes that the scientific advances which bring them to power also induce the requisite change of mentality, so that physical compulsion is superfluous.

Huxley, although he describes certain developments now becoming familiar, assumes the necessary political changes, and concentrates on the human results. It has become a cliché to say that this or that phenomenon is a piece of *Brave New World*, and it has become evident to the point of banality that certain aspects of the story have started their fulfilment in the West. We have the first steps towards test tube babies and genetic engineering; the hallucinatory drug cults and their 'trips', as the inhabitants of *Brave New World* took a 'holiday' with 'soma'; mechanical attitudes to sex; the mutability of the past, and the worship of technology. But to find the vision closing in, with its various facets drawn together in a system, is a rather harder thing.

And yet, many of the scientific necessities are already with us. We have foolproof contraceptives, illimitable communication, electric energy and gadgetry in abundance. Their proper application waits only upon the correct social machinery: science, as always, is several lengths ahead of politics.

The victory of technology over man, says Huxley in a foreword to one of the later editions of his novel, requires only a highly centralized totalitarian government. But, he says,

> There is of course no reason why the new totalitarianism should resemble the old. Government by firing squads . . . is not merely inhumane . . . it is demonstrably inefficient, and in an age of advanced technology, inefficiency is a sin against the Holy Ghost. A really efficient totalitarian state would be the one in which the all-powerful executive of political bosses and their army of managers control a population of slaves who do not have to be coerced, because they love their servitude.

Of all people, it is the Swedes who have come closest to this state of affairs. They have the necessary background and predilections. Outside Russia, they alone have grasped the necessity of adapting politics to technology, untroubled by doubts or reservations. They offer the first example of a system that fulfils Huxley's prophecy. Historical accident and national idiosyncrasies have pushed Sweden ahead on the road to *Brave New World*. But even if she is isolated, inbred and incompletely western, her present state cannot be dismissed as something alien and eccentric, curious to examine, yet with no portents for the rest of us. All that stands between ourselves and Sweden is a certain protective shell granted by the Western European heritage. But it is fragile, and it is being eroded from within and without. To watch present Swedes may be to watch our future selves.

To begin with, says Huxley, *Brave New World* depends on economic security; without it, the love of servitude is impossible. And in this, the foundation of the 'new totalitarianism', Sweden is well advanced. She has solved the problem of permanent security and abolished enclaves of distress within collective prosperity. She has been helped in this by a century and a half of peace, isolation and neutrality, by being small and easily governed, and by being populated in proportion to her natural resources.

Economic security by itself does not necessarily imply a love of servitude. Other conditions are required: on the side of the rulers, a thorough understanding of the interaction between economics and power; and on the side of the ruled, submission to authority and a reverence for the expert. Also, in both cases, an aversion to individuality, an instinct for the collective, a suspicion of parliamentary institutions, a worship of the State, and a preference for government by bureaucrat rather than by politician.

All through their history, the Swedes have consistently fulfilled these specifications. Thus it is that the techno-political establishment which has been brought to power in Sweden by a scientific and industrial revolution, found a singularly malleable population to work with, and has been able to achieve rapid and almost painless results. Sweden of 1971 bears as little resemblance to herself of 1930, as the Soviet Union of today to Tsarist Russia. It is in the past forty years, and particularly since 1950, that the Swedish metamorphosis has taken place.

It is the product of the Social Democratic Party which has held unbroken power since 1932. Their system has proved to be an incomparable tool for applying technology to society. They have altered the nature of government by making it a matter of economics and technology alone. Politicians have lost their significance in Sweden, supplanted by a form of technocratic oligarchy, which is apparently unassailable, because its tenets are universally accepted. Henceforth, changes of political complexion are unlikely to mean changes in circumstance, and the same development is to be expected, whatever the party in office.

To view this is a sobering affair. It is not as if the Swedes were endowed with originality in politics. They are imitators and assimilators. They possess no magic keys. They have shown that the means already exist to build the political foundations of *Brave New World*. In this sense, they have demonstrated that Huxley did not see far enough.

Security [he says in the aforementioned comment to *Brave New World*] tends very quickly to be taken for granted. Its achievement is merely a superficial, external revolution. The love of servitude cannot be established except as the result of a deep, personal revolution in human minds and bodies. To bring about that revolution, we require, among others, the following discoveries and inventions. Firstly, a greatly improved technique of suggestion through infant conditioning and, later, with the aid of drugs, such as scopolamine. Second, a fully developed science of human differences, enabling government managers to assign any given individual to his or her proper place in the social and economic hierarchy. (Round pegs in square holes tend to have dangerous thoughts about the social system and to infect others with their discontents.) Third (since reality, however utopian, is something from which people feel the need of taking pretty frequent holidays), a substitute for alcohol and other narcotics, something at once less harmful and more pleasure-giving than gin or heroin. And fourth (but this would be a long-term project, which would take generations of totalitarian control to bring to a successful conclusion) a foolproof system of eugenics, designed to standardize the human product and so to facilitate the task of the managers.

It is the achievement of the Swedes to have shown what can be done without these expressions of perfection. They have shown that the 'revolution in human minds and bodies' can be carried through, to a remarkable degree, by available methods. They have demonstrated, for example, that the relatively crude indoctrination offered by television and conventional education holds tremendous possibilities, pro-vided only that there is effective centralized control of both. They have proved how powerful are the existing agents of inducing love of servitude. They are the first of the new totalitarians.

In the search for prophecies fulfilled, it is useful to make one excursion into *Nineteen Eighty-Four*. The Swedes have demonstrated the power of that form of semantic manipula-tion Orwell called Newspeak: the changing of words to mean something else. In this way, thought can be directed, and undesirable concepts eliminated, because the means of expressing them have been removed. 'Freedom' does not yet in Swedish, as in the brainchild of Orwell's Ministry of Truth, mean exactly 'slavery', but it already implies 'sub-mission', and a powerful word in the vocabulary of opposi-tion has therefore been effectively neutralized. Similarly, it is exceedingly difficult to speak in any but favourable terms of the State, because the words in that field have been positively loaded.

But otherwise, *Brave New World* is enough. 'Industrial

civilization is only possible,' says Mustapha Mond, 'when there's no self-denial. Self-indulgence up to the very limits imposed by hygiene and economics. Otherwise the wheels stop turning.' This is precisely what the rulers of Sweden are always saying, although of course not so directly, and with rather greater verbosity.

The Swedes have found other devices, extremely useful for inducing the 'love of servitude', in the manipulation of sexuality and the official sponsorship of changes in morals. It is a mistake to believe that the Swedes are particularly advanced or emancipated. The English are no less sexually liberated. But what distinguishes Sweden is that morality has become the concern of the government, where elsewhere it is something independent, growing out of changes within society.

The ultimate crime in *Brave New World* is to deviate from a norm. That norm is innocent of ethics and morality, and decided on grounds of expediency alone. The situation is already a doctrine of Swedish law. Gone is the idea of right or wrong, or the moral content of an action. Crime is now defined as social deviation. The test of whether an offence is punishable, however, is solely whether it has awkward effects on the collective. Analogously, in non-criminal spheres the worst solecism is to be different. Sweden, like Soviet Russia, belongs to that group of countries in which 'individuality' has a derogatory ring.

All this is not because Sweden is so far advanced but because, in all senses except the purely technological, she is so extraordinarily backward. Sweden is a relic of the Middle Ages, a State of corporations and communes, and the Swedes are medieval people living only as members of a group. It is an ideal situation for the incarnation of *Brave New World*.

Like the rulers of *Brave New World*, the managers of Sweden have abolished history, in order to cut off the past and, by disorienting their time sense, to make people easier to manipulate. But the Swedish leaders, at any rate, act historically and, like Huxley's privileged Controller, they at least are aware of their historical roots. To understand the new totalitarians of Sweden, then, it is best to start with Swedish history.

2. The Historical Background

The true distinction of the Swedes is not that they have successfully married technology and man, but that they have done so with so little apparent difficulty. The process which, in other countries, generated both modern technology and resistance to its political demands, had only the first of these effects in Sweden. As a result, the conflicts normally associated with the technological revolution have been all but absent. This is very different from the discomforts of the Western world; but Sweden is not quite of the West.

To begin with, the Scandinavian peninsula is not so much a part of Europe as an extension of Siberia and, encased in that northern fastness, Sweden was a late starter. The Ice Age lingered, so that man arrived rather later than he had done elsewhere on the European mainland. The Swedes were barbarians while Rome fell and the Dark Ages gathered. Until almost the threshold of medieval times Sweden, with all Scandinavia, remained primitive, unchronicled, inaccessible and unknown. One of the last European countries to be christianized, Sweden was finally admitted to the Pale of the Church in A.D. 1103, five centuries after Britain. The country still bears the marks of its early retardation.

The Swedes enter history with the opening of the Viking Age in the eighth century A.D. That fascinating period established the future division of Scandinavia. Where the Vikings of Denmark and Norway turned westwards overseas, those from Sweden pushed overland to the east. The Swedes advanced into Russia, and since then the Danes and

Norwegians have belonged to the West, where Sweden has had one foot in eastern Europe.

The early Swedish colonists established the medieval state of Kiev out of which modern Russia grew: the very word Russia perpetuates their memory in the form of *Rus*, their ancient name. Inland Vikings, the Rus, like their ocean-going colleagues in the West, were essentially merchants, and it was the trade routes along the great rivers to Constantinople that drew them to the Russian hinterland. For about a hundred years, until the middle of the tenth century, the Swedes dominated trade between northern Europe and the east. But as the Rus declined, the Slavonic Russian empire rose; and as the Arabs lost their grip on the Asian approaches, shorter southern routes were opened, the roundabout way via the far shore of the Baltic fell into disuse and the Swedes were by-passed. By the beginning of the eleventh century, Sweden had turned into a cul-de-sac, facing east.

The Viking age was the greatest of the sallies made by the Swedes into the outside world: their natural state has been one of isolation. Except for one or two inconsequential Danish incursions in modern times, they have been free of foreign invasion descending with singularly little alien infiltration from prehistoric Teutonic arrivals. They remain outstandingly homogeneous. The roots of their language are immaculately Germanic. Where English is haunted by Celtic, and Italian by Etruscan, all research has failed to shake the original purity of the Swedish tongue. And Swedish history lacks the tension provided elsewhere by the feud of Saxon and Celt, Slav and Teuton, Latin and Goth.

The Swedes have been excluded from most of the formative experiences of Western Europe. They were never occupied by the Romans. They escaped the convulsions succeeding the fall of Rome. They stood aside from medieval power struggles. Continental military adventures in modern times hardly relieved their fundamental isolation; they were scarcely touched by the intellectual currents of Europe. For centuries Sweden led a sequestered life on the outskirts of the West.

Nowhere else did the Pope exercise so little influence and, alone in medieval Christendom, the Swedes possessed what amounted to a national Church. As a result, their horizons have been narrowed. By escaping the papacy, the one universal power of the age, Sweden was deprived of the internationalism which became the great medieval civilizing force. She was precociously nationalistic, and her untimely isolation sent her into the twentieth century with little more than a peasant culture she could truthfully call her own. She has been left intellectually defenceless and, when cultural invasions finally penetrated her borders after the late eighteenth century, she swallowed the successive waves hook, line and sinker. Even today Sweden resembles some retarded society hurriedly assimilating a stronger civilization.

Originally divided among petty warring kings Sweden was unified by A.D. 1000. But provincial rivalry died hard, and the country had to wait until the fourteenth century for a fixed capital and an ordered succession to the throne.

A series of dynastic marriages united Sweden, Norway and Denmark under the Danish Queen Margrethe in 1397. Rivals for the mastery of Scandinavia, Sweden and Denmark were, however, unhappy bedfellows, and the union was ill starred from its birth. It was finally destroyed in 1523 by Gustav Vasa, the founder of modern Sweden. In that year he drove out an invading Danish army and secured Swedish independence. But it is as an administrator, not a soldier, that he is honoured among his countrymen.

The best Swedish kings have been royal bureaucrats, and Gustav was the first of that breed. He was a born organizer, devoted to administration, who brooked no delegation; no detail was beneath his notice. He turned Sweden into a centralized State of a kind that was only equalled almost three centuries later in Napoleonic France. And he met little of the opposition that faced Western European rulers. *They* had to overcome an adverse mode of thought and feeling in establishing central rule: *he* had the help of a favourable mentality. The reason is partly to be sought in a peculiarity of Swedish history. Sweden was never feudalized, where Western Europe very largely was.

In its true sense, feudalism was something deeper than merely serfdom and military service. It was an attitude of mind from which have emerged the Western civic virtues. The heart of it was a contractual relationship between man and master. It limited the prerogatives of a superior, and insisted on the rights of vassals. Its heritage has been a suspicion of the central power and acceptance of that aristocratic state of mind we misname democratic.

Feudalism dominated England, France, the Low Countries and western Germany. It was imperfectly established in Saxony and Spain. It was absent from Prussia, the Scandinavian countries and Russia. At one extreme of constitutional development, there was England, where civil liberties and parliamentary supremacy directly grew out of feudal limitations on the sovereign: at the other, Russia, where Duma and people were impotent before monarchs devoid of such restraints. There were many gradations in between, but Sweden leant towards the Russian end of the scale. Where the lower orders of society had no defined rights, autocracy and absolutism were the natural consequences. The heritage of that situation has been submissiveness to authority.

The other characteristic of feudalism was a parcelling out of sovereignty. Where it ruled, the notion of a unified state was rudimentary, the country organized as a pyramid of vassalage with the king or emperor sitting uneasily on top. It was an extreme kind of decentralization.

Subject from the Middle Ages to a form of centralized rule Sweden, on the other hand, was saved this fragmentation. In the feudalized countries of Europe there was conflict in the transition from the Middle Ages to modern times, because it meant the replacement of local rule by a central bureaucracy. With no feudal age to colour their habits of thought, the Swedes escaped that conflict. In Sweden most of the peasantry were under direct royal control, so that the Swedish kings had the economic power to check the land-owning aristocracy. Royal functionaries had established a centralized administration, when England, France and Germany were still divided among independent magnates.

The reasons for this difference are complex and contentious. But geography must have played a part. Protected from invaders by the Scandinavian watershed, and a long, labyrinthine coastal archipelago that even in modern times has been a formidable barrier, Sweden did not need the defensive mechanism of independent military barons that evolved in the anarchy of the Dark Ages on the European mainland. Moreover, communications in Sweden were better than on the Continent. Roads were admittedly non-existent, but an indented coastline and a honeycomb of natural inland waterways were there for the sailing. The country is ice- and snowbound for several months of the year, but travel has always been easy by sled and ski. Thus nature discouraged baronial autonomy and promoted the exercise of central power.

From early times, therefore, a Swedish king was able to control the nobles. They sometimes fought him, but they served him just as often; by the reign of Gustav Vasa, they were staffing a central administration, and their tradition became that of the civil service.

Since the early Middle Ages, many of the Swedish nobility had been dutiful royal functionaries. In the seventeenth century, it became their principal occupation. Charles XI, one of the great reforming kings, then decimated their estates by recovering alienated royal lands. To retain their position, while submitting to the new order, they converted themselves from a class of land-owners to a class of titled bureaucrats. They devoted themselves to extending the power of the State, and brought Sweden firmly under bureaucratic rule.

The identification of aristocracy and civil service has conferred on the Swedish bureaucrat a unique supremacy and esteem. For centuries he has been honoured with deference and respect. He has never had to bear the scorn, dislike and suspicion poured on the State functionary in so many other countries. He is considered greater than the politician, the lawyer and the industrialist. The senior official remains, true figure of a mandarin, at the top of Swedish society. The chief civil servant in a ministry has more prestige than his minister. *Generaldirektör* – Director-General – the title of such a position, rings better in Swedish ears today than the title *Statsråd* – Cabinet Minister.

When Gustav Vasa came to the throne, the remoteness of the influences then forming modern Western man preserved medieval attitudes among the Swedes. As indicated above, this meant unquestioning submission to authority. In the West, for better or worse, that has not held uniformly, but in Sweden it has been preserved intact until the present day. Clearly, the Swedish attitude, by creating acquiescent subjects, is more favourable to strong government; it is particularly useful when rapid social changes have to be carried out.

In consolidating his authority, Gustav possessed yet another advantage. Unlike England and other Western European states, Sweden had no urban middle class to obstruct royal despotism. The country has always been divided into a mass of peasantry, and a thin crust of merchants and bureaucrats at the top, subservient to the monarch.

Gustav approved wholeheartedly of the idea of the despotic prince perfected in Italy; he imported Germans to teach him the new politics of the Renaissance. In taking German intermediaries, he was continuing an old tradition. Since the Scandinavian decline that followed the end of the Viking

Age, the Germans had carried advancement to the Swedes. With one Francophile interlude in the late eighteenth and early nineteenth centuries, German influence dominated Swedish life until the Second World War.

Gustav, although he was glad of German tutelage, resented German suzerainty. He disliked the economic stranglehold which the Hanseatic merchants had acquired, and he broke their power once and for all. He did so with a conscious desire to establish a nation-state. He was a nationalist ahead of his time.

As a nationalistic despot, Gustav was always open to innovations that would extend his power, and it was in that spirit that he introduced the Reformation to Sweden. He was perhaps the first monarch to grasp properly the political implications of Luther's doctrine. He saw, more clearly and rationally than Henry VIII, the uses to which a national Church could be put. If Henry knew only that he had to break out of the domination of Rome, Gustav from the beginning had the aim of better controlling his subjects. Gustav's purpose in accepting the Reformation was to make civil servants of the clergy. He and his successors became truly their own Popes. The Swedish Church was made identical with the State, a situation comparable only with the Russian, the Byzantine and the Mohammedan worlds.

The Swedish Reformation subjected the priesthood to the State. This, of course, happened elsewhere, but with the important rider that the nature of the Reformer's doctrine weakened the sacerdotal power. In Sweden, the clergy increased the hold on the population that they had exerted since the Middle Ages. Sweden, then, became that unique phenomenon, a priest-ridden Protestant society.

What Gustav did, almost alone among his contemporaries, was to nationalize the Church without undermining the dominion of priest over parishioner. The theology of the Reformation was anathema to him, since it implied the rise of individual responsibility and the weakening of the clergy. What he strove for was the politics of the new movement, without its religion. For the awakening of the religious spirit, the emotional core of the Reformation, Sweden had to wait until the nineteenth century. It then became confused with the rise of Social Democracy, which has inherited its evangelical content.

Gustav Vasa used the Church deliberately to foster the concept of Swedish nationality; 400 years later, a Socialist Minister of Finance, Mr Gunnar Sträng, confessed to identical aims. When Catholic immigrants came to Sweden after the last war, a bishop approached the government for fiscal concessions in church building. Mr Sträng refused, saying that, although he himself was no believer, he preferred the new arrivals to turn Protestant, 'So that they would become good Swedes'.

Gustav's successors completed the work of incorporating the Church into the State by the beginning of the seventeenth century. The Church was deprived of its economic independence, all property (including churches) and income being transferred to the Crown. The clergy obediently turned into ordained bureaucrats. Ruled directly by lay officials and royal secretaries, the Church became a government department.

Since the Middle Ages, the Church had kept population records, and its parochial system, built on the 'cell' pattern, was admirably adapted to civil administration. The State simply took this apparatus into its own service and, by the beginning of the seventeenth century, had acquired, ready made, by deed of transfer, the kind of centralized administrative machinery that Napoleon had to build for himself two centuries later. The Church issued permits to move and organized conscription, doing all the work of petty officialdom in keeping a check on the citizen, aided by ingrained subservience to the clergy. Only in 1970 was the last of the major bureaucratic functions, the keeping of population registers, removed from the Church: it was then transferred directly to computers.

It is one of the striking aspects of Swedish history that there has been no religious strife, no visible desire to keep the old faith. The Reformation triumphed easily and bloodlessly. In the century of religious passion, the Swedes are distinguished by the meekness and alacrity with which they changed creed. Political unity and personal convenience seemed of more importance than conviction.

In various forms, this attitude has persisted through the years. There have been very few fights over principle; men have seen the greatest virtue in submission and acquiescence. Today, a Swede will most often show the same reluctance to suffer for an idea as his sixteenth-century predecessor.

The absence of persecution need not necessarily imply toleration; it may equally well suggest that force is redundant where submission is willing and conviction weak. This seems to have been the case in Sweden. Rulers have long understood that their subjects will not stand more than a certain rate of change. An official of the Social Democratic party said in 1969 that reforms had to observe a speed limit to avoid opposition; the kings and chancellors of the sixteenth and seventeenth centuries acted on exactly the same principle. The Reformation was carried through in Sweden over about a century, at a comfortable pace, but with the final goal always in sight; 'One people, with one Lord and one King', to quote a Swedish bishop of the time.

If any Swedes were anxious for the martyr's crown, their rulers were unwilling to oblige. The Swedes had discerned, before most Europeans, that martyrdom only perpetuates the ideas it is designed to suppress, and that opposition is best disarmed quietly. The eradication of the Catholic faith from Sweden was accomplished without dungeon, stake or block. Sweden had been severed from Rome for over sixty years before, in 1595, Catholics were prohibited from publicly holding services, but not, immediately, from worshipping privately. In 1617 the old Faith was finally banned, but a Swede could still turn Catholic without risking life or liberty; exile was the sole and inexorable punishment. One of the first to feel this was Queen Christina, the great-granddaughter of Gustav Vasa. In 1654, during the twenty-third year of her reign, she adopted Catholicism, and was forced to abdicate and leave Sweden immediately, never to return. In few other countries did the Reformation triumph, or Catholicism disappear, so swiftly, completely and effortlessly.

By the end of the seventeenth century not a single Catholic remained in Sweden. Occasionally, a Swede would convert, usually as a result of contacts made abroad, and deportation would invariably follow. It was not only Rome that had been the enemy; Geneva was equally so. Calvinism, and Protestant dissent of all kinds were suppressed by law as well.

The rigours of Swedish religious legislation were maintained until the last half of the nineteenth century. In 1848, Baptists were forced by religious persecution to emigrate to America. The last deportations for turning Catholic were carried out in 1855. In 1860, the laws against apostasy were finally repealed. In 1870, the Free Churches were legalized.

Until 1970, when adopting a religion was made voluntary, all Swedes were automatically born into the State Church, whatever the convictions of their parents. Permitted since 1860, withdrawal was only converted from a privilege into a right in 1952. Before that, anybody wanting to leave the State Church had to submit to a personal examination by the clergy, who had the power, periodically used, to refuse the application. These examinations continued until the late 1940s.

The continuous supremacy enjoyed by the Church from the Middle Ages to the nineteenth century gave it an unchallenged hold on the population. Its educational monopoly upheld cultural isolation and a monolithic structure of intellectual life. A few pundits prescribed the lines of thought by a kind of informal ukase, and the rest obeyed implicitly. It was a Protestant, and more humane, version of the Inquisition.

Isolation, ignorance and hierarchical tastes made the Swedes easy to control, and identity of Church and State presented politicians with the benefits. Although the religious background has now grown faint, the legacy of the Church remains in political submissiveness and intellectual servitude. If the various reorganizing governments of Sweden, from the Liberals of the nineteenth century to the Social Democrats of the 1960s, have been able to execute rapid and often uncomfortable changes virtually unopposed, it is because conformity has been made a cardinal virtue, and dissent a mortal sin.

Ecclesiastical hold over the population was never disturbed until a workable political substitute was available. However scornful of Christianity, the rulers of Sweden tolerated the Church as a means of controlling the population. And the clergy, being civil servants, still enjoy, by virtue of their bureaucratic status, a respect that they could never assure for their cloth. Men may abjure Christ, but they cannot bring themselves to drive out the priests. Sweden is one of the rare countries in which men are often anti-religious, but rarely anti-clerical.

When Gustav Vasa was reorganizing the country, he had no time for foreign affairs, adopting a policy of isolation. That, in his opinion, was the future of Sweden. But his sons thought otherwise. They started expanding eastwards, and periodically for the next 250 years, Sweden battled with Russia and Poland for the mastery of the Baltic. Until well into the eighteenth century, Sweden belonged to Eastern Europe. Today, Stockholm remains unmistakably an Eastern European city.

Possessing Finland before the twelfth century, Sweden had a common frontier with Russia, and early began to feel the expansion of the Muscovite State, as it drove towards the sea. Until well into the fifteenth century, the pressure was contained with ease. But in 1478, Tsar Ivan III captured Novgorod and attacked Finland. With great difficulty, the Swedes managed to fend him off. Russia was gathering strength, the balance of power along the Swedish border was dissolving and the arrival of the tsars at the sea was only a matter of time. At the end of the 1550s, the Russians acquired their first foothold on the Baltic by the capture of Narva on the Estonian coast.

That was the situation facing Erik XIV, Gustav's eldest son, when he succeeded to the throne in 1560, and started the Swedish drive to the east. His first aim was to blockade Narva and obtain a stranglehold on Russian trade with the West. Unfortunately, this antagonized Lübeck, a Hanseatic city with considerable Russian interests, and Denmark, then a rival for control of the Baltic States. The Danes, allied with Lübeck, attacked Sweden, and there followed the Great Northern War. Lasting from 1563 until 1570, its only visible result was to consolidate the Danish grip on the outlet of the Baltic to the open sea. Erik had started off to encircle Russia, but had ended by being bottled up more securely by the Danes.

In the meantime, Erik's half-brother, Duke John,* had developed ambitions on the Swedish crown. To enlist the support of Poland, John married Catherine Yagellonica, the sister of the Polish king. John crossed to Finland to raise a rebellion, but was captured by Erik before he could do so, and removed to Sweden, where he was thrown into prison. John, having been forgiven and freed, deposed Erik in 1568, and, in turn, imprisoned him. The king was supposed to have gone mad, but whether this was really the case, or whether a charge of insanity had simply been trumped up in order to

---

* Although in most systems of nobility 'Duke' was a territorial title, in the Swedish royal house it was a personal one, conferred on the younger sons of the king.

serve as a pretext for the deed, has never been satisfactorily decided. What is certain is that Erik died in prison in 1577, reputedly poisoned at the order of John.*

Assuming the throne, John in his turn continued the drive to the east. His adversary was that autocratic tsar, Ivan the Terrible. After ferocious campaigns in the Baltic States, the Swedes captured Narva, once more isolating Russia from the sea.

Sweden had now clearly immersed herself in Eastern Europe. John persuaded the Polish Diet to adopt Sigismund, his son by Catherine Yagellonica, as king. With Sigismund also heir to the Swedish throne, John was working towards a union of Sweden and Poland which could then take up arms against Russia.

After John's death in 1592, Sigismund went to Sweden. But Sigismund, a Catholic, found no sympathy among the unbending Lutherans ruling the country. After a few unhappy years, he returned to Poland, and the union lapsed. His uncle, Duke Charles (a son of Gustav Vasa), ascended the throne in 1603 as Charles IX, and continued his brothers' attacks eastwards. Defeated by the formidable Polish cavalry, Charles turned from Poland to Russia.

At that time, Russia was going through one of her recurrent periods of anarchy, civil war and rival pretenders to the throne. It was a propitious moment for outsiders with fingers in the Russian pie. Sweden and Poland each advanced a tsar. Swedish and Russian troops entered Moscow in 1610 to help the Tsar Basil. Soon afterwards, the Swedes were defeated, and Basil deposed, by a Polish army. In 1613, the Russians, revolting against the indignity of foreign pretenders, rallied round the national figure of Michael Romanov. They attacked the Swedes, who, sensing difficulties ahead, immediately opened negotiations. The result was the Peace of Stolbova, in 1617, by which Sweden acquired Ingria and

---

* The state of Sweden, and the manners of its kings, may be gauged by the legend that the poison was administered in *pea soup*.

Kexholm, the territories at the end of the Gulf of Finland. Sweden was now a leading Baltic state, and a force among the Slavs; she was about to become a European power.

Gustavus Adolphus, the eldest son of Charles, had succeeded his father in 1609, and was now king of Sweden. One of the most efficient and truly militaristic of European sovereigns, he was an extraordinary combination of soldier and civil servant. He lived for fighting and organizing: under him, Sweden became the first of the modern war machines. He was helped in this by one of the great bureaucrats of history, Axel Oxenstierna.

Oxenstierna was the Chancellor, the highest officer of the realm. In day-to-day affairs, he was the real ruler of Sweden. He was a great reformer, and a bureaucrat to the depths of his soul. He consummated Gustav Vasa's modernizing work; modern Swedish government is his brainchild. While in England, for instance, Parliament was then undergoing those convulsions which were to give it sovereignty, Oxenstierna was consolidating the power of the bureaucracy.* Among Swedes, he remains the most honoured of men.

Oxenstierna was a nobleman, and executive office was a monopoly of the nobility. It remained so until late in the nineteenth century. The nobility acted as a corporation or guild with the function of ruling. The attitudes of this thoroughly medieval survival persist in the modern civil service, the fundamental change being that whereas in the past entrance to the guild was by birth and ennoblement, now it is by competitive examination. The members form a caste of dedicated and incorruptible bureaucrats, devoted to the service of the State as something great and mystical, existing above the citizen and beyond Parliament.

Oxenstierna gave form and permanent strength to the

* His almost exact English contemporary was Sir John Eliot, the member of the House of Commons, who, defying Stuart absolutism, died a martyr for parliamentary rule.

bureaucratic establishment that has since ruled Sweden. He devised an administrative system that still functions today. Before Cromwell, he consolidated the hold of the central government on the provinces by a species of Major-General, evolved from medieval bailiffs. He perfected the centralized institutions of a modern State. The first Central Bank and the first national ordnance survey in Europe were his projects. He created a State building directorate, which still exists under the original title, and which is the direct historical reason why present Swedish governments have a control of the housing market unknown in most democracies.

The immediate services of the Chancellor were in mobilizing the resources of Sweden for the king to fight his wars. Oxenstierna reformed the system of conscription, and devised a method of rapid mobilization which gave Gustavus Adolphus a strong and supple army. The economy was harnessed to the central will. Political propaganda was conducted through the Church. Not until the present century can Europe provide a like example of total mobilization for war.

The outbreak of the Thirty Years' War in 1618 posed a threat to Sweden because of Habsburg designs on the Baltic. To forestall an Austrian invasion, Gustavus decided on a preventive Continental campaign, on the side of the Protestant states against the Catholic League. In 1621, he crossed the Baltic, invaded Poland and captured Riga. He advanced into Germany, as far as Munich, victorious all the way. For a short while, Europe was at his mercy, and the Protestant powers seemed about to triumph under Swedish leadership. But in 1632, at the battle of Lützen near Leipzig, Gustavus fell, and the ambition went out of the Swedes. It was no longer Europe they wanted to conquer but the Baltic they had to save. In the peace of 1648, Sweden obtained part of Pomerania, the State of Bremen and Livonia.*

* Livonia was a state made up of Lithuania, Latvia and adjacent Polish territory.

Now turning on Denmark, Sweden conquered the maritime provinces of Bohuslän, Halland, Scania and Blekinge, thus moving her south-western border to the coast, and wresting from the Danes control of the outlets to the open sea. Until the early eighteenth century, Sweden ruled the Baltic.

The reign of Gustavus's daughter, Christina, was devoted to the war with Denmark, an interlude to secure Sweden's rear, before the continuation of the proper business of the Swedish kings: campaigning in the east. In 1655, the year after coming to the throne, her successor, Charles X, marched on Poland. He got stuck in the morass of Eastern Europe, and his reign was a succession of futile engagements with Poles, Russians and Danes, ruinous to the internal economy of Sweden. His son, Charles XI, succeeding him in 1660, kept peace abroad, reorganized the country and repaired the damage. When Charles XII came to the throne in 1697, Swedish ambitions were backed by domestic strength.

Now thoroughly alarmed at the power of Sweden, Russia prepared to invade the Swedish Baltic provinces, and eliminate her rival in the north. So urgent did Tsar Peter the Great consider this task, that he stopped a war with Turkey in order to free troops for its accomplishment.

A celebrated duel was about to begin. Across the battlefields of Eastern Europe, Peter the Great faced Charles XII. Peter was a great soldier, statesman and reformer; Charles a general in search of a political leader. Despots both, they dominated their countries and, for a moment, their age. War started early in 1700. Peter besieged Narva, and Charles crossed the Baltic to relieve it. There were 10,000 Swedes to 35,000 Russians. Charles's army was untried, and cut off from home; Peter's troops were battle-trained, well entrenched and close to Russia. But the Swedes, flouting the rules of contemporary warfare, charged the centre of the Russian line instead of the flanks, and won a quick and crushing victory.

The battle of Narva made Sweden once more the arbiter of European affairs, an ally worth the courting. Charles now attacked Poland, the long-held goal of Swedish ambitions, annihilating the Polish army. In 1707 he turned on Peter once more, and became the first modern leader to know the discomforts of invading the endless plains of Russia. The king of Sweden chased the Tsar's armies towards Moscow. But the Russians replied with the same scorched earth policy that broke Napoleon and Hitler. Baulked on the direct road eastwards, Charles turned south into the Ukraine. In the summer of 1709, he attacked the Russian army at Poltava, a fortress on the Vorkla, a tributary of the River Dnieper. He was repelled, with the loss of almost 10,000 men. But he still had 15,000 troops with his cavalry intact. He withdrew his army from Poltava to Perevelotchna, on the Dnieper. Crossing the river with a skirmishing force, he set out to fetch reinforcements. A day or two later, the army capitulated to the Russians without firing a shot.

It was one of the swiftest and most absolute collapses in military history. At Poltava, Charles's soldiers had sustained their first setback; and it destroyed their morale. At Perevelotchna, they could see Turkish country and safety on the other bank of the Dnieper: reinforcements were not far away; the pursuing Russian troops were inferior, in numbers and equipment, yet the Swedes, the wonder of Europe, neither fought, nor fled, but meekly gave themselves up.

From that moment, a thread was woven into Swedish history of capitulation at the first approach of difficulties. When, in the Second World War, the Swedes allowed German transit traffic to the detriment of their neutrality, and when they succumbed to other Nazi demands equally humiliating, it was in a sense the echo of Perevelotchna.

After Perevelotchna, Charles spent five years in Turkey, first trying to organize another attack on Russia, and then as a prisoner, because the Turks found him an embarrassment.

Finally, he escaped, returning to Sweden in 1714. In his absence, the Tsar had invaded the Swedish Baltic possessions, establishing a permanent foothold on the Gulf of Finland, where he built St Petersburg.

Charles now tried to capture Norway, then a Danish possession, as compensation for his Russian failure. But his countrymen followed half-heartedly. By defeat, he had forfeited their loyalty. It was probably a Swedish bullet that killed him at the battle of Fredrikshald in Norway in 1718.

Leaderless and disheartened, the Swedes retreated from Norway: the Russians raided the Swedish mainland unchecked. At war's end, in 1721, Sweden signed away most of her foreign possessions and part of Finland. Perevelotchna was the end of Sweden as a great power. Swedish history thenceforth becomes an unrelieved tale of capitulation and withdrawal into neutrality and isolation.

In 1742, a Swedish army again capitulated to the Russians without firing a shot. This time it was at Helsinki, after a failed attempt at recovering the lost Finnish provinces. After a somewhat inept essay in neutrality, the Swedes then tried equally ineptly to manoeuvre among the European powers at the beginning of the Napoleonic wars. Finally, in February 1808, the Tsar attacked Finland and, in Helsinki a few months later, a Swedish army once more capitulated without fighting. Finland was then annexed by Russia, obtaining its independence in 1917, after the Bolshevik Revolution.

Charles XII had died childless and unmarried, leaving a disputed succession, which the Russian Empress Elizabeth, daughter of Peter the Great, exploited by forcing on Sweden a monarch of her choice. He was a German prince, Adolf-Frederick of Holstein-Gottorp. The accession of Adolf-Frederick's son, and successor, Gustaf III, in 1771, opened the final act of Sweden's relegation to the world of minor states. Perevelotchna was in 1709; only in 1788, when Gustaf essayed the last, disastrous attempt to regain Swedish ascendancy over Russia, did the Swedes finally begin to understand that their military genius had deserted them. Thenceforth they have looked on Russia with obsessive fear as an hereditary tribal enemy.

Gustaf's son, Gustaf IV, presiding over the disasters of the Napoleonic wars, was made scapegoat for the national misfortune, and deposed. The crown was then offered to Jean-Baptiste Bernadotte,* one of Napoleon's marshals. This was a device to acquire the protection of France against Russia, for Napoleon was still the ally of the Tsar, and theoretically able to shelter a dependent. In 1810, Bernadotte landed in Sweden, and declared war against England. In 1812, Bonaparte broke with Russia. Bernadotte, foreseeing the collapse of France, refused to follow his erstwhile master, made friends with the Tsar instead, and joined the coalition against Napoleon, being granted Norway by the Allies as reward. Bernadotte also foresaw the expansion of Russia, and decided that the safety of Sweden depended upon her abandoning Eastern Europe. Finland was irrecoverable: by acquiring Norway he hoped to accomplish the necessary reorientation, and avert Russian suspicion.

Norway had belonged to Denmark since the fourteenth century, but the Danes made the unfortunate mistake of supporting Napoleon after Sweden changed sides. In 1814, Bernadotte invaded Denmark, forcing her to cede Norway and join the Allies.

The 1814 campaign was the last occasion on which Swedish troops went into battle. At the Congress of Vienna, Sweden gave up Pomerania, her last Continental possession. Deprived of the bonds which, however tenuously, had given her some connections with the outside during the previous centuries,

---

* Bernadotte ascended the throne as Charles-John. All subsequent monarchs are descended from him, and the present royal house of Sweden still bears his name.

Sweden was now, as she had been three centuries earlier, obscure and isolated.

Norway was her only burden. The Norwegians had never really accepted Swedish overlordship, and for most of the nineteenth century were preparing their secession. They achieved independence in 1905, after a crisis which might have culminated in war, if the Great Powers had not tactfully threatened to intervene.

Unlike Switzerland, Sweden never adopted neutrality of her own volition, but allowed it to descend on her, *faute de mieux*. If the Swiss abdicated from history, the Swedes allowed themselves to be forced out. At the Congress of Vienna, in 1815, Switzerland pleaded for neutrality, and was guaranteed it by the Great Powers; the Swedes did not make their profession as a neutral until the outbreak of the First World War in 1914.

Perhaps non-belligerency, meaning the bare avoidance of hostilities, more aptly describes the Swedish condition than neutrality, which implies an attitude of mind as well. During the first half of the nineteenth century, Sweden vacillated between France and Russia. With the rise of Germany, Swedish sympathies veered accordingly, and after the French defeat at the hands of Prussia in 1870, Sweden became in spirit a German colony in the north. In 1914, Sweden supported the Central Powers, and members of the government suggested a policy that they dubbed 'active neutrality', by which they meant helping the Kaiser by all means short of fighting. Exactly the same phrase was resuscitated half a century later under similar circumstances, in this case to describe an anti-American posture during the Vietnam War.

At all events, Sweden kept out of the Great War and, in 1939, declared herself neutral once again. Until 1943, however, she permitted the Germans to send troops and supplies across her territory. In 1943, when the tide had turned in favour of the Allies, the transit traffic was stopped, and supply of iron ore to Germany pared down. The Swedes had avoided the Second World War and achieved a century and a half of uninterrupted peace and isolation that enabled them to develop in their own way, without unwanted foreign intrusions to disturb them.

★   ★   ★

One of the gravest obstacles to the fulfilment of Utopia has been the development of individuality. It brings too much incertitude and too much resistance to the calculations of authority. But the Swedes have been spared that burden; among them the concept of individuality and the development of personality have been grossly retarded down the centuries. The Swede has never emerged from behind the veil of the group; he is conscious of himself only through some general category, as a member of a people, a clan or a party. He has preserved untouched a devotion to an hierarchical order of things and an unprecedented devotion to corporate organization. Sweden has remained a country, not of individual citizens, but of groups and guilds. The industrial revolution found a receptive environment in Sweden and did not have to grapple with the inappropriate mentality of Western Europe. Sweden is a country in which modern institutions have been grafted onto a medieval frame of mind.

This is connected with the absence of the Renaissance from Sweden. The Renaissance is all things to all men. It is an art movement, the revival of classical learning, the rise of humanism, the advance of knowledge or the opening of the age of exploration. The sum of its parts is that force which has created modern Western man. Its heart is the discovery of the individual.

That is the real distinction between the Renaissance and the Middle Ages. Medieval man, with his instinct for the collective, existed solely as a member of some group. Renaissance man discovered that he was an individual, with an identity all his own.

In that sense, the Renaissance was confined to Western Europe. It was absent from Sweden, as it was absent from Russia, and Swedes share with Russians the distinction of undeveloped individuality. Escaping the discovery of the individual, the Swedes continued to think and act in groups. They have preserved their medieval core intact, where Western man is heir to the Renaissance. In this lies the fundamental difference between Sweden and the West.

The hierarchical view of society was a vital part of the medieval mind. It was sapped in the West by the Renaissance, but in Sweden (as in Russia) it had survived more or less intact. Related to this, personal pride was the most reprehensible of medieval sins and, in Sweden today, it remains one of the worst transgressions. Self-effacement is the obligatory virtue.

The writers of the European Renaissance cultivated individuality to the point of affectation and whimsy. No Swedish comparisons can be drawn, because there were in Sweden no contemporary writers. Before the eighteenth century, there was no Swedish literature; before Strindberg, in the nineteenth century, there was no drama. But Swedish authors have always given an oddly anachronistic impression. Carl Michael Bellman, the national poet of Sweden, lived in the eighteenth century, but his world, with its pessimism and its melancholy panegyrics to drinking, is that of the medieval song. And yet the modern Swede says that Bellman still expresses his feelings as nobody else is able to.

Indeed, most Swedish writers and poets are steeped in a morbidity and cruelty that is recognizably medieval. They reduce mankind to stereotypes, treating their characters, not as individuals, but as formalized symbols. To read a modern Swedish novelist, or see a modern Swedish film, is most often to feel a nearness to the world of the Middle Ages. Thus *The Seventh Seal*, Ingmar Bergman's medieval morality film, is in fact a typical example of modern Swedish cinema. Individual values and spontaneity are overshadowed by a dark, oppressive sense of destiny. It is as if Boccaccio, Cervantes, Shakespeare, Rousseau and the apostles of the European personality had never been born.

Throughout the history of Sweden, among all classes, personality is curiously elusive. This is as true of the figure of St Erik in the twelfth, as of King Charles XII in the eighteenth century; or in the nineteenth century Alfred Nobel, the man who invented dynamite and founded the most famous of literary prizes. They had singularly undeveloped characters, and their chroniclers did not help. It is in a long tradition when today a Swedish educational official can say that, 'We are not interested in a man's personality, only in his actions'.

The Renaissance in its completed form had within it the seeds of conflict, almost by definition. It brought forth not only the discovery of the individual, which led to the concept of personal liberty, but also the invention of 'The State as a work of art', which demanded servile underlings. Moreover, out of the Renaissance as the revival of learning and the discovery of the world, there issued technology which, in its application to society, also requires submissive people and, ideally, the immersion of the individual in the group. Out of these innate contradictions, it can be argued, grew the tensions plaguing the industrialized Western world. The same process that generated the scientific and technological revolutions also created opposition to them.

It would obviously have been preferable to accept the one and reject the other. That is what happened to Sweden. While the Swedish rulers from the sixteenth century onward imported Renaissance ideas to perfect the centralized State they had inherited, the absence of the Renaissance as a revolution in personal development, spared them opposition. Individuality means, almost by definition, resistance to authority. Neither grew up in Sweden. Retaining an instinctive submission to hierarchical organization, acting and thinking in groups, ever reluctant to oppose orders from the top, the Swedes have eased the task of their reformers and administrators down to the present day.

Spared the penalties of individuality, the Swede, by remaining within the embrace of the group, has also been spared the personal anguish caused by change. Lacking the instinct of personal rebellion, he has followed his herd. Besides, social change has been made smooth and painless by the peculiarities of the Swedish political system. It is a specialized mechanism adapted to the swift enactment of the intentions of the central bureaucracy. The legislature is weak, the executive strong, and, for centuries, real power has lain in the government administrative machine.

Only once in its history has the Diet, the Swedish parliament, ruled supreme. That was during a period, known as the Age of Freedom, which lasted from 1718 until 1772; from the death of Charles XII until the reign of Gustaf III; an interlude of parliamentary supremacy in an alien environment. The Diet was then a medieval assembly of the Four Estates: nobles, clergy, burgesses and peasants. Not only did the nobility hold the power in the Diet, but they had a prescriptive right to rule, government office and the higher ranks of the civil service being reserved for them by law.*

Since the Middle Ages, the executive power had been vested in the Council of State, a committee of nobles appointed by the king. The Diet was partly an advisory,

---

* Comparisons may be odious, but to grasp the singular development of Sweden, it is worth remembering that an edict of this kind has never existed in England, and that the Commons, long a power in the kingdom, had established its primacy by the seventeenth century.

partly a confirmatory body; its main function was to approve royal ordinances. But it had one important constitutional rôle: it decided the powers of the king. Provided he ruled successfully, the king obtained the privileges he desired.

Charles XII was given unlimited powers: the Diet knew a strong king when they saw one. His death, opening a period of disputed successions and weak monarchs, was a signal for the Diet to assume supremacy. Two aristocratic factions, known as the Hats and the Caps,* struggled for power, and complex and disorderly party politics flourished throughout most of the Age of Freedom.

When Gustaf III came to the throne in 1771, the Estates assumed that he would accept the situation. But Gustaf liked neither the restrictions on the royal prerogative, nor what he called the aristocratic despotism that was ruling Sweden. In 1772, with the help of the army, and some disaffected nobles, he carried out a *coup d'état*, and substituted his own brand of royal despotism. In the constitution promulgated the same year, the Diet was degraded to a subordinate assembly with a vestige of its former prerogatives. The legislative and executive powers were appropriated by the king, who delegated it to the Council of State and the Civil Service.

Gustaf was widely applauded for eradicating parliamentary corruption. Although he had all but got rid of parliament in the process, his subjects were unworried. Few people cared about the form of government, as long as it functioned properly, a recurrent theme in Swedish history.

Gustaf derived his strength from an alliance with the bureaucrats, reinstated in the authority lost during the Age of Freedom. But as his reign progressed, he became infected

---

* The Caps got their name because their policies were said to be so stupid and inept as to be fit only for men in their night caps. Their political opponents adopted the label hat, as an obvious contradistinction.

with the ideas of the Enlightenment, toying with a return to parliamentary rule. He was assassinated in 1792* after a conspiracy among bureaucrats who felt their prerogatives once more threatened. The last of the few attempts in the history of Sweden to break the power of the bureaucracy had been forestalled.

For a long time, the Age of Freedom was condemned as an age of falsehood and inefficiency, proof that parliamentary supremacy meant political corruption. The bureaucracy was widely regarded as the only reliable guarantor of public honesty and it was this principle that guided the development of Sweden from royal despotism to a form of constitutional rule. If the bureaucrats were anxious to retain their traditional power, they had the support of a nation that mistrusted politicians.

After the assassination of Gustaf III, the modern form of Swedish government was hammered out in a process that led to a new constitution in 1809. Montesquieu's dictum on the separation of the legislative and executive functions was incorporated, but in such a way as to shackle the Diet and entrench the powers of the bureaucracy. The Executive was made strong, the Diet debarred from interfering directly in its affairs. Hedged about with restrictions the Diet was slow to act, and its rôle was established as the negative one of obstruction.

The Diet had no direct control over the administrative machinery of the State. In order to give it some insight into the conduct of the bureaucracy, the new constitution established the Ombudsman. The title means literally 'Agent'. He was to be a parliamentary watchdog, with the duty of ensuring that civil servants kept to their rules. He was a necessary

---

* The king was shot at a masquerade in the Stockholm Opera House by Captain J.J. Anckarström, a former officer in the household regiment. Verdi wrote his opera, *Un ballo in maschera*, around this incident.

link in a system that had taken the separation of legislative and executive powers to extremes.

It was a unique anomaly of the 1809 constitution that, although it incorporated principles of modern political thought, it yet persisted with the forms of a medieval assembly. The Estates lasted until 1865, when the first modern legislature in the history of Sweden was established. It was a bicameral model borrowing something, like the constitution itself, from American and French models.

The late survival of the Estates meant the preservation until the nineteenth century of the corporate political life of the Middle Ages. Each Estate was a corporation with privileges entrenched by law. Nobility and clergy established their claims by birth and royal appointment. Admission to the Peasants' Estate depended on the ownership of privileged land. But the Estate of Burgesses offered perhaps the clearest example of medieval form. It was an assembly of city trades and professions, the qualification being membership of a guild. Such membership was compulsory in most professions; in all, it was restricted, and the right to vote was therefore a privilege awarded by a *corporate* organization, not by the State directly.

Hats and Caps had been an interlude; they had no antecedents and left no heirs. Swedish political parties in the modern sense first appeared at the end of the nineteenth century, and were not firmly established before the first decades of the twentieth century. That was about two centuries after the foundation of Whigs and Tories that gave Britain her party system, and some decades later than the evolution of similar institutions on the Continent.

After the abolition of the Estates in 1865, two factions appeared: Liberal, representing the urban middle classes, and Agrarian, the enfranchised farmers. Liberals and Agrarians were no true parties; they were the old burgess and peasant Estates adapted to modern parliamentary forms.

The nobility retained their power for another twenty years, partly through dominance in the Upper Chamber of the Diet (indirectly elected through local government bodies, like the early United States Senate), partly through their preponderance in the Executive. They monopolized the premiership until the appointment in 1884 of Robert Themptander, the first commoner to hold the post.

The first true political party in Sweden, in the sense of professing certain ideas and having a definite programme, were the Social Democrats, who appeared in the last decade of the nineteenth century. To a certain extent they retain that distinction today. The non-Socialist parties are really interest groups or class factions. For this reason, ideology is a virtual monopoly of the left.

During the first three and a half decades of the twentieth century, Swedish party politics evolved their present form. On the one hand were the Social Democrats, who early came to dominate the country and the Diet; on the other, Conservatives, Liberals and the Farmers (later Centre) party. Broadly speaking, the Conservatives represent business and the professions; the Liberals, small shopkeepers and the urban middle class, and the Centre party, the farmers and agricultural workers.

Although class privilege disappeared with the abolition of the Estates in 1865, the right to vote and sit in the Diet was based on property and income qualifications which kept most of the population unfranchised for decades.* In 1909, universal male suffrage was introduced and, in 1921, women were given the vote.

The Social Democrats, the first advocates of universal suffrage, were originally not a parliamentary party, and the

* By comparison, the English working classes were partially enfranchised by Disraeli in the Second Reform Bill in 1867; Bismarck did the same in Prussia in 1866. Sweden followed suit a quarter of a century later.

fight for the vote was therefore *against* the legislature, instead of *within* it, as in other countries. As a result, the extension of the franchise in Sweden had the paradoxical effect of diminishing respect for the Diet, leaving a permanent stain on parliamentary institutions.

Just as the Estates survived in politics, so in agriculture the persistence of strip farming had conserved a medieval institution until modern times. Strip farming, which reigned in Western Europe during the Middle Ages, had disappeared from most countries long before it did so in Sweden. In the Swedish case it lasted until the first half of the nineteenth century.

Under this system, the farmer, instead of working a continuous holding, had his land distributed over a maze of disconnected narrow strips. Clearly he could not work such fragmented property on his own and, as a result, fields were collectively tilled.

Strip farming was finally abolished, and enclosure decreed, in 1827. Unlike the English enclosures of the sixteenth and eighteenth centuries, the Swedish version resulted in neither the enlargement of the big land-owners' estates, nor the creation of a landless peasantry that migrated to the cities to form an urban proletariat. It was carried out with more equity. Farmers were not dispossessed; they simply changed the form of their holdings, and their manner of work.

If, despite its high material standards and technological advancement, Sweden was, until the 1950s, a mainly peasant land, it was because of a unique form of industrial organization. This was the *bruk*, an industrial settlement lying away from the towns, out in the countryside. There were hundreds spread over central and southern Sweden. In the isolation of these small colonies, there grew up a powerful sense of community. It was in the *bruk* that many of the institutions of modern Sweden grew up; it was the cradle of the Swedish Welfare State.

The *bruk*, unlike the village, belonged to one man. He owned their houses, and tenancy was tied to the job. Until late in the nineteenth century, a *bruk* worker could not change employers without permission, and if he was in debt to his master, was legally bound to stay.

If the *bruk* worker was not wholly free, he was at least looked after by his master. Provided he worked satisfactorily, he would be cared for in his old age, with a roof over his head and a small pension. The *bruk*-owner also provided free medical care and schooling.

The work of the *bruk* required profound cooperation and devotion to the needs of the group. Whatever the industry, whether iron-working, copper mining or timber, the men were organized in gangs that could ill afford the luxury of personal independence. A sense of the collective weal developed. In this environment, the trade unions flourished naturally, and out of its disciplinary pressure grew the extraordinary hold that the Swedish labour movement has over the population.

Within the *bruks*, ancient Swedish attitudes were preserved without interruption, providing the emergent industrialized society with a firm, historical foundation. If, in England, the industrial revolution meant a break with the past, in Sweden it was a continuation.★

With the advance of industrialization, manufacturers acquired more political power, and the *bruk*-owners began to influence lawgiving with their paternalistic traditions. For this reason, Swedish industrial legislation always had a heavy streak of welfare.

The worker felt an ingrained loyalty for his *bruk* and

★ The *bruk* survives, many Swedish firms retaining the ancient form in a modernized version, still working away from the cities in rural manufacturing colonies. In these industrial outposts in the forest, the social organization and the mentality of the old *bruks* lives on, virtually untouched.

everyone in it. It was the fidelity of the clan, with the *bruks-patron*, the *bruk*-owner, looked up to as the chieftain.★ There were, of course, bad masters and dissatisfied workers, and there were conflicts enough and to spare. But bitterness and resentment between man and master were absent. Instead, there was mutual respect which has survived tension and crisis to temper present labour relations.

The Swedish industrial revolution was carried out after 1880, much later than in England and a little later than in the rest of Western Europe. Nevertheless, manufacturing in its pre-industrial form has a long history in Sweden. The *bruks* took their final shape in the seventeenth century, but the industries on which they were based had existed long before. Sweden is a country of forests and rivers, rich in iron, and modestly favoured with copper. Iron-working was known from about 500 B.C.; bronze 500 years earlier. Abundant wood gave the fuel to smelt the ores.

The early miner was part peasant and hunter; so too was the *bruk* worker, cultivating his own plot of land, and allowed to shoot for the pot. Until the end of the nineteenth century, industrial cities and an urban proletariat were of little importance. The *bruk* was the cradle of the Swedish industrial revolution, and the working class were peasants. The change in Swedish society has been based on a peasant mentality.

Industrialization was carried out almost painlessly. The collective mentality and corporate organization inherited from the old agricultural communities and the *bruks* was exactly what was required to cope with the technical and

★ These attitudes still flourish. The *brukspatron*, however, no longer exists, his place being taken by the managing director. The contemporary Swedish managing director is not only a man of distinction (or infamy) among businessmen, but a father (or stepfather) to his workpeople. I once met a taxi driver, a rabid Socialist and trade unionist, who boasted how once he had been chauffeur to one at a certain *bruk*. It was like hearing a simple Catholic peasant talk reverently of an audience with the Pope.

social upheaval brought by the new times. Capital and labour soon organized themselves in order to negotiate efficiently. The trade unions started in the 1880s. In 1897, the L O,* the Swedish trade Union Confederation, was formed, and was soon delegated substantial power by its members, so that it early appeared as the leader of a strongly disciplined and monolithic organization. The employers riposted in 1902 by founding their own national federation, S A F,† and, by 1908, central wage bargaining had been established.

Employers early acccepted the right of workers to organize themselves in the defence of their legitimate interests, and Swedish trade unionism, therefore, escaped the suppression that has embittered industrial life elsewhere. From the start it was desperately anxious not for militance but for respectability. The early trade unionists were bureaucrats at heart, patently more at ease behind a desk than at the barricades. They disliked the idea of strikes, preferring civilized negotiation with the bosses; and the bosses, on the whole, wanted to reciprocate.

But at the beginning of this century, unions and employers manoeuvred themselves into a position over wage demands from which retreat was impossible and which, in 1909, led to the only General Strike in Swedish history. The unions soon capitulated before the strength of the employers, and the strikers returned to work, their demands unsatisfied. The strike had weakened the unions and discredited the LO. The employers, however, magnanimously refrained from attacking the unions and undermining their influence. With the respite thus granted them, the unions reorganized and purged themselves of any belief in the strike as a practical weapon. It became for them a deterrent, which had failed if

* The initials L O stand for *landsorganisationen i Sverige*; literally, 'The national organization in Sweden'.

† S A F – *Svenska Arbetsgivareföreningen*, 'The Swedish Employers' Confederation'.

it had to be invoked. The employers feared not trade unions, but anarchy, and they therefore accepted with equanimity the resuscitation of the LO, because this gave them a single, disciplined body with which to negotiate. Since the General Strike, both labour and capital have regarded conflict as pestilential and unprofitable.

At most times during the past seven centuries, the Swedes have been lucky enough to supply Europe with what it wanted. During the age of sail, Sweden provided the maritime countries with pine pitch for caulking hulls and tall spruce for masts. When the price of copper rose in the seventeenth century, Sweden was able to oblige with supplies. Steel is always in demand for war and, since the late Middle Ages, Swedish products have been much sought after. When the elementary education of the nineteenth century created a demand for reading, the forests of Sweden were ready to provide the wood pulp for newsprint.

Except for a transitory episode in Delaware during the seventeenth century Sweden was involved neither in the original colonization of America nor in the carving up of Africa. But during the late nineteenth century, there was a wave of emigration to the United States which sent a million Swedes across the Atlantic. It was a peasants' exodus, caused by land hunger and bad harvests in the 1860s. It induced the first cultural invasion of the Swedish lower classes.

Alien borrowings had been the exclusive concern of the upper classes, and the mass of the population had, until the exodus to America, been steeped in a national tradition alone. Now repatriates and letters home brought American influence to Sweden.

The lower classes of Sweden were learning about America, while their rulers were returning to German domination. Gustaf III, a single-minded Francophile, had imposed French cultural supremacy, but it waned as Prussia rose. By the victory of Prussia in the Franco-Prussian war of 1870–71, the

Swedish upper classes had once more turned to Germany for everything. Modern politics were German imports, from imitations of Bismarck, exponent of the strong paternalistic state, on the right, to Social Democracy on the left. Education copied Prussian models; the arts shed their Gallic clothes, taking a German mantle instead.

This continued unrelieved until the defeat of Germany in the First World War brought some Anglo-Saxon influences. But German culture still held sway and German remained the second language of Sweden until the Nazi collapse. The emergence of the United States as a super power swept German culture from Sweden, substituting Americana instead. Within five years of the end of the war, English replaced German as the principal foreign language, and Sweden was thoroughly Americanized. Culture follows the sword.

Today, Sweden is one of the richest and technologically most advanced states in the world. It is a remarkable achievement, considering her backwardness until little more than a hundred years ago, when she was among the poorest of European countries, comparable only with Russia and the Balkans. In the seventeenth century there were four doctors in the country; at the end of the eighteenth, less than a hundred. Sweden entered the nineteenth century three hundred years behind the times, she left it ready for the twentieth century.

Isolation and absence of native culture delayed the progress of Sweden. It was not until the eighteenth century that a Swedish culture began to emerge. In the arts, it took the form of classical and French imitations. In the sciences, there was more originality. The Age of Freedom produced Linné, the botanist who devised the modern system of classification, and Polhem, an engineer who anticipated later inventions, notably water turbines and conveyor belts.

Uncomfortable with metaphysics, the Swedes are genuine materialists in a way that it is hard to match elsewhere. They are literal minded to a fault, and their considerable talents have been concentrated on engineering, applied science and the systematizing of available knowledge. The prosperity that has appeared in Sweden over the past century is due to inventiveness and a bent for adapting new advances made abroad. And an ingrained ability to see the world in economic terms alone made the Swedes devoted worshippers of technology far earlier than was the case in most other countries.

The other great fount of Swedish talent lies in administration. That has had an incalculable effect on the country's development. In business, it has meant superb management; in public affairs, a State that has adapted its institutions to exploit the economic and technological power of modern times.

In Sweden, then, the technological revolution of the twentieth century was exceptionally favoured. It had come to a country with little political feeling, but a love of bureaucracy, where the population submitted to an hierarchical order of things and accepted autocratic rule. They were well adapted to a centralized administration, and had uniform attitudes controlled by a monolithic educational system. They were steeped in a collective mentality, and the individual was at a discount. They were completely materialistic, and unencumbered by spiritual baggage. Culturally undeveloped they accepted what was put before them, and adopted whatever was new. Other people's wars benefited them commercially, but they escaped hostilities themselves. Geographically and intellectually isolated, they were spared conflicting influences from abroad, subject only to one trend at a time. The situation might have been tailor-made for the system that was to come.

3. Industrial Peace and the Rise of Modern Sweden

Like Soviet Russia, contemporary Sweden is the creation of a single political faction: the Social Democratic party. Its long rule has coincided with the onrush of technology and the achievement of a belated industrial revolution. In the West, industrialization has passed into history and responsibility for its accomplishment has been obscured by the passage of time. But in Sweden, as in Russia, the process is within living memory and is clearly the work of an unchanging regime. In both cases, one faction can therefore claim exclusive credit for the modernization of a backward society. As in Russia it is the Communists, so in Sweden it is the Social Democrats who have presided over this singular metamorphosis.

The Social Democratic party has dominated Sweden since the beginning of the century. Their advance was made easy by the multi-party system of the Diet. Sweden has escaped the splendid duels and dramatic simplicity of the two-party system. In England, the advance of the Labour party was blocked by the more or less cohesive mass of the Conservatives; in Sweden, there was no such unified opposition. Their enemies divided, and the Social Democrats were able to advance swiftly and unhindered.

They were helped further by the rigid class structure of the Swedish parties. The appeal to the working classes was unchallenged and, since 1918, they have been the largest single party in the Diet. Between 1920 and 1970, the Social Democrats have ruled alone or in coalition for forty-five years;

since 1932, they have held power continuously, except for a voluntary interregnum of six months in 1936.

In a constitutional state with free elections, so consummate a hold on power is something extraordinary. The reason is to be sought in the historical roots of the Swedish Social Democratic Party. Its devotion to collectivism and the corporate State* appeals to something very deep in the Swedish character. It is the political expression in modern form of the group thinking nurtured by Swedish history. It is a thoroughly native institution, even if its ideology has been imported,† and there lies the peculiar advantage enjoyed by the Social Democrats. Their main opponents, the Conservatives and Liberals, have not appealed to Swedish feelings, but have adopted alien ideas that resist acclimatization. Both, in latter years, have sought their inspiration in their English namesakes. That is to say, they accept, by implication, a political creed that holds Parliament sacrosanct and (broadly speaking) puts the individual above the collective. Nothing could be more foreign to Swedish tastes, and the disastrous record of Conservative and Liberal parties over the past four decades is eloquent confirmation. It is interesting to note that the Centre Party has the same native collectivist foundation as the Social Democrats and has been the most successful of the Opposition. On the other hand, it isn't really of the Opposition; it is merely out of office. The Centre Party nearly always helps the Social Democrats out of tricky situations; from 1952 to 1956 it ruled in coalition with them, and it usually joins the government in undermining the Liberals and Conservatives. In this way, the Social Democrats have a foundation that goes deeper than politics, and above this they have built a privileged kind of power. It hasn't come of this naturally; they have had to work single-mindedly for it.

* See Chapter 5.
† See page 90ff.

When the Social Democrats succeeded a Conservative government in 1932, they were faced with heavy unemployment and a languishing economy. It was the Swedish corner of the Great Depression and, since the parties of the centre and the right seemed unable to offer a remedy, the voters had given the left a mandate to try instead.

Since their appearance, the Social Democrats had professed an orthodox Socialist creed of immediate nationalization, levelling incomes and all-embracing social welfare. But that was an ideological sop to the faithful. Behind the electoral demagogy, the party was directed by sober economists who believed that reforms without resources courted economic disaster; that to talk about the distribution of wealth was meaningless rhetoric, until there was more to go round in the first place; and who therefore considered their first task the creation of prosperity, leaving radical innovation until the country could afford it.

With industry mainly in private hands, the enforcement of State ownership would be bound to interrupt the march of progress. To build the Welfare State too fast would be living beyond the country's means. Therefore, the Social Democrats exploited the existing capitalist system without prejudice, and restrained the expansion of social benefits to a speed justified by the rate of economic growth.

The architect of recovery was Ernst Wigforss, the Minister of Finance. By a Keynesian invocation of expansionist budgets, spending money on public enterprises, such as roads and municipal housing, he absorbed the workless and induced the economy to move. By generous company taxation and State loans, he encouraged manufacturers to produce more and invest more. It paid to build factories and expand production. In December 1932, unemployment reached its apogee at thirty-one per cent; two years later it was halved, and at the end of the decade it was nine per cent. Exports in 1937 were twenty per cent above those in 1929; the comparable in-

crease in the output of wood pulp, foundation of national
wealth, was forty-three per cent. Industrial production for
1939 was sixty-five per cent more than in 1929: world trade
stagnated during the same period. Sweden had done better than
most countries in mending her fortunes. By 1940, she had not
only overcome the Depression but, making up for her late
start, had overhauled the rich industrial states of the West.

Imposing as the immediate achievements of the 1930s
might have been, the real significance of the decade lay in
the ideological groundwork for what was to come. The
spectre of poverty and fear of unemployment enabled the
government so to guide development that the nation worked
hard while sacrificing immediate benefits for future prosperity. A planned economy was so obviously successful that,
although Socialist policy, it was rapidly accepted by all
camps. And therein lies the crucial importance of those years
for Sweden. The Swedes were indoctrinated with the ideas
of State direction and intervention in the economy. These
became part of the national political canon so that when,
in later years, more radical measures were introduced, opposition was absent and the controversy known in the West
was avoided in Sweden.

In all this, there lies a curious parallel with Russia. In both
countries, the 1930s saw the establishment of basic industries
and the execution of the groundwork for future progress
by regimes that, driven by a compulsion to overcome national
backwardness, were obsessed by the priority of economic
advancement. In each case, the tasks were accomplished, with
the obvious difference that whereas the Soviet Union employed despotic rule, the Swedes enjoyed a constitutional
form of government.

Lenin once said that 'Electricity plus Bolshevism equals
Communism', which was a way of explaining that his aim
was to modernize Russia in a hurry, and to use an amalgam
of politics and technology to do so. Swedish Social Democrats,

in a similar way, see their movement as the political arm of the technological revolution, its purpose that of transmitting and distributing to the population the benefits of what scientists and engineers have achieved. To do this properly, the Social Democrats believed in the necessity of a planned economy. But they also understood that, while the planners propose, the producers dispose, so that their schemes would be futile until the economy gave the wherewithal to manipulate. While beginning the erection of the apparatus of central planning, they were also vigorously engaged in breathing new life into Swedish industry. It was one thing to encourage investment and build new factories but, unless the workers agreed to work, plans for expansion were so many empty words. At the end of the 1920s, and the beginning of the 1930s, strikes and lock-outs were ravaging Sweden. Industrial peace was seen to be vital for industrial progress, and it was pursued with the same urgency as the purely technological and economic prescriptions for putting the country on its feet.

In May 1931, strikers had been shot dead by the army at Ådalen, in northern Sweden. Neither employers nor trade unions had wanted to invoke force, both considering the incident a lamentable failure of the civil authority which they would have preferred to avoid. Troops had been called in by the provincial governor who feared that the police were unable to control militant demonstrations organized by the Communists among the strikers in Ådalen. The order to open fire was an understandable reaction to a crowd that was beginning to be aggressive. Since the riot act had been read, the fusillade was indisputably legal, but it was a shocking aberration of national behaviour, the first and last of its kind. Five demonstrators were killed. Their deaths gave a taste of violence that horrified Sweden and aided the peacemakers. The country wanted an end to conflict, and the Social Democratic government was elected in 1932 on a promise of peace. If it was to remain in power, it had to redeem its pledge.

Industrial peace was entrenched within six years. It was not a radical innovation, but the fulfilment of a long historical process. The Ådalen shots obscured the powerful underlying forces of Swedish society that were driving labour and capital into each other's arms. The trade unions, even if their leaders spoke with the tongue of intransigence and class warfare on ceremonial occasions, saw the futility of strikes. Impelled by the tradition of loyalty and understanding nurtured in the *bruks*, they sought to negotiate with the employers. And the employers, heirs to the same tradition, shrank in their turn from sustained confrontation.

Devotion to corporate thought had ensured the early birth of collective bargaining. The first Swedish wage agreement was negotiated in 1869, between Stockholm masons and builders, *acting as two groups*. Individual approaches, each man getting what he could out of his master, had never been popular with either. By the first decade of this century, collective bargaining was a common habit. At the end of the 1920s, it had been extended to national agreements for particular industries. But it was not enough. If the miners made peace, but not the dockers, the country was little better off. The complexity of an industrial nation required conciliation all along the line, and the only way of ensuring it was by centralizing the whole process of wage bargaining. A unified, national system became imperative.

The impulse for its establishment came, oddly enough, not from the Social Democrats, but from the last non-Socialist government to hold office. In 1928, the Conservatives passed legislation prohibiting industrial conflicts during the validity of a collective agreement. It was a peculiar hybrid of civil and criminal law in which an act was made illegal, but offenders could not be prosecuted. By definition, a strike under these conditions was a misdemeanour, but punishment was excluded. It is a concept well embedded in Swedish law. A man may be found guilty but escape penalty. The stigma of conviction is supposed to be its own punishment, but the effect is to condemn the crime, rather than the criminal. Applied to industrial relations, it discredits unauthorized action without stigmatizing the participants as criminals, and thereby presenting them with a martyr's crown. And it is a fact that, today, Swedes have an instinctive horror of wild-cat strikes (which are usually termed 'illegal'), without considering the individual strikers as malefactors. It is a particular application of a Swedish propensity to deny personal responsibility, and to separate the man from his act.

The remedy for contravention was established as civil damages for breach of contract. Both strikes and lock-outs are proscribed, with workers and employers allowed impartially to bring a suit. A special industrial court was established to administer the new law.

At first the trade unions were infuriated by the legislation, which they inclined to see as a device to shackle themselves. But they were mollified by the discovery that the bosses, whom the new arrangement might be supposed to favour, turned out to sympathize with them. Both sides disliked the prospect of the law's obtruding itself into their disputes; they both disliked even more the underlying threat of government interference. When the Social Democrats came to office in 1932, the unions wanted to keep the State out of the labour market with perhaps more urgency than under a Conservative regime. Before, it had been a question of repelling the employers, enemies from the outside; now what was at stake was the containment of an internal rival, the party, for the control of the labour movement. The employers were equally anxious to keep the authorities at bay. Self-preservation drove both sides together and, they conscientiously devised a system of central bargaining which enabled them to settle their disagreements privately – or at least be seen to do so.

Collective bargaining had long been accepted as demonstrably rational and efficient. Unions and employers accepted the principle; what remained was to centralize it, so that the LO and the Employers' Confederation could negotiate for the whole country. They conferred on and off for five years and, in 1938, codified their ideas in the Saltsjöbaden agreement, named after the Stockholm suburb where it was signed. It was the peace treaty between labour and capital. The signatories agreed that their interests were the same, and that antagonism would get them nowhere. They committed themselves to the peaceful settlement of industrial disputes. Strikes were outlawed as long as the agreement was in force. The right to strike was not, however, abolished; it was regulated. In order to strike without breach of faith, it was necessary to repudiate the agreement, which required at least a fortnight's notice. Under the guise of rules of procedure, a cooling-off period had thus been built into the system.

Both the unions and the employers were led by men with the tastes of councillors, and an instinct for the conference room. Saltsjöbaden was not a cockpit of politicians, agitators and prophets, but a consistory of lawyers and administrators. The agreement bore their stamp. Both sides had agreed to treat its drafting as a matter of defining procedure and organization. Their only problem was to arrive at a mutually acceptable code which would take care of any conceivable dispute, and specify methods of negotiation and arbitration so that strikes and lock-outs would be superfluous. Both unions and employers were preoccupied with methods of settling disputes over the interpretation of texts. A central agreement, specifying wages for a whole country, is of necessity a complex document, and what appears clear and unequivocal at the conference table can turn out to be obscure and ambiguous by the time it is applied to a particular factory.

The Saltsjöbaden agreement abolished the confusion of

individual unions and employers negotiating separately and at cross-purposes, substituting the order of two parties facing each other across the table; it was the duel instead of the brawl. The LO and the Employers' Confederation, assuming sovereign power, divided Sweden between themselves, and industrial peace was enshrined as a national institution.

If central bargaining was to be anything more than empty words, each party had to monopolize the representation of its side of industry, so that it could talk with real authority. It is one of the most telling indications of the Swedish condition that, although the Saltsjöbaden agreement obviously depended on universal trade union membership, it does not specify the closed shop. Enunciation of that principle is absent, because it is unnecessary. The Swedish trade unions have never had to press for a closed shop: it was voluntarily presented to them. Not for nothing are they numbered among the heirs of the ancient collective mentality of the farms and the *bruks*: its legacy is a fearful sense of guilt at not belonging.

Belonging to an organization remains second nature to a Swede, and joining a trade union can therefore be taken for granted. It is an important act, without which a working man cannot really attain his full stature. It is a psychological necessity, since the historical background continues to force upon the Swede the necessity of joining a group in order to acquire a sense of identity. Trade-union membership covers over ninety-five per cent of the working population, almost all of it genuinely voluntary. In the few cases in which persuasion or intimidation is necessary, it almost always concerns people who deviate from the norm in their personal lives.

Inviolable discipline is obviously another vital condition of wage bargaining. Again, this follows automatically as a consequence of the nature of the Swede. Swedish workers obey their leaders implicitly, and accept almost without question the hierarchical structure of their unions. The LO commands obedience before the individual unions, as the bishop before the parish priest. Sweden has escaped the antagonism between unions and the central organization.

Sweden has also escaped the antagonism of man and master over new machines; modernization has never been obstructed by the unions. The Swedish trade unions share with the Social Democratic party a sense of mission as agents of the technological revolution. From their birth, the unions have supported technical progress because they have never seen in it anything but a means to raise wages and create work. It is a corporate expression of a national admiration of efficiency and a long tradition of mystical belief that all innovation must necessarily be for the better. Ludditism was unknown in Sweden; however badly off, the working classes saw in the advent of machinery, not a threat to their jobs, but a promise of less drudgery and a better future. In after years, this tradition has smoothed the way for automation. The unions have never jibbed at the replacement of men by machinery. If a new device means that one factory hand can do the work of three, this is perfectly acceptable, because it is interpreted as an aid to profits, and hence better wages. The attitude, celebrated among English trade unions, that a machine must be tended by a certain number of men, whatever its actual requirements, would scandalize a Swedish trade unionist. He would say that, since full employment reigns, there is always work elsewhere and, if it means moving to another town, that is something that has to be borne for the good of the community.

Full employment, or at least the avoidance of idle hands, has been the keystone of Swedish policy since the 1930s. Unemployment declined steadily until, in 1950, it fell to two per cent, the level it has held since then. Much of this is simply due to the general progress of the world. But the

Swedes went beyond the usual remedies of fiscal and monetary policy in the establishment of special devices to counteract business cycles. The main ones are these. In the fat years, firms may set aside part of their surplus which, deductible from taxable income, is placed in a blocked bank account. When the lean years arrive, the money may be withdrawn for investment and expansion. The government decides when this is to happen, and what schemes are to be financed. Then, the Labour Market Directorate, the official body supervising questions of employment, has contingency plans for road building and other public works which are started when a recession appears. Furthermore, the Directorate has a device to mop up surplus labour when the country goes through a bad patch. This is a scheme for vocational retraining, partly financed by an industrial levy, and always in readiness. Its total capacity is about 7,000, which was invoked to the full in 1971 for the first time for over a decade.

Full employment and mobility of labour are, in the Swedish system, half the battle. The two remaining impediments to industrial efficiency are demarcation disputes and the proliferation of unions.

Demarcation disputes were quelled early in the history of the Swedish trade-union movement, because the LO saw in them the threat of internecine strife that would sap its strength and handicap collective bargaining.

Modern industrial society requires the large trade union covering a whole industry, instead of the exclusive one representing a craft. Since the beginning of the century, the LO has gradually realized this ideal, engineering the necessary amalgamation of its constituent bodies. It has been accepted without protest because most trade unionists understood that modernization cannot rationally be confined to employers, but must apply to themselves as well. Efficient central bargaining demands few, but large and firmly led unions, and not many Swedes were willing to dispute this proposition.

As reorganization proceeded, people obediently transferred their union membership as directed; mostly the change was carried out collectively, so that the individual was not bothered by unnecessary paper work. From 1900 to 1970, the number of LO unions was reduced from 120 to forty, and it happened with little more than the pinpricks of administrative reform. The rank and file understood the advantage of size in bargaining; their leaders approved, because it gave them greater power. It is better to serve a large organization than to rule a small one.

To function efficiently, the LO and the Employers' Confederation have been devised as mirror images of each other. As the one sits on top of unions covering whole industries, so the other has directly under it corresponding trade associations. The levels of hierarchy are matched, so that they can all negotiate authoritatively as exact counterparts with identical domains. This is essential in wage bargaining, because a central agreement is not an exhaustive specification, but a generalized framework within which each industry has to establish the details for its own territory. The central agreement concerns a total national wage increase in the form, not of a percentage, but of an absolute amount, and this has to be suitably apportioned all along the line. It is not necessarily an easy task.

The Saltsjöbaden agreement guaranteed employers peace to build up their factories and expand their business. It ensured proper distribution of the benefits of technology, and the efficient utilization of a small country's resources. It mobilized the industrial power of Sweden in a way normally open in peacetime to a dictatorship alone.

In the meanwhile, the Welfare State was gradually being erected. It is not by origin a Socialist institution. The paternalistic *bruk*-owners had, for at least two centuries, held decent notions of looking after their workers, while the old village communities had cared for the poor and the aged. The concept of social welfare was sufficiently well imprinted on the Swedish mentality to make its legal codification a foregone conclusion under any party. Old-age pensions, debut of the modern Swedish Welfare State, were introduced in 1913 by a Liberal government. They had been delayed for years, not because of any opposition on principle, but because the Diet wanted to be doubly sure of the details. Following a long tradition, the Swedes insisted on studying how others had done the same thing in order to avoid their mistakes. Before acting, they thoroughly examined conditions in Germany, Denmark and England, all of whom had already established national pension schemes.

The first Swedish old-age pension was contributory, dependent on the total paid and partially subject to a means test. When first granted, in 1914, it was 56 kronor annually. At the contemporary rate of exchange, it was equivalent to £3, £23 in terms of 1971 purchasing power. As incomes rose, and whole working lives were passed under the scheme, payments increased correspondingly, reaching 728 kronor* in 1947. The following year, the Social Democrats made the first basic alterations in the system since its inception by granting a fixed pension irrespective of the contributions paid, and by abolishing the means test. It was a recognition that the country was now on its feet, and what the Social Democrats called 'the harvest era', or the reward for past deprivation, was about to begin. The new pension was 1,000 kronor† annually: in 1951, it was given its present form by being tied to the cost-of-living index. The pension at the beginning of 1971 was about 5,000 kronor‡ per annum. Since the introduction of the pension, the age of retirement has remained sixty-seven.

In 1937, the Social Democratic government introduced

---

* £50 ($200) at current rates; £118 ($280) in 1971 terms.
† £70 ($310) at current rates; £186 ($450) in 1971 terms.
‡ £400 ($960).

maternity grants and children's allowances. When first paid, the maternity grant was 110 kronor* per pregnancy, irrespective of income, and a supplement of up to 300 kronor†, subject to a means test, was paid. Children's allowances, also conditional on a means test, were a maximum of 100 kronor ‡ annually. In 1947, the means test was removed from this field too. A children's allowance of 260 kronor** annually per child was then introduced. Both maternity grants and children's allowances have been periodically raised to compensate for inflation: at the beginning of 1971 they were 1,080 kronor (£88, $210) and 1,200 kronor (£98 or $239) per annum.

Strictly speaking, maternity grants and children's allowances were not social welfare. They were explicitly conceived as a means of counteracting a falling birth rate. Outside Nazi Germany, Sweden was the first country to subsidize fecundity. The Swedish maternity benefits were established as the direct result of a book called *Crisis in Population*, published in 1934 by Professor Gunnar Myrdal and his wife, Alva, both socialist economists of international repute. The Myrdals at that time had intimate connections with the German academic world and their study was based on similar work carried out in Germany by Nazi ideologists. Both Myrdal and his German mentors were perturbed by the dangers to their respective nations of a falling birth rate, seeing in it a threat of depopulation.

The professor was then a Nazi sympathizer, publicly describing Nazism as the movement of youth and the movement of the future. In Myrdal's defence, it must be pointed out that, whatever his other propensities, Hitler did have advanced ideas on social welfare, and that the social ideology

---

* £35.5 ($72.5) in terms of 1971 buying power.
† £92 ($220) in terms of 1971 buying power.
‡ £30 ($720) in terms of 1971 buying power.
** £45 ($108) in terms of 1971 buying power.

of the German Nazis and the Swedish Social Democrats had much in common. Until the mid 1930s, Nazism had considerable attractions for those who favoured a benevolent and authoritarian state and the Swedes, traditionally subjected to German intellectual domination, were prone to such influences. Nazi thought, often incognito, permeated Swedish life.

Medical care in Sweden was provided from the beginning of the century by private benevolent funds, attached to the popular organizations, particularly the trade unions, and enjoying public subsidies. In 1950, these funds were taken over by the State and used in the establishment of national health insurance. But even before then, membership had embraced most of the population, so that such insurance already existed in fact if not in law. In nationalizing the funds, the government was simply transferring a public service from one form of corporate organization to another.*

Swedish socialists look back on the first twenty years of their regime as a period of establishing prosperity and creating what they call 'a strong society' which is a euphemism for a powerful centralized State. Only with both goals achieved could social security be perfected. The electorate accepted the delays in erecting the Welfare State, because they accepted without question the economic arguments advanced in explanation. The national bent for seeing the world exclusively in economic terms smoothed the way of the politicians. It also assured the naturalization of a Marxist way of thought and feeling.

The Swedish Social Democrats are the only existing party inside or outside the Communist world able to claim an

---

* Unlike Britain, Sweden does not yet have a free dental service. Dentistry was specifically excluded from the health services, because Sweden was judged unable to afford it. Free dentistry cannot be expected before the middle of the 1970s. Health insurance provides free hospitals, reimbursement of doctors' fees, except for 7 kronor (£0.58 or $1.35), the cost of medicine above 15 kronor (£1.25 or $3) and compensation for lost earnings.

apostolic succession from Marx. Swedish Socialism is a German product. The first Swedes to encounter a Socialist ideology were apprentices in the nineteenth century who, handicapped by backwardness at home, went to Germany in order to learn a trade. There, Marx was then trying to organize the working class. Socialism was in the air, and the Swedish visitors, fresh from the intellectual vacuum of their own country, were suddenly exposed to an unaccustomed onslaught of agitation and ideas. Many became fervent and uncritical Marxist disciples. Most returned to Sweden with little more than personal conviction. One of them had the true proselytizing fervour, and brought Socialism to his countrymen: August Palm, a tailor.

In May 1875, the German Social Democratic party was formed, promulgating as its constitution the Gotha Programme. This was a compromise between the radical ideas of Marx and the more moderate ones of his opponent, Lasalle. Roughly, the difference was that Marx wanted quick and thorough-going changes whereas Lasalle was prepared to hasten slowly. The synthesis had been dictated by the need to heal divisions within the Socialist movement and allow the formation of a single party. Marx subsequently attacked the compromise in his *Critique of the Gotha Programme*, which is now part of the Communist canon. Nevertheless, the programme was thoroughly Marxist. Its main deviation was that it left the form of government open, the future Socialist State conceivably existing under the same Hohenzollern monarchy then ruling Germany. Apart from that, the basic tenets of Marx were propounded, including the class war, the inevitability of capitalism's demise and the appropriation by the working class of the means of production. Palm brought the Gotha Programme back to Sweden, adopting it *in extenso* as the manifesto of the society that he formed in 1881, the first socialist organization in Sweden. The programme was badly translated, probably because it was imperfectly under-

stood. It was nonetheless taken over by the Swedish Social
Democratic party when founded in 1889.

For some time, the Swedish Social Democratic party considered itself a branch of the German Socialist movement. In
1897, the Swedes followed the German Socialist Workers'
party, by adopting the Erfurt Programme in place of the
Gotha Programme. The one was an alteration of the other in
a Marxist direction, mainly in the sense that the party aimed
to take over the country and change the form of government
to what we would call a one-party State. But, like the Gotha
Programme, the Erfurt Programme eschewed revolution on
the assumption that the march of history would inevitably
achieve the party's aims, so that violence was superfluous. Too
restrained for the East, too radical for the West, the Erfurt
Programme has by now been abandoned, except in Sweden,
where it remains the manifesto of the Social Democrats. It
has often been modified but never replaced. Continental
socialists have acquired their own non-Marxist doxologies;
English Socialism is a national product; the Communist
world must approach Marxism through the intermediary
of Lenin, Mao or Stalin; alone among them all, the Swedish
Social Democrats can trace a direct and undefiled descent from
Marx himself.

After flirting with ideas of revolution, the Social Democrats at the beginning of this century committed themselves
to parliamentary means of achieving their ends. In 1917, the
Bolshevik Revolution in Russia put new life into the radical
Social Democrats who, defying the party line, had continued
to harbour ambitions of invoking force to overthrow the
existing order. They broke away to form the Swedish
Communist party. A small faction that has never had a chance
of taking over the country, the Swedish Communists have
been burdened with the peculiar inhibition of being Social
Democratic schismatics. When a Swedish Prime Minister,
Mr Olof Palme, in 1970, described them as 'radical Social

Democrats', he was no more than speaking the historic truth.

Long ago, the Swedish Social Democrats abjured Marx. And in the sense that they have discarded his ideological paraphernalia, and now rarely study him, this may be taken at face value. But in the way that they think and act, they suggest a deep and pervasive Marxist streak in their intellectual make-up. Professor Herbert Tingsten, a Swedish political economist, and former Social Democratic ideologist, puts it in these words: 'The historical-philosophical concepts, from which Marx developed his more detailed economic and social theories, have maintained their authority to a far greater degree than the theories themselves. The materialistic interpretation of history is still, as a rule, accepted as a significant and true dogma, even if there is rarely any attempt to explain with any exactitude what exactly it consists of. A general mood of economic determinism has surrounded the economic debate. It is enough to mention the continuous reference to "progress", as some kind of independent, motive force. A reform is sufficiently justified if it is said to be in line with "progress".'

The Swedish Social Democrats interpret the human being exclusively in behaviouristic terms. From this, follows their Marxist doctrine that, by altering his surroundings man can be moulded in a certain, predetermined way. Like the orthodox parties of the Communist world, the Swedish Social Democrats have acted on their belief by manipulating the environment of their citizens in order to create the new man for the new society.

In so doing, they have shown that it is not necessary to apply Marxist economics in order to realize Marxist social theories. As will appear from the next chapter, the Swedish Social Democrats have acquired the requisite economic control of the country by oblique methods, and the more rigid forms of State direction have been superfluous.

In accepting economic determinism as their principal article of faith, the Swedish Social Democrats not only subscribed to Marxist orthodoxy, but followed a national habit of thought. Marxism, at least in the form in which it is practised, is rooted in materialism and a sense of expediency. Both have been historically imprinted on the Swede, and he therefore lacks the spiritual core that gives moral resistance. In this, Sweden is quite extraordinary. The Russians, to make a comparison, are possessed by an intense spirituality that has been the bane of their revolutionaries, so that the Bolsheviks found more opposition in Russia than the Social Democrats in Sweden, to the application of Marxist doctrine. In the first case, the new influence fought, in the second, it followed, a native tradition. In this sense, Sweden is one of the most truly Marxist countries in existence.

4. A Planner's Promised Land

Most essays in planned economy have been obstructed by administrative deficiencies and popular resistance. But Sweden might have been designed especially for central planning. A monolithic State with a powerful centralized administration rules a submissive population that respects authority, and prefers civil servants to politicians. The whole tradition of the country has been *dirigiste*; when the Social Democrats assumed power they were not required to introduce new ideas, but to coax existing ones to their own purposes. There had always been State supervision of industry, and even the businessmen who carried through the Swedish industrial revolution at the end of the nineteenth century believed, not so much in *laissez faire*, as in the solemn duty of the government to encourage, protect and, where necessary, finance their activities. Planning as such had no enemies in Sweden (which is rather different from the case, say, in England) and the only dispute has been over the form it is to take and, occasionally, the purposes for which it is used. It is because of the peculiar nature of her political and social institutions that Sweden has achieved things out of all proportion to her size.

The *bruks* have instilled in workmen great loyalty to their firms, while Swedish industrialists have always been gifted organizers. Industrial peace ensured the full exploitation of these qualities. But perhaps the most valuable asset of Swedish industry is that its workers have been historically conditioned to think in groups. They adapt instinctively to the large teams and intricate processes involved in modern production. To this they add a remarkable submissiveness and discipline, implicitly obeying their employers. Instructions are followed to the letter: it is easy to translate managerial decisions into action. Sweden is the organization man's promised land.

With willing material, and no opposition, Swedish industrial management is like the general staff of a well-trained army. Waste, of men or materials, is rare. Swedish industry has advanced tremendously since 1930. Companies have arisen on a scale, and with a prestige, that would flatter a country many times the size.

Thirty-two firms have an annual turnover of more than £50,000,000 ($120,000,000). The great concerns originated in the invention or adaptation of new devices by Swedes; they are still associated with these products, and are often household names abroad. Among the most famous are SKF, for self-aligned ball-bearings (annual turnover £30,000,000 or $733,000,000: 62,900 employees), Alfa-Laval, for centrifugal separators (annual turnover £11,000,000 or $270,000,000: 17,500 employees), AGA for automatic lighthouses (annual turnover £70,000,000 or $169,000,000: 13,000 employees).

A population of 8,000,000 contrives to support two motor car manufacturers – Volvo and Saab – of international repute. It also maintains a profitable aeronautical industry, turning out military jet aircraft that can stand comparison with the products of the Great Powers. The dedication that has gone into all this has a cold intensity reminiscent of a war effort.

But, of course, Sweden is devoted to peace. The Gross National Product has soared splendidly; the standard of living has risen appropriately. In 1968, the Swedish GNP was £1,350 ($3,230) *per capita*, runner up to the USA with £1,791 ($4,305) and narrowly ahead of Canada with £1,260 ($3,025) in third place. Britain, having a GNP of £704 ($1,690) lies twelfth in the world. Other figures relating to prosperity tell the same tale. Of telephones, Sweden has 49.9 per 100* in-

* All figures for 1968, the latest available.

habitants, against 54.1 for the US; of TV sets 296 per 1,000 inhabitants against 409. Sweden uses 168 kilograms of newsprint *per capita* per annum; the US 409. And so on, *ad nauseam*. By most statistical definitions, only the United States is more affluent. But if to the accumulation of national wealth is added the concept of equitable distribution, then Sweden must be allowed the lead. The Swedes possess no slums, they know no malnutrition. Millions of Americans, it is generally acknowledged, live in poverty; there are no poor in Sweden. Only the Swedes have abolished enclaves of destitution in the golden fields of prosperity; only they have managed to establish true economic security for the average citizen.

While private enterprise has been allowed to exploit its genius for technical progress, the State has spread the benefits. It is a way of enjoying the material fecundity of the capitalist system while avoiding its inequalities. The capitalist produces; the State distributes. To do so, the State acquired considerable powers over private enterprise without altering the formal tenets of ownership.

Nationalization, although the most obvious, and in some ways the simplest, means of controlling industry, has been spurned for a number of excellent reasons. In the first place, it is demonstrably inefficient. 'You've only got to look at the British coal and steel industry,' in the words of an impeccably orthodox Swedish Social Democrat, 'to get cold shivers down your back. We've looked hard at that kind of nationalization, and it's not for us.' Politically, there are more profound reservations. To own is possibly to take the credit for success, but it is inescapably to suffer the consequences of failure. The Swedes have devised a system in which the State, while it controls, does not own industry, so that while it takes the kudos as the general source of prosperity, the responsibility for particular failure descends upon the owners. It is the blessings of possession without the odium; power without responsibility.

A number of economic devices enable the government to steer industry. Credit is rigorously controlled by the central authorities. Taxation is so designed that companies find it increasingly difficult to finance themselves, and investment and expansion depend on State loans. Since these, in their turn, depend on whatever conditions (and they need not necessarily be economic) the government decides to impose, there is considerable scope for direction. To take one example, placement of factories can be steered. When Volvo, the motor car manufacturers, expanded their plant in 1970, they were compelled by this means to transfer some production to Umeå, in northern Sweden, about 800 miles from their headquarters in Gothenburg. Left to themselves, the directors would scarcely have done so, since economically the move was indefensible. But politically, the government required it, in order to bring employment to a depressed area.

Such control, while reasonably efficient, leaves much to be desired, particularly in the supervision of daily business and insight into company affairs. The next step is, obviously, the State in the boardroom. This is Social Democratic policy. It started in 1971 with the major banks, who now have government directors on their boards. Shipyards are the next in turn, and doubtless large industrial concerns will follow not long after. Only one or two State directors have been appointed to each bank and, being in every case a small minority, they cannot exercise formal control. But their words carry weight; they are the commissars. It is not the intention, at least during the 1970s, to have a majority of State directors on private companies. One agent on each board is enough; he can relay government orders, and report back on private company matters. By his presence, power has been transferred from the shareholders and directors to the government, without altering the forms of ownership. The arrangement gives the State all the control it needs, while ensuring local autonomy, allowing market forces to work within prescribed limits, and avoiding the horrors of merciless centralization. It is not so very different from liberal reforms mooted in the Communist world.

What the Swedes are doing is to exploit the managerial revolution. 'Since the managers have taken over,' to quote Dr Rudolf Meidner, a leading Social Democratic economist, and a State director on the board of Stockholms Enskilda Bank (one of the 'big four' Swedish banks), 'the nature of ownership is immaterial. The point is, capital is now divorced from management. Shareholders don't exercise power any more, they just draw their dividends. The real control now lies with the expert manager, and he's a paid employee. To him, it's immaterial where his salary comes from.' The Social Democrats are working towards a future in which private ownership of industry will be like a constitutional monarchy; the pale relic of an ancient institution. Company directors appointed by the shareholders will probably continue as figureheads, in order to reassure the public with the appearance of the old order, and to avoid the distress and possible opposition caused by naked change. But the real power will lie with the State and the managers if, by then, any distinction can be drawn. In Swedish parlance, this is 'functional socialism'. A Marxist might call it 'state capitalism'.

In certain cases, the State has entered trade and industry directly in order to influence prices and development. Most iron mining has been nationalized. Building is a favourite field of intervention. For example, the State now controls about half the output of wall insulation, an important product in a northern country. Then, hotels and restaurants are largely State-owned. Furthermore, the government has extensive influence through the cooperative and the trade-union movements, both of which are so intimately allied with the Social Democratic party. About one fifth of all building is in the hands of companies owned by the trade unions. The cooperatives have roughly twenty per cent of all retail trade in Sweden, and are given priority by the authorities when granting permission to establish new shops.

The State, then, has thorough control over the economy. And yet, the statistics say that ninety-five per cent of Swedish industry is privately owned. It is perhaps one more reminder of the distinction between statistics and reality. It is a comforting figure, not infrequently quoted by officials in Sweden to reassure those who doubt government intentions.

The powers sketched above are the very sinews of planning but, for satisfactory control, one condition is wanting: isolation, so that the authorities may keep outside influences at bay, and reign unhampered. And it is noticeable that the Social Democrats, although they pay lip service to 'international solidarity', have nevertheless pursued a strictly isolationalist policy. They have preserved the country's historical introversion and isolation. It came out with particular force in work for European integration and relations with the EEC.

Since 1963, the Swedes had flirted with ideas of approaching the EEC, forced by the necessity of preserving export markets. They were vague in their intentions for a long time but finally, in 1971, they rejected full membership on two main counts: that it was incompatible with their neutrality, and that it would interfere with their particular brand of development. In particular, the government was unable to accept free movement of labour and free movement of capital. That the free movement of capital was not condemned on principle had been demonstrated in the abortive negotiations with Denmark, Finland and Norway for a Nordic Common Market in 1969, when the Swedes made this a condition. But in that situation they were the biggest nation, and clearly wanted to extend their economic power to their neighbours. Dealing with the EEC, however, Sweden was a small nation and therefore at the receiving end of capital movement, implying the intrusion of alien influence. As far as the movement of labour was concerned, the Swedes, to quote Mr Olof Palme, the Prime Minister, 'could not give up the powers of the trade unions to regulate immigration'. He was referring to the mechanism of granting entry and work permits, in which the board making the decisions contains L O representatives, and in which the L O has the last word.

It is true that certain Swedish industrialists favoured the EEC, but they were a tiny minority involved in large companies with international connections. By and large, Swedish businessmen, like the Social Democratic government (not to mention the trade unions and the general public), were morbidly afraid of foreign influence, and were fervid apostles of economic nationalism. EEC was not for them.

About 4.5 per cent of Swedish industry is foreign-owned, and in no sector do foreign interests dominate. But, warned by the advance of the multi-national companies, and fearing the invasion of international capital, the government has intensified the already stringent control of foreign investment, repelling it where required. There was a representative incident in the case of a firm called Billman. This is a manufacturer of electrical control equipment, and a Swiss company in the same field, Landis & Gyr, wanted to buy it. There was at the time no legal impediment to their doing so, since the brokers had circumvented the current regulations. Behind the scenes, however, Mr Krister Wickman, the Swedish Minister of Industry, stopped the deal, more or less forced certain large shareholders to sell their holdings to the government and kept the company in Swedish ownership, with a substantial State interest.

Fundamentally, the Swedes want to import technology and extend trade, but keep out foreign influence. Thus, Sweden has been a keen member of EFTA, which in essence is an *ad hoc* organization to abolish import duties and which, now this has been done, has become moribund. It has certainly not had the influence on the life and government of its signatories that the EEC has had among its own members. And EFTA has not eroded the sovereignty of national governments as the EEC most definitely has. And there is the heart of the matter. The Swedes are jealous of their sovereignty and refuse point blank to renounce one jot of it. The Europeans may point to all the advantages of integration, but the Swedes see absolute control of their own society as the most valuable of possessions. They know that to mould the country according to their plans they must be isolated from external interference. Their rulers understand that to open their borders to foreign ideas would be to undermine a unique system that needs isolation for its survival.

Control of a modern industrial society ideally demands an efficient and easily manipulated central administration protected from external interference. The rulers of Sweden have inherited a system that might have been shaped with their needs precisely in mind. They have a strong bureaucracy and a weak Diet. They have an administrative machine immune to parliamentary influence, with considerable powers of government by decree. They have extensive constitutional means of evading both the political and judicial process.

In its original form, the 1809 constitution placed the executive power in the hands of the king, acting through Ministers of State, whom he chose without consulting the Diet. They, however, had no direct influence on the administrative organization that ran the country. That organization was independent. Ministers gave it general directives, but the precise way in which these were to be carried out was left to the bureaucrats. The administration was free of parliamentary control, and ministers were not responsible for its action before the Diet. The Government was a committee of bureaucrats. National policy was usually decided in the administrative organization, afterwards being accepted by the government and *then* presented to the Diet for approval. The

Diet did not originate legislation; it passed or rejected measures formulated elsewhere.

All this holds still today. The 1809 constitution has been periodically amended as circumstances changed, but its fundamental principles have remained unquestioned. As the franchise grew and the position of the monarchy declined, a Cabinet system evolved. But there was still nothing in the constitution that compelled the government to have a majority in the Diet. The appointment of the government continued to be a royal prerogative. Ministers were not then, as they still are not, required to sit in the Diet. Until the beginning of this century, the king could and did force governments on the country, against the will of the Diet, and against the verdict of the electorate. Only since 1917 have the principles of a constitutional monarchy been fully accepted, and the government required by custom to enjoy the confidence of the Diet.

In 1865, the Estates were abolished, and a bicameral legislature substituted. In 1970, a unicameral legislature and a new constitution came into force. The changes have been confined to parliamentary and electoral procedure; the new constitution, like the old, maintains the same distribution of powers within the State and the spirit of 1809 still reigns unchallenged. The Diet remains weak, the executive strong, and the administrative machine preserves the extraordinary power conferred on it in the seventeenth century.

Although the Diet, after the enactment of the 1809 constitution, had begun to grope towards modern parliamentary forms, the power of the bureaucracy continued unabated, spilling over from the administration into politics. Civil servants still dominated the Cabinet. In the 1850s, when loose Diet coalitions of a Liberal and Conservative complexion appeared, the forerunners of genuine parties, they both courted the civil service. A Liberal Minister of Finance, J. A. Gripenstedt, thought it vital for his political survival in 1858 to raise the salaries of the bureaucrats, although he was able to neglect with impunity the interest of everybody else in the country.

The tradition of Gustavus Adolphus and Axel Oxenstierna, codified in the constitutions of 1809 and 1970, has been to entrench the powers of the bureaucracy. The Diet has neither a say in the running of the civil service, nor the ability to influence the administrative process. Cabinet ministers and senior bureaucrats are privileged to rule by administrative orders, which the Diet is prohibited from debating and over which it has no say. Most of the rules and regulations that have governed Sweden have been beyond parliamentary control, and the power of the bureaucracy has been extended by a pervasive system of *droit administratif*.

To the Swede, the Diet is not the fount of power. It is wrong to talk about disillusionment with parliamentary government, because he has never held any illusions. Unlike the Englishman, he has never (except in the Age of Freedom) believed that the legislative assembly actually rules, since he has long accepted that its proper function is to register the decisions of the executive. Political controversy does not lie in the nature of the Swede. His interest is in good administration alone. He understands that the one excludes the other, and when, therefore, his system of government muzzles politicians in favour of bureaucrats, it is only in recognition of popular tastes.

This promotes central planning and the efficient direction of the State. Politics are an impediment to the planner; it is far easier to deal with people interested only in smooth functioning and good organization. The Swede fulfils this specification. He is an apolitical animal. He wants his rulers to administer without political interference. It is in answer to that desire that he has been given a strong administrative machine, with the Diet kept at arm's length.

A Cabinet minister has the function of giving force to

Cabinet policy. But he may only issue general directives, and their execution is delegated to autonomous public service directorates. These directorates are not only free of parliamentary control, but they are independent of ministerial supervision as well. They are required to follow the directives of their ministers, but are allowed great discretion in doing so. Not the minister, but the director general, as the head of a directorate is titled, is the ultimate authority in administering the country's affairs. It is the directors general who are the everyday rulers of Sweden.

A director general is selected by the Cabinet and, even if his is a civil service position, there is nothing to stop it being a political appointment. Since the 1940s, most of them have been Social Democrats. The Diet has no say whatsoever in selecting a director general: it is exclusively the concern of the government and that means, ultimately, the party caucus. This makes for great efficiency in the translation of policy into action, because it links the civil service to the party apparatus. If political power changed periodically, a balance of injustice would be ensured but, holding office for four decades continuously, the Social Democrats have acquired a thorough and permanent grip on the bureaucracy. This has been of great value in those fields where society is moulded, and for that reason the directorates of housing, town planning, social affairs, of the labour market and, above all, of education, have become the preserves of the governing party.

The directorates establish their own budgets independently, their sole limitation being the amount of money granted by the Ministry of Finance. Only their total spending is subject to control; the apportioning of funds is their concern alone, not even their own Cabinet minister having any say in the matter. This formidable economic independence gives them considerable influence in the process of government. At the same time, the directorates are used by the Cabinet as expert advisers, and in this way they have become creators of policy. Since the party has taken over the directorates, this means that it rules much of the national life without parliamentary control. As the bureaucrats have become more deeply involved in both the execution and formation of policy, not only the Diet, but even the government seems to have taken a back seat.

The bureaucratic machine lies outside the purlieus of the judiciary, pronouncing judgement on its own actions by a system of administrative law. Many issues concerning the liberty of the citizen are the prerogative of the civil service. Exempt from parliamentary supervision, and immune from due process of law, the Swedish administrative machinery has been protected from the most prolific sources of delay, to become a most effective instrument of technocratic rule.

Planning in its widest sense is the kernel of economic progress, and in this field the Swedish system gives tremendous power to the expert. Town planning, for example, is the monopoly of local government, and the concern of a municipal bureaucracy. Expropriation, keystone of public control of land, is a simple administrative process, outside the jurisdiction of courts of law. An expropriation order may not be contested; once it is signed, it is final. Only the amount of compensation may be questioned, and decision is in the hands of the administrative courts.

The proper use of human resources demands a mechanism of control to regulate the supply of work and workers according to the oscillation of depression and boom. This is in the hands of a body called the Labour Market Directorate. It creates public employment, such as road construction, and all private building requires its endorsement. A clear distinction is drawn between planning approval, which ensures that all construction conforms to official rules, and permission to start building, which depends on the economic situation. The one is the concern of the planning authorities, the other of the Labour Market Directorate, which bases its decisions exclusively on the supply of labour and the state of the economy.

Since the Diet cannot influence, or debate, the activities of the Labour Market Directorate, and since its director general has for long been a Social Democrat, its activities can be steered according to party policy. The advantages are manifold. Industry may be directed to chosen parts of the country by economic and political specialists working without extraneous interference. Building may be retarded or accelerated, and employment created or pared, according to whether the economy needs heating or cooling. If inflation or deflation are not exactly at the beck and call of a civil servant, at least he has the ability to encourage either at the stroke of a pen. A reversal of economic policy which, in England or America, would be the subject of parliamentary debate, and stand in danger of parliamentary sanctions, is simply a matter of administrative order in Sweden.

The Swedish planners have been fortunate in their industrialists. In England and America, economic direction has been delayed, and sometimes frustrated, by the liberalism that gave political expression to the personal independence demanded by the capitalist ethos. Where control has been tentatively enforced, it has not infrequently been undermined by private sabotage without compunction. In the 1960s, for instance, the Labour government in England saw its financial restrictions undermined by private manipulation of a sophisticated credit system. A bank manager could then say to a customer that 'our aim is to protect our customers from the authorities', and remain honourable and honoured. None of this holds in Sweden. It is not only that the government has more power, but that businessmen want to submit.

Capitalism, in the sense of free enterprise and competition, has never existed in Sweden. The nineteenth-century entrepreneurs who built up Swedish industry believed in State help and control, a belated form of mercantilism. The firms that then grew up were, in all but name, monopolies. The Swedish economy has in consequence preserved a quasi-monopolistic nature. It has led to a degree of concentration which in the West is probably only equalled by Belgium.

Four or five families dominate Swedish economic life. Shipping, for example, is chiefly in the hands of the Broströms of Gothenburg; the Johnsons of Stockholm conduct nearly all the engineering trade with the Soviet Union. But the most celebrated of these merchant clans is the Wallenbergs, whose interests are spread over the whole of Swedish industry and who dominate banking and finance.

Under these circumstances, it might be imagined that the Swedish capitalists would profit by their strength to fight the government. In fact, this has never happened, because they have always by tradition identified themselves with the State, even after the accession of the Social Democrats and the ultimate threat they posed to the independence of the businessmen.

If the Swedish Central Bank exercises a unique and absolute control over financial affairs, it is not entirely due to its very extensive powers, which, in effect, make private banks its branches. It is also a consequence of the quasi-civil servant attitude of bankers.

'I admire the independence of English bankers,' said Mr Tore Browaldh, sometime managing director of Svenska Handelsbanken, one of the three major Swedish banks, 'but it could never happen here. Swedes *like* State control. It would never occur to a Swedish banker to help a customer against the State; his instincts are the other way: to carry out the orders of the Central Bank. He identifies himself with the State. I suppose it's a result of the Corporate State. I would say there are no conflicts of loyalty; between the State and the customer, the State always wins. Even if we know we're cutting our own throats.'

This interplay of bureaucratic control, acquiescence and

private identification with the State, smooths official control in most fields. Much of the development of Swedish society, for example, lies with the Directorate of Social Affairs which deals with social welfare, medicine and health services, housing and, to a certain extent, education as well. For some years, the director general was Professor Bror Rexed, who also happens to be one of the Social Democrats' leading ideologists. He frequently announced future policy, before his own minister had spoken, and before the party had officially made its decision. But, speaking as a senior bureaucrat, his words were accepted as a rescript which, in due course, would be formally endorsed. To take two important examples, he it was who announced in 1970 that the transplantation of organs was to be reviewed, and the law modified, and that, until the results of further research were available, the fluoridization of drinking water was to be suspended. Both were questions of public interest but, because he dealt with them, they were removed from political controversy. By the time the Diet was allowed to discuss these issues, what might have been a matter of parliamentary debate turned into the consideration of received truth. It is in this manner that controversial subjects are removed from politics.

The Directorate of Social Affairs enjoys untrammelled power in the custody of children. An administrative order issued by a party official is sufficient to take any child away from its parents and have it brought up by any person (or institution) and in any way seen fit. This is no modern contrivance; it is an old arrangement brought up to date.* In the last century, it was not infrequently used to ensure that the

---

* Illegitimate children are automatically wards of child welfare boards, the local agents of the Directorate of Social Affairs. They have to be brought to child care centres regularly for inspection, and their mothers are legally compelled to undergo any cross-examination which the officials see fit to carry out to retain custody. Unmarried mothers are particularly exposed to the removal of their children.

children of religious dissidents were brought up in the State Church. Courts of law have no say in the matter, and there is no way that a parent can oppose an order depriving him of custody of his own child. The only redress is after the fact, and concerns the way in which the order is carried out. For example, if the police use excessive violence in removing the child, a complaint may be lodged, but only to an administrative committee. At no point is it possible to invoke the due process of law, and parents may not be present at the civil service boards which discuss the removal of children from their homes. In the last resort the Ombudsman may be approached, but he has no power to rescind a decision on custody; he can only reprimand an official for not acting with proper decorum.

Custody of children, then, is in the hands of bureaucrats. Child welfare officials may enter any home to investigate family conditions. They have power to order the police to force an entry and remove children without recourse to the judiciary. This is a daily occurrence, and it is only mentioned in the press if something unduly dramatic occurs. For example, in Gothenburg in 1970, six policemen entered a flat to remove a teenage girl from her father because she had repeatedly run away from foster parents to whom she had been committed, since she preferred to live at home, and she refused to leave of her own free will. Her father also wanted her to stay. In local eyes, the sensational part was that half a dozen constables had been considered necessary to remove a child, where two ought to have been enough.

Child welfare authorities are in contact with every citizen at one time or another. By law, every birth must be reported to the local child welfare centre. A representative will then visit the home to assess conditions and report findings to the doctors at the centre. It is unwise to resist entry, because that will arouse suspicions of maltreatment, with consequent danger of official action. Moreover, there is a legal compulsion on the citizen to report all suspicions of maltreatment to the child welfare centres. Anonymity is guaranteed, so that the suspected parent, like the victim of the Spanish Inquisition, need never know who his accuser is.

The danger of arbitrary action is obvious and, indeed, perfectly reasonable parents, mainly in the countryside, walk in constant fear of having their children taken away if their methods do not conform absolutely to the accepted ideas of the day. This is at least partly due to the popular acceptance of the child welfare board, the local body administering the field, as one of the authorities that direct everyday life. The board is one of the citizen's overseers, rather than his helper. In 1968, 21,000 children were removed from their parents' custody. This is about 1 per 350 inhabitants. Sometimes children must be removed for their own good, usually from the violence and neglect of alcoholic parents. But not infrequently action is taken because children may be a little scruffier, or parents somewhat more happy-go-lucky than is considered acceptable. The important point is that parents *fear* arbitrary action. A hard-working, respectable divorcée in a country town, for example, was reluctant to travel away from home, although her eldest daughter was eighteen and capable of caring for the younger children, because she feared that the child welfare authorities would use her absence as a pretext to break up the family. She felt defenceless. The point is not so much that her fear was justified but that it exists. An official of the Ministry of Justice admits in confidence that there are grounds for such fears, and that child welfare boards do act arbitrarily.

The intention of the Swedish child welfare arrangements is to protect children from maltreatment. But the form which they take is obviously a gross violation of the integrity of the citizen. Yet native disapproval of this state of affairs is rare in the extreme. I once asked a man, a schoolteacher, university graduate and supporter of the Liberal party, whether he was not worried at what could be construed as a breach of the rule of law. After all, his rights as a father were at the mercy of bureaucrats. His answer was this: 'I don't see that there is anything to worry about. A civil servant is to be trusted more than a judge, because he is an expert in the matter, while the judge is not. And anyway, I've got more important things to worry about than theoretical matters like these; I've got two children, and I've got to see that they have a decent standard of living.'

Such is the control, and such the public mentality, enjoyed by the Swedish planners. The rulers of the Soviet Union, although favoured by despotic power, are not so fortunate. Obstructively resentful of officialdom, the Russian, in the words of the Spanish saying, has always known how orders are 'to be obeyed but not carried out'. To the Swede, that sort of compromise is downright immoral. His elected leaders have received those political blessings denied the autocrats in the Kremlin: compliant citizens and an unopposed bureaucracy.

5. The Corporate State

The Swede considers the Diet as the least of the five components that make up his State. Of the others, government, bureaucracy and the party in office are familiar in Western countries, but the fifth is peculiar to Sweden. It is a branch of public life known as the popular organizations.

The popular organizations are mass movements, representing interest groups, that dominate national life. Far more than pressure groups lobbying clandestinely in parliamentary corridors (although that is part of their work), they are corporative bodies, like medieval guilds, with a quasi-legal status, and a prescriptive right to speak for their segment of the population. They influence the process of government directly, by-passing the Diet. They are agents of authority. They deputise for the State in whole sectors of public life, and they have had duties delegated to them that properly belong to the civil service.

In the hierarchical structure of Swedish society, the popular organizations occupy an intermediate level, like a bulkhead between the rulers and their subordinates, dividing among themselves the conduct of affairs in most spheres of everyday activity. The country is adapted to dealing, not with the individual, but with corporate bodies and the citizen is therefore expected to belong to some organization catering to his occupation and interests. 'The broad masses,' to quote a Swedish poet, 'live in the depths of the popular movements.' Like Fascist Italy, Sweden is today a corporate State.

But the Swedish version of the corporate State is far more

complete than the Italian one. Corporatism sat uneasily on the Italians, with their individualistic tradition, and it only affected the country superficially; in Sweden, it has permeated all corners of national life. The difference is that, whereas in Italy corporatism was an alien contrivance imposed by a ruling clique, in Sweden it is the natural inheritance of every-man. No revolution or *coup d'état* was necessary; it grew up with modern Sweden and, to the present-day Swede, appears perfectly natural and desirable.

Its roots lie in the agricultural system. Until well into the nineteenth century, the Swedish peasant had preserved the archaic system of strip farming. Although nominally his own landlord, he was not his own master. His holdings were not continuous, but distributed over a maze of disconnected patches so narrow that it was impossible to cultivate them separately, and the land of each village was therefore worked collectively as one large farm. The villagers worked together in gangs, with precise regulations governing their actions. Economically, each village was considered as a unit, and book-keeping and sales were handled communally. It was collective farming, centuries before the Bolsheviks imposed it in Russia. The only difference was that, rather than having managers imposed by a despotic central power, the ancient Swedish collectives were ruled by elected village councils. But once in office, councillors exercised dictatorial powers, to which the villagers submitted abjectly.

The old Swedish farming system required absolute sub-mission to the demands of the collective. Its origins lay in an idea of levelling individual differences. By dividing the holdings, no man could monopolize the best or suffer the worst land, but all would share burdens and favours equally. Not only farm work was regulated, but private lives too. Church attendance, morality and everyday behaviour were supervised by the village council, with punishment of whip-ping, fine and imprisonment meted out for transgression. The individual was required to behave as the community demanded, and no personal deviation was permitted. More than a thousand years of such conditioning produced a collective mentality and a view of personal identity exclusively in terms of membership of a group. Individuality could not develop in this environment, and conformity was the highest of virtues.

The collective village system was compulsory, except in parts of northern Sweden. Those were frontierlands, where the colonization of virgin soil was not finished until the beginning of this century, and where a sparse population and the requirements of a pioneer life made the system useless. But, over most of the country, and among most of the peasantry, collective farming ruled. In 1827, the Diet abolished strip farming and redistributed land to form the consolidated holdings of modern agriculture. The peasants were given six years to demolish their old homes in the village and move out to their new, enclosed farms. Thus the ancient villages were destroyed, the face of the countryside altered and collective farming eradicated at the stroke of a pen.

The reform turned the life of a whole nation upside down. Yet there was no resistance to it: Sweden is one of the few countries in which agrarian reform has not caused unrest. The peasants meekly razed their homes, and built new ones, more or less within the prescribed time limits. Although they disliked the change, the population submitted without protest to the dictates of authority, because that is what they were used to. The government had demonstrated that reform, however profound, could be imposed without trouble.

The scattering of the villages and the disruption of a traditional pattern of life caused great hardship. Before, the peasants had huddled together in companionable villages at the centre of their fields; now they were separated from each other in lonely farmhouses. The scattering of their homes destroyed the contact and community that were part of the old villages, and that had become necessary for their well-being. But the change was forced through by the Liberal faction in the Estates, because, as one of their number expressed it: 'The old system encouraged a conservative point of view.' It was an early example of the acknowledged use of environment to influence attitudes.

Although the old village collectives had been destroyed, their mentality persisted. Deprived now of full use in everyday life, it sought other outlets instead, and out of this need was born the popular organizations. Unknown in Sweden before, they were called into existence by the changes in the countryside.

When the villages were destroyed, the inhabitants were driven to seek some method of preserving the contact they had known before. At first, they gathered for no other purpose than the prolongation of camaraderie. But it was not enough; some other spur was necessary for the emergent movement. An ideological push was needed: it had to be imported from the cities. Various men came preaching causes, to gather cohorts of adherents, not because they necessarily had something compelling to say, but because they acted as focal points around which to rally. Associations thus formed, which rapidly grew into national organizations. Their professed aims were irrelevant; their original function was to provide a substitute for the village community and to satisfy cravings for belonging to a group.

Temperance societies were the first to appear. Drinking is a historical Swedish obsession, and it is perhaps only to be expected that, in a country with a puritan background, organization would begin over a national vice. Temperance organizations advanced as the old village disappeared from the face of the countryside and, by the middle of the nineteenth century, when enclosure was completed, they had 100,000 members in a total population of 3,800,000.

For some time, the temperance movement was alone in

providing the solace of the group. Driven by a compulsive longing for the collective, many Swedes took the pledge, while drinking clandestinely, in order to gain admission. After 1850, the revivalist movement, offering social activities in addition to purely religious meetings, displaced temperance as the main outlet for a collective mentality that continued with undiminished vigour. A revivalist fervour swept the country during the latter half of the nineteenth century, the belated arrival of the devotional content of the Reformation. After 1860, the introduction of freedom of worship released pent-up religious feelings, and there was an explosion of free churches. But by the end of the century, religious enthusiasm was spent, and the temperance societies regained their supremacy. In 1900, the temperance movement claimed a third of the Diet members of all political parties, imposing restrictive drinking laws. The temperance movement had developed into a popular organization of the modern Swedish type; it not only satisfied a group mentality, but exerted political power as well.

Preserved in all their medieval force by the temperance movement, the corporate attitudes of the old Swedish peasant communities were handed down to modern Sweden. As if dropping into an instinctive pattern of behaviour, the Swedes distributed themselves naturally among the organizations that proliferated with the development of the country. The corporative sense was not confined to the peasants. The upper classes were also arranged in a corporate form. While the Estates still existed, they took the form of medieval corporations. The bureaucracy has never ceased to act as one. A collective mentality dominated the rulers as much as the ruled. Neither tolerated deviation within their own ranks, and one of the most obvious characteristics of Swedish life has been an unrelieved and willing conformity. When, towards the end of the nineteenth century, the trade unions arose, their work had in a sense been done for them. They did not, as elsewhere, have to preach solidarity and the advantages of collective organization, because they were dealing with people who had inherited a taste for both. Acquiring members was easy since, like the temperance societies, the unions satisfied powerful group instincts.

If a powerful sense of the collective accompanied the old agricultural system, it was also fostered by the *bruk* form of industrial settlement. Isolated and self-contained, the *bruk*, like the old agricultural village, had a vigorous organization that welded the inhabitants together.

The form of habitation encouraged a sense of community. Houses were huddled wall to wall along a single street. Privacy was not respected and anybody was permitted to enter a home unasked. Until the middle of the nineteenth century, a *bruk* contained on average about 300 inhabitants. Within the confines of so small a number, it was impossible to escape public scrutiny, and the usual pressures of Swedish society were magnified, so that conformity seemed like a law of nature. The *bruk* did not, like the old agricultural village, have the law behind it in imposing conformity but, in the power of consensus, it possessed compulsion enough. Demanding a highly developed sense of the collective, the work of the *bruk* generated a pattern of living that left no place for the individual. Out of this developed a profound sense of corporate identity.

There was an illustration of the power of this environment in northern Sweden during the 1960s. Workmen refused to move away from a small sawmill *bruk* that had closed down, although offered excellent positions elsewhere. The security of the *bruk* collective meant so much to them that, rather than lose it, they preferred to stay and scratch a living or exist on social welfare. They were explicit in their dependence on the sense of community for peace of mind.

The collective mentality of the *bruks* and the old agricultural communities was transferred to the cities as urbanization progressed and a new style of living supplanted the old. Swedes required no inducements to join a corporative organization, because they had a natural urge to do so. Opinions in Sweden are allowed no validity if maintained by an individual as his own, but, if they are to be accepted, they must be professed as the representative view of a group. It is as if the individual is allowed no right to exist outside a collective body. 'How can you have an opinion of your own?' asks a Social Democratic intellectual. 'It doesn't make sense. You've got to get your ideas from a group.'*

Out of this soil, Saltsjöbaden grew spontaneously. It required no ideological motivation, or political argumentation, but fulfilled a natural requirement. The most obvious effect of the Saltsjöbaden agreement was the entrenchment of industrial peace, but its most profound consequence was the establishment of the corporate State. And in this lies the key to the facility with which the expert, the organization man and the political manager were able to assume power. Saltsjöbaden was only a stage – albeit a critical one – in a line of development that had been in the air for at least a decade. Nor was this atmosphere confined to the Social Democrats; they were merely the exponents of the idea who happened to hold office as it was materializing.

Between the industrial legislation of 1928 and the Saltsjöbaden agreement in 1938 some employers, frightened by the advancing power of the trade unions, turned to thoughts of legal restraint. In 1934, they persuaded the Conservative party to bring before the Diet a proposal for legislation guaranteeing the right to work without belonging to a trade union, and making any form of coercion a criminal offence. The unions and the Social Democrats naturally expressed hearty disapproval. But, apart from the predictable cries from industry, there were reservations of a deeper nature. A number of Conservative politicians had seen with misgivings the rise

* No irony intended.

of the trade unions as a powerful monolithic and independent corporation. They feared that a pact between capital and labour might lead to a situation in which the individual citizen was ignored, and the direction of his working life placed exclusively in the hands of collective organizations. Admittedly only a small minority of the educated classes reasoned this way; those who had been influenced by liberal ideas from the West. But, through their position in the non-Socialist parties, they carried political weight, and allied themselves with the representatives of industry. In a short while, however, most of these altered their viewpoint, to support the Social Democrats on the issue. The reasoning behind that change is well illustrated by an incident in the Diet.

When, in 1934, the legislation guaranteeing the right to work without trade-union membership was first debated in the Diet, a Professor Westman, of the Agrarian party, gave his approval, but the following year decided to oppose it. Originally, he felt that the rule of law required protection for the individual. 'But what, after all, is the rule of law?' he said in a speech to the Diet explaining his change of mind. 'Many of us, perhaps all, have carried over, without any modification, opinions from the old liberal, individualistic time, into the new era of collectivism and organization to which Progress has carried us.'

The professor had correctly interpreted the direction that Swedish society was taking, and it is hard to doubt that his change of attitude was a sound reflection of the views of most of his countrymen. Saltsjöbaden was to take Sweden into 'the new era of collectivism and organization'. Although the government kept out of the Saltsjöbaden talks, its presence hovered, unseen, but everlastingly felt, in the conference rooms. It secured, by the agreement, a tacitly prescribed say in the wage-bargaining mechanism that had been established.

Saltsjöbaden was ostensibly an armistice between labour and capital; in reality, it was a concordat defining the powers and jurisdiction of the employers, the trade unions and the State. The written clauses committed the signatories to the maintenance of industrial peace: the unwritten ones laid down the principle that, in return for freedom from State interference in the conduct of their affairs, both sides of industry would enforce the economic policy of the government. Apart from the obvious desirability of avoiding strikes, industrial relations are of principal concern in their effect on wages. Wages* run wild bring the threat of inflation; conversely, to hold them under control, if it does not necessarily mean to be in control of the national economy, at least means that a frightening source of economic danger has been tamed. It is this that the Swedish government needed for the execution of its policies, and Saltsjöbaden gave it to them.

The government required the power of establishing the total cost of industrial wages; the unions and the employers promised to supply it. From the start, the Saltsjöbaden partners loyally observed their side of the understanding. Before each round of central bargaining, the government specifies the greatest tolerable increase in the national wage bill, and it is within the limits thus laid out that negotiations then proceed. Beyond that, there is no overt State intrusion. The LO and the employers' confederation are left alone to settle the details of the industrial wage structure as a private matter. The effect of this was that the government had delegated control of a vital sector of national life to a pair of non-

---

* In 1938, the average monthly salary of Swedish office workers was 290 kronor (£15.40 or $70 at current rates of exchange; 1,080 kronor or £87 or $200 in terms of buying power in 1970). The comparable salary in 1970 was 1,900 kronor (£154 or $380). In 1970, the average weekly pay of a Swedish factory worker was 414 kronor (£34 or $80). The comparable figure for the United States was $143 (£59); for Great Britain, £27.50 ($66). Since 1965, Swedish industrial wages have risen by about seven per cent annually.

official bodies. The advantages were manifold. In matters touching the Labour Market, the government now had to deal with only two monolithic organizations. All contacts were centralized, and spheres of influence defined.

Through the Saltsjöbaden agreement, unions and employers had, in effect, coalesced into a single corporate structure in order to regulate the Labour Market. This was precisely what Mussolini had attempted to impose on Italy at about the same time. But *his* compatriots had shown little enthusiasm for the idea, the employers being singularly cool, and he failed in this, as in many other of his intentions. The Swedes had voluntarily accomplished what the Italian dictator had been unable to enforce.

In a corporate State, non-official organizations carry out official duties. The Swedish trade unions provide a good example, unemployment insurance being entirely in their hands. They collect premiums, make payments and administer the necessary public funds. The local trade-union branches serve as unemployment insurance offices and, in the exercise of this particular function, they do not require membership as a condition of service. They are, in fact, specifically prevented from doing so because, in this instance, they are acting as a government agency. This practice is justified by the State on the grounds that a local union official knows the population better than any civil servant could. Most likely, he will be personally acquainted with applicants for unemployment benefits. He will also know exactly what work is to be found and where, and he can detect malingering far more readily. In a word, it is more efficient.*

---

* In spite of the paper work, the unions display considerable anxiety to keep unemployment insurance in their hands. In the words of an LO official: 'The administration of unemployment insurance is psychologically good for us. We get a lot of prestige, and our members see an added concrete and good cause for their unions' continued existence.'

At intervals varying from one to three years, the LO and the Employers' Confederation negotiate a new central wage agreement. The government conveys its wishes, partly in public statements, and partly in private contacts. It is a mistake, however, to suppose that this is a ukase from above, to be obeyed blindly, if resentfully. It is the nature of corporatism that each constituent organization, or at least its officials, consider themselves a branch of the State, so that no fundamental antagonism exists between the two. In the particular case of wage bargaining, the unions, the government and employers, whatever their ostensible sectarian interests, share an earnest desire to ensure the success of the national economy. Each of the three possesses its own body of formidable economic expertise, more than capable of calculating the rise in wages that the country can afford. By a process of continuous consultation (in which, to ensure the best possible advice, the private banks are included) a suitable figure is hammered out in advance and, when the government presents its specification, it is in fact not conveying a Cabinet decision, but speaking for the consensus between itself, industry and the unions.

Neither the employers nor the government have any difficulty in accepting the limitation of wages. The system stands or falls by the ability of the unions to resolve the dichotomy of representing their members at the same time as guarding the interests of the State. They have to uphold industrial peace while enforcing wage restraint. Much has been achieved by the group mentality of the Swedes, aided by continuous instruction which has drilled into the average workman the notion of renouncing some personal benefit in the collective interest. Nevertheless, there is a considerable residue of working-class feeling which, if it is not to turn into rank insubordination, must be conciliated by a show of fighting the bosses.

In order to do this, the employers, by tacit agreement,

act the whipping boy. Central wage bargaining has taken on the form of a charade in which the LO pretends to be a militant defender of the working man's rights, attacking the niggardly offers of the employers. To judge by their public statements, the LO and employers' representatives are at daggers drawn. In fact, behind the scenes, they are on the most amiable of terms. At the top, to take one example, Mr Arne Geijer, the secretary-general of the LO and Mr Kurt-Steffan Giesecke, managing director of the Employers' Confederation, got on very well with each other, regularly meeting out of the public eye. Such contacts are pursued at various levels and in the intervals between the formal negotiations both sides exchange views quietly, rather as the *condottiere* of the Italian Renaissance were supposed to do in order to arrange convincing, but not too bloodthirsty battles.

Each side will often try to help the other out of difficulties. For example, in 1969, a high official of the Employers' Confederation was told by a LO acquaintance that a certain firm was paying its employees more than the central agreement prescribed. This is quite as serious a breach of contract as cutting wages, and the LO man was concerned because of the threat it posed to the structure of the Labour Market. In the first place, it implied that the company had tried to improve production and attract labour by using wages as a bait. Under the Swedish system, that is heresy, because it means introducing competition, which is inconsistent with order. It also weakens the power of the central authority by allowing freedom of action at the periphery. The theory of central wage bargaining is that the principals establish norms for the whole country, and regulate any local variation. There must be uniformity and monolithic control, since bidding for labour, the natural consequence of full employment, introduces elements of disorder.

The LO man was further perturbed because the incident demonstrated a lamentable initiative on the part of a local union branch, which meant a challenge to the prerogatives of his own central organization. Thus it was that he appealed for help to his ostensible enemy on the employers' side of the fence. To reprimand a union for obtaining higher wages was clearly impolitic, whereas it was perfectly conceivable to reproach an industrialist for paying too much. The man from the Employers' Confederation agreed with the LO point of view, and promised to bring the errant company to heel – with little success as it transpired.

In very private moments, men of the LO and the Employers' Confederation will admit that they like and understand each other, and that it is something of a strain to have to go through a ritual quarrel demanded by political rules. Sometimes the mask slips. In 1971, the placidity of the Swedish Labour Market was seriously disturbed by a strike of civil servants. They belonged to a splinter group beyond the power of the LO, and the government countered with a harshness unknown since the beginning of the century. The purpose was to crush the mavericks and re-establish the monopoly of the LO, a goal much desired by both the LO and the private employers. Nevertheless, the appearance of conflict horrified them and, although engaged at the time in a particularly stiff round of public negotiations, the LO and Employers' Confederation rapidly dropped their mask of belligerency to treat each other with unwonted public courtesy.

But under normal conditions, the same bellicose ritual is re-enacted. There are interminable and acrimonious negotiations, during which open rupture is threatened, only to be averted at the last moment by what appears to be the retreat of the capitalists. The unions can then show that they have forced the employers to increase their original wage offer. But since that offer was adjusted in order to make the final compromise what the Minister of Finance would like, the necessary display of aggressive bargaining can be mounted without damage to the economic situation of the day. The consequence of this is that the man on the factory floor will accept as a righteous triumph the kind of wage increase which, if it were communicated as a simple decision by his employer, would raise his spleen and drive him to strike.

It may be objected that a device of this nature is bound to be seen through. A few leaders of society do understand the situation, but the man in the street does not. There are a number of reasons for this. In the first place, the average trade unionist has long been indoctrinated by the Labour move-ment, so that he believes, more or less, in the authenticity of militancy in the central wage bargaining. The mass media also keep up the pretence, because the Labour Market is tabu. An exposure would never be tolerated, because the communicators, by instinct and conditioning, protect the institutions of the State. There is also the propensity of the Swede to take appearance for reality. As long as he has the correct scenery and sound effects, he is perfectly happy. And yet there may be limits to his credulity. An outbreak of wild-cat stoppages in 1969–70, culminating in a miners' strike in northern Sweden, had its roots in alienation from the official trade-union leadership, and an inchoate suspicion that the LO was in league with the government and the employers.

At first sight, the Swedish Labour Market appears to be a conspiracy. And, to a great degree, that is undoubtedly true. It is not so much that the conduct of wage negotiations and the imposition of suitable restraint are hatched by a few men in smoke-filled rooms, but that the rules of self-preservation demand mutual consideration of each other's interests. The government needs a healthy economy to remain in office; the trade unions need it to keep a hold on their members, and the employers need it for profits and the avoidance of State interference. It has been government policy that, as long as industry works efficiently and plays the game in

maintaining peace with labour, private ownership will not
be threatened by nationalization.

Yet the nature of the corporate State may impose public
control in another way. Industrial democracy is a trade-
union demand and government policy. This means that the
employees in each major enterprise are to be represented in
the boardroom. For decades, works councils have existed
in which the men have been able to make their voice heard,
but these organizations have by definition been consultative
and restricted to the discussion of working conditions. But
now the trade unions and the government want the workers
to have a say in the running of the firms by which they
are employed. Each company board is to have a director,
elected by the staff. However, the trade unions have no intention of permitting indiscriminate elevation from the shop
floor. They insist that the workers' representatives must be
trade-union officials and, in the case of large plants and major
industries, LO appointments. The LO says in private that
independent representatives would not be tolerated because
they would threaten the domination of the trade-union
movement, although the reason openly advanced is that the
complexity of modern industry requires specialized economic
and technical knowledge that the man on the factory floor is
unlikely to possess. The trade unions consider industrial
democracy as a means of extending the power of their
organizations into the management of industry, which means
the invasion of one corporate power by another. In this way,
the government will have secured the penetration of industry
by a branch of the State more sympathetic to itself, thereby
expanding its influence.

The corporations which, in the manner of the LO and the
Employers' Confederation, serve as the vicars of the State, are
described in Swedish political terminology as central organizations. They are monolithic institutions, administering zones
of national life. Their strength is that they have not been

imposed by political theorists, but have grown naturally out of the collective instincts of Swedish society. Mostly, they are extensions of the popular organizations. Sometimes, as with the Employers' Confederation and certain professional organizations, they can trace their lineage from the medieval guilds which were only abolished in Sweden in 1846. They have been formed by the linkage of tributary bodies under a central management which, far from being contrived, emerged spontaneously in a natural process of topping off an hierarchical structure.

Finding it more convenient to deal with collective bodies than with individuals, the State has parcelled out society among the central organizations. Through them, it upholds contact with the citizen in many spheres. These organizations are so pervasive that the Swede today finds himself most often dealing with the authorities, not directly, but through the agency of some corporate institution.

There is scarcely a field of life in Sweden today which is not the concern of a central organization. Nobody disputes the desirability of the system on principle: the main concern is to avoid clashes of jurisdiction. Overlapping, attended by demarcation squabbles, is abhorred as the essence of inefficiency.

For this reason, the L O has declined responsibility for the white collar workers. Instead, their unions have been gathered into a separate central organization, called the *Tjänstemännens Centralorganisation* – T C O. English experience has taught the Swedes that it is impossible to represent both white collar and manual workers without a conflict that weakens the body trying to do so. The interests of the two groups are so different that they are best served by each having its own representation.

University graduates, exporters, motorists and lawyers are some examples of categories each possessing its own central organization, and therefore a private and direct channel to the rulers of the State. Besides nursing the interests of its members, a central organization secures a quasi-legal status for them without which they do not officially exist.

Without written laws, this guild structure is rigidly maintained by silent understanding. A certain lawyer, employed by the public prosecutor's office in Stockholm, discovered that he was legally entitled to promotion, privileges and a rise in salary. Despite continuous requests for what was his due, he obtained no satisfaction. Eventually, a senior official hinted that he ought to act through his central organization. Despite the absence of a closed shop, or rules on the subject, he did so. Within a week he obtained by proxy what he had failed to secure directly in a year, with retroactive effect from the time of his first application, into the bargain. The lesson driven home was that everything, even that which was of right and a matter of course, had to go through the central organization; that the administration upheld the corporate State.

A persuasive argument for inclusion in a central organization is that, in practice, it is usually the only means of influencing the government. Under the Swedish constitution there is a system of consultation by which government measures must be submitted to public comment before being presented to the Diet. Theoretically, the private citizen has the right to give his opinion; in practice, however, only the central organizations, or subsidiary corporative bodies with relevant expertise, are heeded. Not all organizations are admitted to the process: those that are, acquire the official status of 'consultative bodies'. Strictly speaking, they are only supposed to be involved in measures affecting the working conditions of their members but, in practice, this limitation is meaningless, since virtually all legislation may be so construed. Their comments have the same force as those of the Diet; usually rather more, because they represent expert knowledge, where the Diet only offers political clichés. It is usually easier to achieve an amendment to a new law via a consultative body than through the Diet. The effect is to withdraw most of the important issues from politics, and, elevating the corporate organizations to legislative level, to reduce the Diet to the state of a ratifying assembly.

In Western countries, the normal concept of democracy is that the will of the people is exercised exclusively by an elected parliament, acting through the executive. In Sweden, on the other hand, when politicians talk about democracy they are thinking about the corporate organizations as much as the legislature. This duality is in fact often plainly stated. 'Our democracy,' to quote the words of Mr Olof Palme, the Social Democratic Prime Minister, 'is a democracy of the popular organizations.'

When Swedes talk of the democracy of the popular organizations, they mean a form of direct democracy. Their theory postulates that, since members of a popular movement and a central organization can make their voices heard through their local branches, they have a means of directly influencing the government. Thus a man theoretically has several channels to the government, according to the number of organizations to which he belongs, of which his vote at Diet elections is only one. Therefore, the Swedes believe they are more democratic than other democratic nations which only have their parliaments. That is the myth by which they live. In fact, the corporate organizations are reflections of the State. As the Diet is circumscribed, and the Executive all-powerful, so in the organizations the administration rules, and the representative assemblies are of little account. As a natural consequence, functionaries of the State and the central organizations work together as a kind of freemasonry in the running of the country.

This is accepted by the Swedes as a fact of life. Here is the way in which a leading official of one of the central organizations confesses it: 'Sweden is ruled by a bureaucratic establishment, using the word "bureaucracy" in the widest sense. This means civil servants on the one hand, and officials of the organizations on the other.'

This may be seen in the way that promotion and transfers occur indiscriminately within this establishment, obliterating the distinction between public service and private employment, as if the central organizations and government departments were coequal branches of the State. Thus, in 1970, Mr Otto Nordenskjöld, the secretary general of the TCO, was appointed director general of the Swedish State Broadcasting system. A predecessor of his in the TCO had been appointed a provincial governor, which is a government post. Then, Mr Lennart Geijer, once legal adviser to the TCO, was appointed Minister of Justice, without entering the Diet. In 1969, Mr Bengt Norlin was moved directly from the LO's secretariat to a seat in the Cabinet as Minister of Transport.

Not only has the dividing line between civil service and central organization vanished, but their combined bureaucratic apparatus has spilled over into the political process to take charge of the business of government. The career of Mr Palme provides a notable illustration. At university he was president of the Swedish National Union of Students, both a central organization and a consultative body. From that post, he was recruited directly into the Prime Minister's Chancery, a branch of the civil service maintaining liaison with the Cabinet. After some years' service, Mr Palme entered the Diet, remaining, however, in the Chancery, a kind of bureaucrat with a parliamentary seat, until entering the Cabinet as Minister without Portfolio.

The bureaucratic establishment and the consultative process has degraded the Diet yet further than the subordinate position alloted by the constitution. Since a central organization may influence the government directly and efficiently, it is unwilling to risk the obfuscating deviations of the political process. If its aims are those of the authorities, the matter is simple; if not, delicate negotiations are necessary in which success depends on circumvention of the Diet. Certain formal procedures have been prescribed in the execution of the consultative process. When a government bill has been drafted, and *before it has been presented to the Diet*, representatives of the consultative organizations are called up to have it read over to them. Alternatively the organizations may take the initiative, a delegation waiting on the minister concerned. 'But this,' in the measured words of one central organization official, 'is sheer propaganda. We tell the newspapers well in advance, so that we can get some publicity. It's only to show our members that we're doing something. Also, it's a way of getting our views on record. In fact, by the time we've come that far up, the matter's already been decided. So we've worked out a system of private contacts. As soon as we hear on the bush telegraph that such and such a piece of legislation is in the air, we start making our suggestions. Sweden's a small country, and the whole bureaucratic establishment's also very small – not more than two or three hundred rule the country, and we all know each other. We've got a contact network behind the scenes, and it's there we really work. You might say that we rule by a kind of licensed intrigue.'

The 'contact network' is discreet, informal but elaborate. It exists at all levels, from village council to Cabinet. But it must not be confused with the surreptitious intercourse to be found elsewhere, in which private citizens attempt to suborn public servants. The foundation of that arrangement is the assumption that State and citizen are opponents. If, in a Western democracy, a businessman enters the government, he must accept estrangement from the business fraternity, because once he has accepted the embrace of the State he becomes suspect, whatever the policies of the regime or the nature of his opinions. That is not the case in Sweden. There, the division lies not between State and people, but between governors and governed in the broadest sense of the word.

There is an hierarchic structure, each step of which is composed of people with equivalent power, with no distinction between officialdom and the rest. Thus, a senior Cabinet minister, an L O leader, and the head of a major bank or the representative of a whole industry feel affinity and find it natural to associate. A little lower, it might be a senior civil servant, a leading official of a big trade union, the managing director of a large company and an official of some popular organization, and so on down the scale. These people feel themselves to be the rulers of the country, and they have evolved the contact network because they consider government by stealth the most efficient way of ruling. Meetings are private, and never reported in the mass media. In many ways, the network is the real, if invisible, government of Sweden.

One of the most important coteries in the contact network is that around the Minister of Finance, Mr Gunnar Sträng, comprising some half a dozen of the country's leading industrialists and financiers. By this device, the government can influence business clandestinely; but the traffic is not one way. A saying has it that 'the second Minister of Finance is Dr Marcus Wallenberg' (referring to a leading banker).

The true political dialogue in Sweden takes place within the contact network, and public oratory, not to mention parliamentary debate, is mostly tactical verbiage. The government always lets business know its true intentions. If, for example, the Social Democrats find it necessary to attack private enterprise in order to placate their left wing, they will warn industry in good time. Thus there arises the odd situation of businessmen looking on without alarm while politicians breathe quasi-Marxist fire. Sometimes, however, the conflict between secret conciliation and open attack may grow too great for comfort. An official of the Employers' Confederation confessed in 1970 that he was worried because, although Mr Krister Wickman, then Minister of Industry, was being extraordinarily polite and encouraging in private, his public statements were becoming more bellicose than seemed absolutely necessary.

The existence of the contact network, combined with a corporate State, gives rise to a secret government which, in turn, leads to some anomalies in public life. One is that men will often refuse government office, because more power is to be found elsewhere. For example, the secretary general of the LO (although not in the Cabinet) is one of the most powerful men in Sweden, yielding only to the Prime Minister or the Minister of Finance, and sometimes overruling even them. Again, this is perfectly understood and willingly accepted by the public. The power of the secretary general derives from the position of the LO as a limb of the State; his influence is exerted through the contact network, which may be defined in another way as an informal and extended council of government.

Then, it not infrequently happens that the man with the power need not necessarily be the man with the highest position, and identifying the real chief in Stockholm may be as difficult as doing so in the Kremlin. It is the position within the 'secret government' that counts. To take one example, the real ruler of Sweden since 1969 has not been Mr Olof Palme, the Prime Minister, but Mr Gunnar Sträng, the Minister of Finance. And indeed, in one or two public speeches, Mr Sträng has openly rebuked Mr Palme, in order to establish the order of precedence. Personal advantages aside, the reason for Mr Sträng's superiority is that he is a trade unionist, that he has the LO behind him, and his position at the apex of the contact network as distinct from the formal government structure is unchallenged.

The business of ruling Sweden, then, is conducted not in parliamentary institutions, but in a kind of secret society.

Diet debates are poor affairs, because the central organizations debar the opposition from the pursuit of contentious issues. This is part of the compact of 'licensed intrigue'. The government agrees to treat directly; in return, the central organizations suppress parliamentary conflict. Organizations find that they can achieve their aims by talking privately to the government, where political debate gets them nowhere. Understandably, they keep matters of substance off the floor of the Diet, for settlement in an extra-parliamentary manner.

Under these circumstances, it might justifiably be asked, what functions remain to the Diet and what remains for the members to talk about? After government and corporate organizations have agreed, the result of their deliberations is presented to the Diet for ratification. Debate is confined to empty oratory about generalities, designed to show the electorate that their representatives do, in fact, work. Whatever the question, the assembly is generally in agreement. Issue is rarely taken over principle, the permitted ration of criticism being concentrated on details, and intended to suggest that the government's opponents, while accepting its aims, could realize them better.

The point about all this is not that it exists, but that it is accepted. *The man in the street knows perfectly well that the country is run in this way, and he is happy to let it continue. He trusts his bureaucrats.*

Threat of political trouble is used by corporate organizations as blackmail recognized in the process of 'licensed intrigue'. If the government proves obdurate in a particular matter, it will be raised in the Diet – but not too harshly. Whereupon, to avoid public controversy the government almost always changes its mind, reopening talks. And, in its turn, the organization stops the debate.

Control of parliamentary activity may be exerted by clandestine, external pressure; more frequently it follows from the composition of the parties. Very few Diet members sit as individuals. Whatever their party, they are usually nominated, and elected, as the representatives of corporate organizations. Among the Social Democrats, it may be the trade unions; in the Centre party, farmers' cooperatives; among the Conservatives, the Employers' Confederation. The central organizations command a good proportion of the representation on both the government and opposition benches and, as explained above, they put organization above constituent. In this way, the Diet is the creature of the corporate State.

To take one example of the workings of the system, the TCO in 1968 found difficulty in persuading the government to yield to certain salary demands made on behalf of civil servants. Through their members in the Liberal party, the TCO raised the issue in the Diet. Once was enough; the government repented, and the TCO called off the debate. The party was not pleased, because it had been presented with a question that embarrassed the government, but the central organization it was that ruled.

In another field, the Conservative party is usually restrained by the Employers' Confederation from attacking government fiscal policy to the full. This is not because the Confederation approves – quite the contrary – but because parliamentary aggression would jeopardize its influence in the bureaucratic establishment. To keep their compact with the government, the central organizations must uphold the principle of rule by consensus.

This follows from the nature, not only of the rulers, but the ruled as well. The Swedes have a horror of controversy as something unpleasant, inefficient and vaguely immoral. They require for peace of mind, not confrontation, but consensus. Consensus guides everything: private conversation, intellectual life and the running of the State. The government, although it wants its way, must avoid a fight if it is not to alienate the electorate. It is in response to a deep popular feeling that matters of substance are removed from the political arena and turned over to the bureaucrats.

The nationalization of the chemists illustrates both this

feeling and the functioning of the corporate State. Although the Social Democrats have rejected the dogma of State ownership for its own sake, nevertheless for political purposes they have, from time to time, been constrained to make excursions into nationalization. For some years at the end of the 1960s the party leaders had been troubled by left-wing agitation for more public ownership, and decided that the retail chemists would be the least troublesome sop to offer.

The Apothecaries' Society, the chemists' central organization, had previously decided that their profession needed to be reorganized. The development of the modern pharmaceutical industry, and the spread of nervous stimulants, required centralization for proper control and it was proposed to incorporate all chemists into a cooperative organization, converting independent owners into branch managers. Since the establishment of pharmacies has always been strictly controlled by a system of State concessions granted through the Apothecaries' Society (another ancient example of corporatism), the Society would have had the legal power to impose its wishes.

It was also clear to the Society that, professional considerations aside, the development of the Swedish Welfare State would force radical changes in the chemists' functions. They would no longer run shops whose exclusive purpose was to sell drugs and make up prescriptions, but would have to supervise auxiliary health centres, at which dispensing would only be a part of their work. Moreover, since the welfare authorities provided most of the chemists' income, the State was the biggest customer and, to achieve parity in negotiation, it was imperative to acquire size: one large company would be better than 400 independent chemists. To simplify organization the Apothecaries' Society had already planned to reduce their number to 250.

This was precisely what the government wanted, and the sole point at issue was whether the future organization was to be owned by the Apothecaries' Society or by the State. At first sight it seems odd that ideas of this nature were so readily accepted by a body which might be supposed to exist for the protection of its members' individual interests. Political influence is out of the question since most chemists, and most of their professional leaders, are anything but Social Democrats. But maintenance of the 'contact network' so mingled the officials of the Apothecaries' Society and the officials of the Directorate of Social Affairs that new concepts arose from their combined ranks as if they were one. It might be said that the reorganization of the pharmaceutical profession was hammered out by an informal commission of bureaucrats, whose salaries were partly paid by private levies, and partly by the taxpayer.

On balance, the Apothecaries' Society would have preferred to retain ownership, and they were supported by the Directorate of Social Affairs. But when it was evident that this was politically impossible, the Society's officials started clandestine negotiations to make the transfer as smooth as possible, and to obtain the best possible terms of compensation.

Now all this may read like underhand intrigue; and so it is up to a point. But, constitutionally, there are vital distinctions. Private discussions on the details of nationalization were in full swing before the Diet had had an opportunity to debate the principle. The negotiations were kept secret in order to remove the matter from politics. The government told the Society of the impending nationalization at least a year in advance, long before presenting it to the Diet.

Let Mr Rune Westerling, the man who negotiated on behalf of the Apothecaries' Society, tell the tale in his own words: 'We had to keep the negotiations confidential, because there was so much at stake. I couldn't have let our 400 members into the secret, because you can't stop them talking, and we'd have been embarrassed by the publicity. You know how it is, when it's a question of money, people tend to complain. However much they might have got in compensation, they'd always want more.

'Besides, it's always better to negotiate behind the scenes, because it ensures a constructive atmosphere. The government always appreciate that, and as we kept our members ignorant of what was going on, the Diet was not allowed to know what was going on either.

'Well, about the middle of June [1969] we got down to the final negotiations. We were talking about money, so I was tough' and about the middle of July we had come to a standstill.

'Now, until then, it had been negotiations between equals. That's to say, myself and a few of the Society's top officials against senior officials of the Directorate of Social Affairs. But when the talks had stopped, two ministers immediately intervened. There was Mr Sven Aspling, Minister of Social Affairs (whom I have cultivated, for obvious reasons), and Mr Krister Wickman, Minister of Industry. They rang me, and said they wanted no difficulties, with the risk of controversy leaking out to the press. They also rang the government negotiators, and told them to give us what we wanted. We got it too, and in a few days the agreement was ready; about as fast as it took to get the documents properly drafted and signed.'

That was at the beginning of August. A month or so later, the nationalization of the chemists was announced by the government; not as a measure to be debated, but as a *fait accompli* for the Diet to ratify.

'I certainly see nothing wrong in it – under Swedish conditions,' to return to Mr Westerling. 'You see, we Swedes don't have much feeling for the Diet. We call it the "Transport Company" – you know, it just moves papers. The real work is done elsewhere. I think we prefer it that way. The most difficult problem I had to deal with was how to let our members know. The government, as I've said, was no trouble, and the press weren't interested. We'd kept knowledge of the negotiations to a small circle of negotiators and trusted leaders of the Society. Then, as agreement came in sight, we had a special meeting of the Board of Management, and told them what was happening.

'At first, most of the Board showed irritation. I won't pretend that they didn't resent all the secrecy. But they soon understood that we'd got the best possible conditions under the circumstances, and once they saw that their professional integrity had been secured, they very quickly accepted the deal. The voting was thirty-seven to four, in favour.

'The Board of Management was pledged to secrecy, and we only told our members after the agreement with the government had been signed. Most of them accepted the change on the spot. About ten per cent were angry: they had wanted to fight the takeover on principle. But they were, after all, a very small minority, and very soon all opposition had died away.

'Why should this be so? You see, in the first place, we Swedes don't think of ourselves so much as individuals, but as members of society. And I assure you, the pharmaceutical profession as a whole want to use their knowledge as much as possible for the benefit of society. After all, there are many fields in which people need a local expert with scientific qualifications. You've only to consider matters of pollution, to think of an example. And I think I'm interpreting the feelings of our members correctly when I say that the profession feels that, if it is close to the government, the pharmacies can be used to serve the community properly.

'Then, there's another thing of vital importance, if you want to understand my actions properly. We Swedes genuinely believe in consensus. Once a matter has been hammered out round the conference table, we think it's wrong to go on fighting elsewhere. All you are permitted to do is to discuss the best means of putting decisions into practice. I admit that this does not favour personality. It must repress the individual in order to preserve the consensus. But then, you must agree that individuality is not well developed among the Swedes. It's the way we like it. We've always been like that, I suppose. Anyway, it's the way we work today.

'Well, that's why our members acted as they did. Now, as far as the Society is concerned, the new arrangement has brought nothing but advantages, because we will be relieved of some irksome and unproductive functions. Previously, our duties were of four kinds. We were a trade union, representing the financial interests of our members. We were a professional body, regulating the conduct of our members. We were also a scientific research organization. And finally, we were a business as well, running a number of manufacturing laboratories. Now, when the State takes over, we've agreed to change all this. The union function will be transferred to a division of SACO.★ And our business duties will be taken over by a State corporation.

'That allows us to concentrate on our professional and research duties. I, for one, am glad, because under the previous system we were often faced with conflicts between our various functions.

'The Society's officials will only benefit from the change. They will be able to concentrate on matters of more interest. What is more, their powers will be increased. You see, part of the terms of the takeover are that the Society will be represented both on the board of the new State retail chemists' organization, and also on the board of the nationalized manufacturing chemists. Before, the Society had no direct say in the running of the shops, and now it will. And then, we have been guaranteed large State subsidies for research and professional administration, so that financially we will be better off. Summing up, you could say that the change of

★ *Sveriges Akademikers Centralorganisation* – the Swedish University Graduates' Central Organization.

ownership has definitely been an advantage to the Society, although it might annoy some of the chemists.'

The affair of the chemists' nationalization might be considered a disgraceful affront to the integrity of the Diet, a gross violation of constitutional procedure and the overture to a first-class scandal. But only by an outsider. To the Swedish public and the members of the Diet, it was nothing unusual. They accepted it without a murmur, and the press, which might be expected to cry havoc over such an issue, merely reported the terms of nationalization with the detachment of a bored chronicler. The opposition, which might have been expected to exploit the issue, never acted; to them, it was a matter of vote and be done with it. Thus a Liberal politician in a moment of private confession: 'Strictly speaking, the government had acted unconstitutionally. But it's a moot point. And I don't feel very strongly about it. Oh, I know I'm a parliamentarian, and I should stand up for the constitution and all that. But, well, the Diet's weak, and the bureaucrats are strong, and that's the way things are. Most people are perfectly satisfied. But I must say I prefer the English way of doing things: with a strong Parliament, where M.P.s still have a say in the running of the country.'

And here is what an official of a Social Democratic organization had to say: 'There was no point having a debate in the Diet, because nationalization of the chemists had already been decided in principle. First of all, the Young Socialists had agitated for nationalization, then the other popular organizations agreed, and the party accepted it. That meant the people wanted it. I can tell you that the Ministry of Finance had been working on the details for a long time before we were ready to tell the public. When everything was settled, then we could let the Diet vote.

'I mean, that's what democracy is all about, isn't it? You do things through the popular organizations.'

The popular organizations not only appear as the instruments of democracy, but as the creators of personality. 'You must belong to an organization,' said this same official, 'in order to have a framework of reference.' This very aptly expresses the inner compulsion of the Swede to accept the group. There lies the sheet anchor of the Swedish corporate mentality. It is not confined to any one party, and politicians only decide the nature of the group. Businessmen and industrialists of the most impeccable liberal principles accept the corporate idea as devotedly as the most adamant trade unionists among their employees.

A leading official of the Confederation of Swedish Industries has this to say of his members (if he appears critical, dispassionate, and in some ways an outsider among his own countrymen, it is because he knows Western Europe well, and has lived in the United States):

'In industry, there is a desire among individual enterprises to delegate a great deal, especially civic duties, to their central organization. There is a willingness to turn over most issues to collective treatment.

'I don't like it. There must be some initiative left to the individual company. But Swedes are afraid of owning up to an opinion against the consensus, and for that reason I find it difficult, almost impossible, to get businessmen to speak out. Their attitude is that there is always an expert who can come up with the correct opinion.'

Corporate organizations have burrowed deep into everyday life. It is a condition of sale of all houses built or bought with local government loans (and most are so financed) that the purchaser join the local house-owners' association. It is with this body that the local authorities generally deal, treating it as a town hall annexe. A trivial example from a Stockholm suburb will illustrate how the system works. The question of painting a row of terraced houses had arisen, and the local authorities wanted them all in one colour. Instead of circularizing the householders, some official explained his wishes to the secretary of the house-owners' association and he, in his turn, saw that they were carried out. The secretary had considered it his natural duty to act as an agent of authority; the members all felt it natural to accept the rescripts of their association.

The local house-owners' associations are organized into a central organization, to which practically all suburban house-holders in Sweden belong. Even where membership is not compulsory it is complete because of a feeling that solidarity is a cardinal virtue. There are no rival associations, and the central organization is treated by the government as a corporate body through which to deal with the country's owner-occupiers.

Similarly, tenants of all flats owned by cooperative building societies or public authorities, which means most house-holders, are compelled by the terms of their leases to join the Swedish Tenants' Association. Relations with landlords are conducted exclusively through the association; the individual tenant, if not exactly prohibited, is severely discouraged from doing business directly, and his approaches are invariably ignored. For the managers of such property it is a sensible arrangement, replacing innumerable individual transactions by a few centralized collective deals.

Complaints about the drainage and certainly discussions about the rent must uphold the corporate procedure. This procedure requires that all things take the form of negotiation. When rents are raised, for example, the announcement is made, not as a simple decision of the landlords, but as an agreement with the tenants' association. They meet to discuss the matter, but talk mainly about the economy of the country, not the interests of the association's members. Both sides consider rent increases, not in terms of the tenant's pocket, but as an item in the national budget and support for government economic policy.

On the face of it, the tenants' associations are betraying

their members. But it is misleading to judge Swedish corporate organizations by the standards of pressure groups in Western countries. A pressure group, by definition, implies the exclusive aim of advancing partisan interests. But there is a dichotomy in the Swedish organizations; they exist, not only for the profit of their members, but also for what is usually defined as 'furthering the ends of society'. At first sight, the two functions are bound to conflict with each other, because at some point the interests of the individual member might be supposed to clash with those of the greater collective. In fact, this is not so. Responsible leaders of any organization, whatever its political complexion or social composition, would say that what is good for society is good for the individual, and therefore conflict is impossible.

There is little dissidence. The collective mentality of the Swede, and his historical corporative instinct, make him consider himself as a limb of society, so that he regards communal interests as his own, and sees no conflict between the two. By extension, he identifies himself with the State. He therefore associates himself with the bureaucrat, instead of nursing a sense of estrangement and, in consequence, treats official rescripts, however uncomfortable, not with suspicion, but with a kind of intimate acceptance, as if they were personal resolutions.

The power of the central organizations in public administration has been recognized by treatment equating them with the civil service. Public service directorates maintain so-called lay boards, consultative bodies designed to provide outside scrutiny; membership is drawn from government offices and central organizations. Taking the National School Directorate, the governmental members of the lay board are the University Chancellor's Office (the directorate in charge of the universities), the Labour Market Directorate, the Provincial Government Federation and the municipalities' union (the last two are official bodies representing local government in the hierarchy of the central authorities). The non-governmental members are: the LO, TCO, the Employers' Confederation and the University Graduates' Central Organization. Similarly, the TCO and LO, the boards of management of the State Radio corporation, the iron mines, and other State-owned enterprises.

If the corporative principle has been accepted in administrative practice, it was late being enshrined in the law. It made its debut in 1970, in legislation introduced by the Social Democratic government for consumer protection. It is designed not only to regulate conditions of sale, ensure good quality and abolish the concept of *caveat emptor*, but to influence manufacturers in the selection and design of products. It is, in fact, a means of steering production. Now if the law stopped there, it might be good or bad, according to your point of view, but it would remain a piece of Western jurisprudence. But something has been added to remove that characteristic. It is not the State itself that will enforce the law, but a corporate organization. It did not exist when the law was drafted, but had to be created. In the manner of all Swedish corporate bodies, it is to be a non-governmental agency that will execute government policy. It will be constructed as a central organization, representing the consumers.

In the first place, this will bring the citizen, as a consumer, into the corporate structure. He will not necessarily have to join the organization; it will be deemed by law as acting for him. Furthermore, it will be able to influence manufacturers under the mask of representing the people. Like the House-Owners' Association, and the Tenants' Association, the consumers' organization will give official rescripts the appearance of being negotiated agreements. One effect will be to persuade the public that what the organization has decided is really what they want. It is a means by which the State can influence demand, and *that is the admitted intention*.

There is now scarcely a field of Swedish life in which the

corporate principle does not obtain. In the universities, the agents are student corps, roughly equivalent to English student unions, but copied from German institutions of the same name. With membership compulsory under university rules, the corps are used by the authorities to channel State educational grants, social security and certain university functions. It is as if, at an English university, the Students' Union did the work of the bursar's office, local welfare authorities and the Department of Education and Science.

Student democracy, well established in Sweden, is managed exclusively through the corps. In each university, student representatives on the various academic boards and committees are appointed by the corps, *not* elected by the undergraduate body. Nationally, student representation in the University Chancellor's Office is managed by the Swedish Federation of Students' Corps, the central organization for all undergraduates. Thus, university, for those who want it, is a tutorial class in bureaucratic management. University authorities and government departments insist on dealing with the one approved corporative body. Mr Sven Moberg, deputy Minister of Education, has put the viewpoint of the Social Democratic government in this way:

'Corps membership is an old tradition, the expression of collective thinking, which is consistent with the aims of my government. Now I must admit that there is some dissatisfaction with the corps system because it is old-fashioned, and I dare say we will have to change with tastes and fashion. Some other solution will have to be devised for the organization of the students in a corporate body. But the principle remains that students must be linked through a corporation to the university and the State, and not individually. What we want in the academic world is an analogy of the relationship between the trade unions and the employers' association on the Labour Market. The students, you understand, corresponding to the trade-union side.

'Students must learn to work in some kind of collective organization at university. I admit that this resembles a medieval corporation, but our aim is the establishment of a corporate State. We are aware of the abuses of this system, as in Fascist Italy, and we intend to avoid them. But corporatism has succeeded on the Labour Market, and we believe that it is the solution for the whole of society. Technology demands the collective.'

6. Judiciary and Ombudsman

If the Swede mistrusts parliamentary institutions, he also has a singular concept of the law. In Western countries, the security of the individual derives from the rule of law; but in Sweden it is based on social welfare alone. For this reason, welfare enjoys in Sweden the respect and prestige of the judiciary in England. In Sweden, the law is commonly regarded as a means of putting social welfare into practice. The Swedish attitude resembles the medieval view of canon law as an instrument of divine, or, at least, superior, will. To the Swede, the law is not the protector of the citizen, but the agent of the State.

Mr Carl Lidbom, a former judge of appeal, a Cabinet minister and a prominent Social Democratic theoretician, has expressed the idea in these words: 'The purpose of the law is to realize official policy,' adding in a significant rider: 'It is one of the instruments of changing society.'

A legal official puts her feelings this way: 'The law is *not* there to protect the individual. I feel that very strongly. It is a norm for civil servants, and it has got nothing to do with guaranteeing one's freedom. Somehow, it seems *natural* to me that the law is there to put the intentions of the bureaucracy into practice. It never occurred to me until you brought the point up that it was there for the protection of the individual. The whole of my training suggests the opposite.'

'The law in Sweden,' to quote the deputy Ombudsman, 'is an instrument of the civil service, codifying its decisions.' *

* The Ombudsman, as he is seen abroad, is a legal officer with the duty of protecting the citizen against administrative injustice.

This dictum has a constitutional foundation. The judiciary in Sweden is not perfectly independent. Judges of appeal, although appointed for life, are subject to review by a governmental committee which has the right to dismiss them. The usual justification offered by legal theorists is that, since these powers have scarcely ever been invoked, judicial independence is *in practice* guaranteed.

It is an interesting illustration of the Swedish attitude that it is not the principle but the practice that counts. Yet principles may in fact affect popular opinion, for all that they are minimized by professional advocates. There is a very widespread feeling in Sweden that the judiciary is politically directed, and that it hands down politically coloured judgements. This may not be entirely justified; the important thing is that it is believed. In other words, the law is considered to be not the protector of the citizen but the servant of the State. The attitude of the judges bears this out to a certain extent. Men of tremendous integrity in the administration of justice, they nevertheless look upon themselves as civil servants, rather than as guardians of an independent institution. Their loyalty is to the State as such, not to the law. Justice to them means upholding the interests of the State, not primarily guaranteeing fair play to the citizen.

That the government regards the judiciary as a political instrument has been periodically suggested in public. In 1970, Mr Lennart Geijer, the Social Democratic Minister of Justice, declared that, 'The social composition of the bench of judges is all wrong. There are too many representatives of Social Group One.★ We must change our means of recruitment so that we can have a better balance, with more from the working classes.'

In the Swedish mind, then, the judiciary takes its place alongside ministries and other institutions as an agent of the

★ The upper classes. The vocabulary of snobbery has been abolished and replaced by that of vulgar sociology.

State. Justice is not associated with the courts. It is expected, instead, from the Ombudsman. To this we will return later.

Some Swedish authorities might regard the idea of the law adumbrated above as old-fashioned, and as uniquely a means of codification. On that interpretation, it is a passive instrument, lacking in ideological content. The more advanced theoreticians see it as an agent of indoctrination. There was an instance of this in certain fiscal legislation. Although the Swede implicitly accepts high taxation* he still cheats the exchequer. Heavy fiscal burdens caused tax evasion to swell during the 1960s. It ceased to be the prerogative of the affluent, and affected all conditions of men. Understandably, the government was perturbed, although not on economic grounds. While the financial losses were noticeable, it was the alienation of the citizen from the State implied by activity of this kind that was the real cause for concern. It threatened the sense of community upon which Swedish society is based, and the control of the citizen founded on that concept. Legislation was invoked to stop this *mental* rot.

All tax evasion was made a felony, to be rigorously punished by heavy fines and imprisonment, where before it had been leniently treated as a lesser misdemeanour. The express intention was to mark with the stigma of serious crime something that had been widely considered venial. It was part of a trend to make offences against the State more serious than those against the person which, in turn, was a result of promoting the collective at the expense of the individual. Quoting Mr Lidbom again: 'The new legislation will equate robbing society with robbing the individual. But its aim is not to make new criminals. It is to make the public realize that there is no antagonism between themselves and society, and to make the individual realize that his interests are the same as those of the State.'

The comment of the Ombudsman, Mr Arne Bexelius, is

* See page 174 ff.

this: 'Swedes on the whole *do* identify themselves with the State, but the aim of the new legislation is to get at the exceptions.'

In the Anglo-Saxon West, the legal profession has a status of its own. A judge, although he is paid out of the public purse, is generally regarded not as an agent of the State, but as an independent creature above government, populace and bureaucracy. He is the servant only of the law and, however imperfect, a guardian of the individual's rights, prepared on occasion to side with him against authority if it exceeds its prerogative. To the Swede, however, the lawyer is the instrument of government; the judge merely another bureaucrat, like all the others, enforcing the ukases of the public administration and subduing the citizen. In consequence, the law is treated with the same obsequiousness by the public as are the other branches of the administrative machine.

At a trial for assault in 1968, the accused, a young man of little means, was given legal aid. He was dissatisfied with the lawyer assigned to him and, as he was entitled to, demanded another. The judge then addressed him as follows: 'Young man, if you persist in your demand, do you know what will happen? It's not an easy matter to change lawyers in the middle of the case. I'll have to adjourn the court, and you'll have to wait a few days, and then the new lawyer will have to spend time reading up the case. *Have you thought about what that's going to cost society?* It'll be a lot of money.' Whereupon the prisoner in the dock apologized for wanting to do anything that would waste public money, and immediately retracted his demand. He appeared to consider it natural that the good of society (i.e. the State) should take precedence over his own interests.

The desire not to oppose and the necessity of giving the State the appearance of omnipotence extend to the judiciary. If it were not so, feelings of security would be threatened; under Swedish conditions, confrontation in any sphere generates unease everywhere else. Even in jurisprudence, the aim is consensus, not controversy.

Acquittal* in Swedish criminal cases is rare; so, for that matter, is a proper legal battle. It is not only that the police, the prosecution and the judge dislike a fight, but so do most defence lawyers. Almost all trials take the form of a plea of guilt, qualified with a request for leniency on personal, humanitarian or psychiatric grounds. Partly, this is a natural consequence of Swedish legal practice, which gives the prosecution great privileges in running a trial. The police are allowed to conduct what is in all but name their own preparatory examination without bringing the accused before a judge. There is no equivalent of the English remand proceedings, and a man may be held in custody for months while the police prepare their case. On the other hand, they rarely take a suspect into court unless they have a cast-iron case, and conviction is a foregone conclusion. Since the aim of this procedure is to make the judiciary appear infallible, acquittal would not only be an affront to the prosecution, but it is a scar on the system.

Sometimes, of course, things go awry. In 1970, there was one case near Stockholm in which a man called Höglund was accused of murdering his wife. The trial had not been long in progress before it became obvious that the prosecution was doing very badly. The evidence was shaky and unconvincing, the public prosecutor was reduced to bullying the accused and, if it had been England and America, the stage would have been set for a splendid and convincing performance by the defence, with a dramatic acquittal as the probable outcome. What in fact happened was that the prosecution abruptly stopped the trial. 'If the case had carried on,' said the national police chief in a newspaper interview, 'it would have had an unfortunate result [i.e. acquittal] and we would have lost

* Acquittal as understood in England and America is unknown in Sweden. See below.

the confidence of the public. Our work would have been handicapped. We depend on cooperation for our effectiveness, and our system works on confessions. Practically all our cases are settled by admissions of guilt. If we didn't get those confessions, it would make things difficult, and our work would be much slower. More policemen would have to spend more time on every case. I don't know what we'd do if our prisoners started defending themselves and refusing to cooperate under interrogation. And one case like this would be enough to destroy our reputation. But I think we managed to stop the case before it could do us any lasting damage.'

This attitude is not peculiar to the police, but is common to the whole legal profession. The exceptions are not frequent, and the lawyer who likes putting up a fight in court is not admired. On one occasion, an attorney of this rare kind was publicly attacked by the prosecutor as 'the disgusting kind of man who defends a client that he knows is guilty'. In other countries, that might be interpreted as arrant bullying, if not a threat to the rule of law. But it is unfair to judge one country by the standards of another. Under Swedish conditions, the outburst was quite understandable. It was saying, in other words, that the lawyer in question had broken the conventions, thus wasting the prosecution's time and endangering the system. Above all, a man was being reproached for the unpardonable misdemeanour of introducing controversy where consensus was accepted.

Consensus is indeed entrenched in Swedish legal doctrine, the relation of judge, prosecution and defence being defined as one of cooperation to ascertain the truth. In most Western systems of jurisprudence, the position is that prosecution and defence confront each other over a question of guilt or a point of law, the judge arbitrating between the two. Even if in most countries judge and prosecution may work too closely for Anglo-Saxon tastes, nevertheless a defending lawyer is firmly on the other side of the fence. This means that his loyalty is unreservedly to his client. That is not necessarily true in Sweden. The relation of defence lawyer to public prosecutor and that of the judge to both is equivocal. The function of an attorney is not to secure an acquittal but to help the court. This in turn implies that his prime duty is not to get his client off but to make the system work.

This is not to say that the sole function of a Swedish lawyer is simply to deliver his client up to the jaws of justice, suitably plucked and pruned. Behind the scenes, he can do a lot, by that 'licensed intrigue' spoken of before, to persuade the prosecution to drop the case. For his only hope lies in keeping the case out of court. As long as he can negotiate privately, he may devote himself to the interests of his client; but once the matter turns into the public display of a trial, his duty is to the system. And that precludes controversy in open court. The Swedish judiciary works in public as a registry of guilt. It stands or falls by the absence of the concept of acquittal.

The function of a Swedish court is not to decide whether a suspect is innocent or guilty, but to put evidence on record and decide on a penalty for guilt established by preliminary inquiry. The only alternatives open to a judge* are to hand down a sentence or refrain from delivering judgement.† The latter is a way of giving a man the benefit of the doubt without admitting the fallibility of the system. The accused is discharged, but with the implication that he was guilty, and only escaped punishment by a quirk of fortune. The 'no judgement'‡ of the Swedish system has nothing to do with

---

* The jury system is unknown in Sweden, except in libel cases. Judges sit alone, or together with assessors.

† This happens in about one per cent of all cases. Appeals are rare, usually concerning the sentence, not the verdict. Reversal of the verdict of a lower court is very rare indeed.

‡ It is less definite than an open verdict: it is no verdict at all.

the removal of suspicion implicit in the Anglo-Saxon idea of acquittal. In Sweden, the only way of obtaining restitution is to sue the Crown for wrongful trial and a pronouncement of not guilty. Such suits are exceedingly rare.

The law says more than most institutions about the political soul of a country. In the Anglo-Saxon world, the existence of acquittal derives from an admission of the fallibility of the State. Conversely, the absence of acquittal from the Swedish legal system implies that the State is always right, and must always be seen to be right. This has certain interesting consequences. Under Anglo-Saxon conditions, a man may be cleared in court, so that he is never considered guilty by his fellows until the verdict is given. It is not only fear of the law of libel that makes the press refer to an accused man as the *alleged* or *suspected* criminal; it is a deep-rooted social instinct. But in Sweden, since the courts may discharge but never absolve, any accusation puts an indelible stain on a man's character. Arrest is automatically taken by the public to be synonymous with guilt. The unvarying practice of the Swedish mass media in calling a suspect *the criminal* is not malice, but simply the expression of the prevailing habit of thought. The instinctive presumption is that, in conflict with the state (or the collective), the citizen (or the individual) must be in the wrong.

Justice may possibly be done in Sweden, but whether it is seen to be done is another matter. It is the inescapable consequence of the Swedish legal system, recognized by the Swedes, that the *real* trial takes place, not in open court, but behind closed doors in the private conferences with the prosecutor beforehand. According to popular belief, the law can only be evaded by intrigue. But corruption is neither suspected nor involved. It is vital for an understanding of Swedish society to realize that public corruption, in the sense of personal bribery, does not exist. Rather, the spur to action is a desire to uphold the system, and those who do the work are frighteningly free of human weaknesses, at least where public duty is concerned.

Public reassurances about the quality of Swedish justice appear from time to time, as if in answer to deep and genuine doubts. For example, after the conclusion of the murder trial mentioned above, the press treated as a sensation (which it was) the discharge of the accused in so serious a case. 'It proves,' wrote *Dagens Nyheter*, a leading Stockholm newspaper, 'that the rule of law is safe in Sweden, and that we have the best legal system in the world.' It is almost superfluous to point out that a statement of that nature has its roots in a sense of insecurity. Doubtless this has much to do with the functions of the legal profession.

As soon as a suspect is committed for trial, his relations to his attorney change. Until that moment, they work together in the familiar manner to avoid conviction. Afterwards, the lawyer is required by his instincts and professional ethics to help the prosecution in guaranteeing smooth proceedings. Once a case comes into court, the duty of the Swedish criminal lawyer lies in coaxing his client to confess. There was a well-known legal practitioner in Stockholm, much respected, who was frequently employed on this errand. It would sometimes happen that the lawyers engaged in legal aid found difficulties in persuading their clients to plead guilty. The judge would then suggest that their celebrated colleague take over. The court would adjourn, and within a short while the necessary admission of guilt would be forthcoming. A newspaper once published a tribute to him, including interviews with former clients. They had all been convicted. 'He was a good fellow', one of them was quoted as saying. 'The judge got a bit shirty, and I thought I'd better take another lawyer, so I took him instead. Well, we had a few words, and he soon showed me there wasn't any point in fighting. I didn't believe the other one, see? But with him, it was different. So I pleaded guilty, and that was that.'

It is worth remarking that, although almost all this man's clients had been convicted, he was not an incompetent lawyer in Swedish eyes. In the same way, skill in obtaining discharges would not necessarily distinguish the accomplished lawyer. Even to the average man, it is the mark of the good lawyer that he makes the system work. The fate of his clients is a secondary consideration. Under these circumstances, it is understandable that in Sweden the man of law is considered, not as the guardian of personal liberties, but as an agent of the State.

As the Swede will accept most political burdens, provided they are dressed in suitable economic clothes, so he will submit to official impositions as long as they follow the letter of the law. His concept of justice is that of legality. To him, right or wrong depend not on a sense of equity, but on conformity with rules and regulations. Whether he is prepared to criticize an official act depends not on its moral propriety, but on whether it is consistent with a governmental rescript. For that reason the lawyer is regarded chiefly as an interpreter of legal texts. He is not (and this is a vital distinction) generally expected to manipulate the law to benefit his client, but to interpret legislation so that the intention of the State is clear. To exploit a legal loophole is considered vaguely immoral. The public prosecutor of Gothenburg once castigated a certain lawyer for doing so in a matter of exporting foreign currency. He did not deny that the law was badly drafted and that the loophole existed, but he reproached the man for daring to take advantage of it. 'He has broken the spirit of the law,' said the prosecutor in a newspaper interview, 'he is a traitor to his country. The duty of a good citizen is to follow the general intentions of the legislators, and not to get round the law by playing tricks with the details.'

The Ombudsman is a good example of the interpretative function of the legal profession. It is a common fallacy that the Ombudsman was created to defend the rights of the citizen. His original function was to exercise parliamentary supervision of the civil service, seeing that it observed its own rules, which is a rather different thing. It will be recalled that the 1809 constitution, in giving the executive great independence of the legislature, also sought to apply a check to the administrative machine by giving the Diet a limited insight into the bureaucracy. It was done through the establishment of the office of the Ombudsman. His full title is *Riksdagens Ombudsman* – the Parliamentary Agent. That exactly explains his function. He is the delegate of the legislature in the supervision of the administrative machine, and a substitute for parliamentary responsibility.

In the beginning, he was, as his name implies, a strictly *parliamentary* agent, acting for the Diet among bureaucrats. His concern was not to prevent injustice to the citizen, but to assert the rights of the legislature. The two were not necessarily identical. A private citizen could not complain to the Ombudsman, nor could a single Diet member, but only the legislature as a body. It was only about three-quarters of a century after the creation of the office that the Ombudsman was permitted to consider individual complaints from the general public. But even in his modern form, the essential duty of the Ombudsman remains that of ensuring that civil servants observe their own rules and regulations.

The Ombudsman is elected by the Diet, but the rules and regulations whose enforcement he checks are the creatures of administrative, not parliamentary, law. That says a great deal about the constitutional division of powers; the subordinate nature of the Swedish legislature emerges from his limitations. The Ombudsman is unable to reverse official decisions or countermand orders; he is only empowered to reprimand delinquent functionaries. He is no impediment to the supremacy of the administrative machine, but he makes sure that due form is observed. In fact, most complaints received by the Ombudsman boil down to a need for assurance that the rules have been followed. Almost all the opinions he hands down are demonstrations that this is the case. And practically without exception complainants are satisfied, even if their suits are dismissed, since they have been reassured that the forms have been observed. It rarely occurs to anyone that perhaps the rules ought to be changed.

To the Swede, the Ombudsman is an office of tremendous importance. It is a surrogate for all other personifications of justice. Both the judiciary and the legislature lack that attribute in Swedish eyes, being merely administrative instruments. A Swede does not look to the law for protection; he would never in his wildest dreams consider approaching his Diet representative for the restitution of a wrong. He looks instead to the Ombudsman, who combines the image that in England belongs to the judge and the M.P. and in the United States to the Congressman and the constitution.

As in extremities of injury or dudgeon, the Englishman will appeal to the courts or approach his M.P., so will the Swede complain to the Ombudsman. Indeed, in Swedish, the Ombudsman is often referred to as a 'wailing wall'. It is an extremely apposite description. The value of the Ombudsman is not in what he does, but that his existence by itself is a comfort. The fact that he is there to receive complaints seems by itself to be a guarantee against abuse. He is invested with a kind of mystic reverence; he is a judicial fetish.

There is a danger inherent in an institution of this nature. People will not be disposed to guard their own rights, because they assume that the Ombudsman will do so for them. He has turned into a standing alibi for the government; as long as he is there, it is felt that all measures must necessarily be right and just. Paradoxically, this is encouraged by the so-called 'publicity principle' of the Swedish administration, by which official documents are open to public scrutiny. Even if this is circumscribed, officially by restrictions where national security is concerned (which makes papers on defence and

foreign affairs inaccessible), and unofficially by keeping matters out of the formal records, there nevertheless remains a
considerable body of material that is open to the public.
Outside Scandinavia there is nothing comparable. In most
countries, official secretiveness generates public suspicion, so
that the authorities have to tread warily. But in Sweden the
attitude is that, since the State is open, there is nothing to
watch. The government can act more or less with impunity
like the men in G. K. Chesterton's *The Man Who Was
Thursday*, who plotted to destroy the world on a balcony
overlooking Leicester Square, waving to the passers-by.
Frankness generally pays.

Any suspicion still falling on the authorities is allayed by
the presence of the Ombudsman. As a result, administrative
abuse is no less, and subservience to the authorities is considerably greater, than in the West. Lulled into complacency
by the thought that their institutions, by their very existence,
provide a defence against official imposition, the population
are induced to drop their guard. Mr Bertil Wennergren, the
assistant Ombudsman, admits that this is so: 'I think you will
find that the Swedes prefer to "drop their guard",' he says,
'since it makes cooperation much easier, and therefore society
functions better. Under the Anglo-Saxon system, where
everybody is on guard, opposition is greater, and society does
not function so well.'

7. The Rule of the *Apparatchik*

As a result of the corporate nature of Sweden, political power is extraordinarily penetrative. Power in this version means not only dominion over the machinery of State, but also direct mastery of the citizen. And power, concentrated in a few points and among a few men, is not difficult to appropriate. Since it is to be found within the confines of the bureaucratic establishment, he who possesses that monolithic institution possesses the country.

With the years, the Social Democrats have acquired possession of the bureaucratic establishment, their private bureaucracy infiltrating the civil service to foster a mechanism of government that by-passes the parliamentary process. The road to power lies, not through the Diet, but in the bureaucracy. The real master of Sweden is not the political campaigner or the parliamentary debater, but the man who knows how to manipulate the bureaucratic machinery. It is the type known in the Soviet Union as the *apparatchik*, the man of the apparatus.

Since the party has enveloped the State, it is the party *apparatchik* who is the ruler of the country. Party is perhaps a misnomer; more correctly it is the Labour movement. This is a huge, variegated organization which, in its control and penetration of society, resembles the Soviet Communist party and, in its desire to be all things to all men, is like the Catholic Church.

The Swedish Labour movement has two heads: the Social Democratic party and the trade unions. Dividing the leadership and sharing duties, they are fused into a monolithic structure with rigid discipline and tremendous strength. The party conducts parliamentary business and administers the government; the unions provide the money, maintain ideological control of the working classes and deliver their votes at election time. The order of precedence is a moot point. The party, admittedly, is the political arm of the movement, but its own bureaucracy is so thoroughly intermingled with that of the unions that it is hard to observe any distinction. Broadly speaking, the branch of the apparatus is immaterial to the *apparatchik* of the Swedish Labour movement; whatever its name, it leads to the top. With certain reservations, this holds, not only for the party and the unions, but for the subsidiary branches of the movement as well.

The corporate form of Swedish society has given the trade unions a status difficult to conceive outside a totalitarian country. In the eyes of the public, and certainly in the eyes of their own people, the trade unions appear to be a limb of the State. If one were to build a model of the Swedish State as conceived by its inhabitants, it would be a structure held up by a row of columns, representing the bureaucracy, social welfare, the corporate organizations dominated by the trade unions, the party, the government and the Diet.* Of these, the first four could each bear the total load alone. The Diet could certainly be knocked away without weakening the edifice.

Party and unions, then, appear as arms of the State. Both reach out into the country and uphold contact with the population by a parallel network of local organizations resembling the Communist 'cell' system. Every village has its party branch and trade-union representatives. The union network has two distinct structures. First of all, there are agents of the trade-union movement, acting as local LO dele-

---

* The judiciary has been deliberately omitted. It means little to the Swede.

gates. These functions are distinct from factory representation, although the same people often carry out both duties. The purpose of the first type of agent is to deal with trade-union interests as a whole, and represent the movement's *corporate* function to the outside world. This is no formality: in local government, corporate organizations must by law be represented on certain committees, with considerable powers.

Trade-union representatives and party agents are matched at every level. This means that the citizen has contact with both the main branches of the Labour movement at all stages of its hierarchy. Moreover, this form of organization allows party and unions to meet constantly at all levels, so that incipient conflicts can be nipped in the bud. Since in this kind of work party members are almost invariably trade unionists as well, and local representation is often united in the same people, perfect union of both organizations is ensured.

The base of the trade-union hierarchy is, of course, workplace representation. This has two functions: the obvious one of looking after members' interests, and what is perhaps the not so obvious one of political agitation. It is due to the unceasing political work of the shop stewards that the Social Democratic party gets its votes.

In a Swedish context, the political function of the trade unions is more important than their purely union role. Nevertheless, the latter is nursed with great care because, in the last analysis, it is as a guarantor of rising wages and better working conditions that the unions draw their popular support. The chain of command from LO to shop steward has been efficiently organized on hierarchical principles. And, to avoid friction between different unions, there are permanent liaison committees at all levels. As a result, almost all disputes are settled long before they can become a national issue.

Next in importance to the party and the unions lies the cultural and educational branch of the Labour movement, the ABF – *Arbetarnas Bildningsförbund* – the Swedish Workers'

Educational Association. A powerful corporative organization in its own right, it has well-defined functions in the working of the party and union *apparat*. It matches the organization of party and unions, so that for each of their 'cells' one of the ABF exists as well. It supervises the political indoctrination of the rank and file; at the same time it trains the functionaries of the Labour movement and provides a recognized entry into the power structure.

New officials receive their first training in local ABF courses, which provide elementary instruction in the ideology, history and administrative structure of the Labour movement, and in the technique of collective bargaining. These courses are not only for officials but also for ordinary party members or trade unionists with ambition or talent for leadership. The ABF will be asked to assess their capabilities and, if worthy, they proceed to advanced courses, possibly getting as far as residential colleges, the private universities of the Labour movement bureaucracy. No talent is neglected. A promising young trade unionist may be sent to an ABF course; equally well an ambitious one may ask to attend. Every novice can see a way to the top: the ABF is the talent-scoop of the Labour movement.

The weakness of the Diet, and its irrelevance to the search for political advancement, are not the arcane discoveries of political theorists, but truths so evident to the average Swede as not to be worth discussing. He knows that, although Cabinet ministers are nowadays expected to sit in the Diet, it is in the bureaucracy that they achieve their position, seats being provided as an afterthought. And he also knows full well that a Diet seat is usually the reward of a party hack or a stalwart of a corporate organization.

This is perfectly acceptable. Personality is at a discount in Swedish politics. Indeed, to say that an election has concerned personalities is to speak in a derogatory manner. Elections in Sweden are not about politicians but parties; that is to say, not about men, but impersonal interest groups or disembodied manifestoes. This is partly a consequence of proportional representation. The huge constituencies involved, with their cohorts of participants, mitigate against personal identity. The average Swedish constituency sends fifteen members to the Diet, and engages 150 candidates at a General Election. On the other hand, most European countries have some kind of proportional representation without necessarily abolishing the significance of the individual candidate: France is a case in point. But the Swede has consciously banned personality from politics; he has done so to obtain peace of mind. As a corollary, he has no respect for the Diet, which he sees as an assembly of nonentities. To him, the Diet's function is to toe the party line, and keep the files moving. The real power lies elsewhere.

All Swedes know that the best way to power lies in the *apparat* of the Labour movement. Ambitious young men do not go into politics; they go into the bureaucracy. Hitherto, the most profitable branch has been the trade unions, because they are rich and powerful, with enormous patronage at their disposal. The party, obviously, has been another fruitful source of promotion and office. But the ABF, which, in a way, is the Dominican Order of the Swedish Labour movement, has also provided an ever-open gateway to advancement. Apart from its function as a talent scout for party and unions, it offers its own organization, a path to the ruling circles of the State for those not robust enough for the cut-throat intrigue of the rest of the Labour movement. An outstanding product of this machinery is Mr Arne Geijer, secretary general of the LO since 1950. Mr Geijer started his career in the administrative division of the ABF, transferring to the LO when he had risen quite far and shown his paces.

Animated by a compulsion for self-perpetuation, the Labour movement has been careful to secure a constant renewal of its leadership. It has attracted the intelligent and the ambitious. There is always a port of entry close at hand in the local citadels of the Labour movement. These are to be found in every town and village, in the form of a building, suitable in size and dignity to the surroundings, called *Folkets Hus* – the People's House. This contains the offices of the local Labour movement: party, trade unions, ABF and, where necessary, subsidiary organizations, of which Socialist Tee-totallers, the Social Democratic Women's Union and the Young Socialists are the most common. The building is a tangible reminder of the power of the movement and a symbol of its equivalence with the State. In the public consciousness, the town hall and the People's House are twin monuments to authority. Often, the two lie in the same building, but its name is the People's House, and the public power is the tenant of the Labour movement. In most villages, and many small towns, the People's House has the only meeting hall, and often the cinema and public library as well. Generations have grown up associating the People's House and, by extension, the Labour movement with the road to power, with entertainment, culture, central authorities and the outside world. It is in the People's House that many a Swede has taken his first halting steps as an *apparatchik*. To the man of the provinces, at least, it is the goal of ambition, his Westminster, Downing Street, Capitol or White House.

The apparatus of the ABF – and the trade unions – is for those who make their way up from the ranks. It has played an outstanding part in the rise of the Labour movement. When higher education was a privilege, the combination allowed the ambitious working-class boy to better himself and reach for power. But it is unsuitable for the kind of person who is now becoming the ruler of the Labour movement. This is the university graduate and, whatever his political convictions, he tends to be ill at ease away from his academic equals. By a natural process of evolution, the academics have provided themselves with a private branch of the *apparat* in the Young Socialist movement.

The Young Socialists have a respectable history as an organization for working-class youth; since the 1950s they have become the private gateway to power of the academic *apparatchik*. It is now a testing ground for those earmarked for office, and a forum for those in search of it. During the 1960s it has rivalled the ABF–trade-union branch as the most certain way to the top. One of the by-products has been to induce jealousy among trade unionists, who fear that *their* organization is no longer a guarantee of power without competition. Feelings have been deep enough to strain the movement noticeably.

Youth among the Young Socialists is relative. Office-holders may be up to thirty years old or more, and they often find themselves transferred directly to the civil service or the Cabinet. To take one example, a Minister of Education, Mr Ingvar Carlsson, obtained his portfolio immediately upon completing a satisfactory performance as Young Socialist chairman.

The following item once appeared in a Stockholm newspaper: 'The public information department of the Ministry of Finance has been reinforced by the appointment of Mr Gunnar Hofring. He is twenty-eight years old, and comes directly from the Young Socialists, where he has been responsible for handling public information. A few weeks ago, he was appointed to the Young Socialists' board of management. In the ministry, Mr Hofring will specialize in contact with the popular organizations.'

That announcement illuminates Swedish practice. The appointment was to the civil service but, as the reporter took pains to emphasize, it was on political grounds. He did not do this to raise a scandal, but simply to put the record straight. It was a routine piece of news, obscurely placed, with comment unnecessary. The appointment was clearly a reinforcement of

Socialist influence in the bureaucracy. It was a question not of somebody entering the civil service who, at the same time, happened to be active in politics, but of political associations generating official employment. It was not consistent with the letter of the law, but there were few who would offer any criticism. Political jobbery has been accepted in the civil service.

It has become a Swedish maxim that there is no civil service advancement without 'the correct party membership', in the words of a cliché. It is essential to be a Social Democrat in order to get to the top, and in Swedish eyes there is nothing suspect about this. In 1970, Mr Kjell-Olof Feldt was promoted from the post of permanent under-secretary in the Ministry of Finance, a civil service position, to that of Minister of Trade, a political appointment. Mr Feldt was the epitome of an *apparatchik*. He began his career in the administrative ranks of the party, before transferring to the civil service. There, it was an open secret that his political allegiance secured rapid promotion.

On the day that Mr Feldt was appointed to the Cabinet, a reshuffle of senior bureaucrats in the Ministry of Finance was announced, the newspapers publishing extensive interviews with both the new minister and the two civil servants promoted to fill the top vacancies caused by his departure from the Ministry of Finance. These interviews were so displayed as to confer more importance on the bureaucratic field. It was clear that the journalist recognized the bureaucrats he was talking to as representatives of the real rulers of Sweden. But it was equally obvious that he saw nothing questionable in it. And, in an equally bland fashion, he reported what his two bureaucrats had to say about the importance of politics in the civil service. Both agreed that they were Social Democrats; the senior being an active party worker, his junior restricting his support to giving his vote at election time. Both said that it was impossible to work in the higher reaches of the bureaucracy without having the same political opinions as the government. Their admission was expressed in a matter-of-fact manner and drew no public comment.

The division of the bureaucracy in which this occurred is distinct from the public service directorates. It concerns the senior officials working directly under Cabinet ministers. Each minister has under him an administrative department and, in addition, the Cabinet has a large chancery, staffed by a hybrid of politician and civil servant, in which policy is formulated. It is in the Chancery and the departments that power is concentrated, and they are in the hands of the party. And, as the public service directorates are also in the 'correct' hands, the execution of Cabinet policy is controlled by the party as well.

The Labour movement *apparat* reaches far. It has not only permeated the civil service; it extends to the universities as well. Or rather, since the universities are directly controlled by the central authorities, they are extensions of the State bureaucracy, and hence under party influence. All professors are appointed by the government and, in that procedure, there naturally lies an opening for political evaluation. Since the 1960s, party bias has become evident in appointments to those chairs affecting the development of society, notably sociology, political economy and education. It is accepted that, to reach the top in those faculties, it is essential to be a Social Democrat.

A few incidents will perhaps illustrate the situation. An applicant for a lecturing post in the Institute of Education at Stockholm University was asked during her interview to reveal her political opinions. She protested that they were her own private concern, but that she was ready to admit that she was not of the left. Whereupon she was given a broad hint that she had put herself out of court and in due course was notified that she had failed to obtain the appointment.

A professor at Uppsala University once talked very freely to me about political bias in the Swedish academic world.

Before he parted, he earnestly requested me not to couple his name with his complaints. 'I'm not a very brave man,' he ended up by saying, 'and my position would be seriously jeopardized if it got about that I had been criticizing the government. You see, I am only a bureaucrat – all Swedish professors are bureaucrats – and I must *not* antagonize my masters. If you want somebody to quote, go to X [mentioning a certain historian] – he's not a university man; he's free, the lucky devil.'

The unity of the bureaucratic establishment gives considerable scope to the academic *apparatchik*. Perhaps the most celebrated example of recent years was Professor Bror Rexed. Professor Rexed, an ostentatious Social Democrat, held a chair of anatomy at the University of Uppsala for many years. Concurrently, he advanced in the administrative machinery of his own university, of the Ministry of Education and of the party. In the end, he was translated from his professorial chair to the post of director general of the Directorate of Social Affairs. There the professor's activities were a good illustration of the ramifications of the party *apparat*, and of the insignificance of the Diet. He set about furthering party policy, not government instructions, let alone Diet decisions. For example, he began to undermine the private practice of medicine by economic pressure and official propaganda and promoted a form of social work oriented towards the well-being of the collective rather than the good of the individual. In this, he executed the recommendations of a party caucus which thus took on the appearance, and exercised the powers, of a sovereign legislature. The analogy that springs to mind is the authority of the Politbureau of the Russian Communist party compared with the impotence of the Supreme Soviet.

Political manoeuvrings have even extended to the officers' corps. It was an open secret that General Synnergren, who became commander-in-chief of the Swedish armed forces in 1970, owed his appointment to his political sympathies. He had let it be known that he was a Social Democrat, and in suitable public statements he supported government defence policy. Slightly disguised, this was broadcast in the press reports of his selection. He was given the copious treatment of a director general (to whom he is roughly comparable in the hierarchy of the State) and he was presented as 'our first commander-in-chief who is a man of the people'. That description, in the allusive Swedish fashion, means a Social Democrat.

As in the universities, so in the armed forces, there is an opening for political influence in senior appointments. As a professor is appointed by the Cabinet, so are officers of the rank of colonel and above. (It is a curiosity that treating a professor as the equivalent of a colonel corresponds exactly to the order of precedence in old Prussia.) Swedish officers traditionally have been on the right in politics, but many of them, for the sake of their careers, have moved to the left. To quote a particularly forthright staff officer: 'If I'd only known what I know now, I'd have got a Social Democratic party card long ago. But it's too late now. If I suddenly join the party, it'd be too obvious, and they'd never fall for it. But if I'd always been a card-carrying member, well, I'd be much better off.'

The general recipe followed by a man in search of success is to exploit the bureaucratic *apparat*. His first step is to rise in the administration of some branch of the Labour movement. At a certain level, he must see that he is transferred to the civil service, preferably in the senior administrative ranks of the ministerial departments and, best of all, to the Chancery. Then, if he is lucky, he may one day find himself elevated to the Cabinet. He will, in fact, do everything but bother with a parliamentary career.

As a natural consequence of these attitudes, the *apparatchik* has emerged as the only kind of person who gets on in political life. To be one is the goal of many an ambitious young man. And the hold that the Social Democrats have obtained on the bureaucratic establishment, added to their long tenure of office, has given them the aura of having a monopoly of power and governing ability. The Labour movement has been identified with the State; Sweden has become what is in reality a constitutional one-party State.

8. Agitprop and the Perpetuation of the Regime

Dominating the machinery of the State is convenient, but it is the fruit of power rather than the fount. Before the Labour movement can secure its position, the party must guarantee continuity of office. In a conventional totalitarian country, this is achieved by force. But even there, indoctrination is vital in order to mould the populace in the image of the party and to restrain opposition below the point at which it becomes uncontrollable. Again, the Russians have a word for it: agitprop.

The task of agitprop in the new totalitarianism of Sweden is far more difficult. It not only has to quell opposition, but to keep the party in office as well. Sweden is, after all, a constitutional State, and the electorate can unseat the government overnight. The problem is to prevent their doing so, and the only way is by constant indoctrination and manipulation, to make them vote the right way. The Swedish government has no bayonets to keep it in power; it only has its agitprop.

Agitprop in Sweden is the duty of the A B F. At first sight this may be odd, but to combine agitprop with the training of party officials is quite logical. It unites the indoctrinators and their human material in the same organization, so that the methods of the one can always be adjusted to change in the other; indoctrinating and being indoctrinated are two sides of the same medal. And, fundamental requirement for political survival, it keeps the rulers in touch with the ruled.

The prime agitprop task of the ABF is to prepare the ground constantly for the issues of the next election. The ABF gives the party programme the appearance of revealed truth. It creates an ideological demand for the politicians to fill, so that electoral manifestoes come, not as the imposition of unwanted ideas, but as answers to a need. The work of the ABF is centrally directed and co-ordinated with the activities of the political leaders. No electoral campaign starts cold; when speakers go out into the country, they know that their audiences have been prepared. Slogans will fall on fertile ground.

The ABF works with the so-called 'study-circle'. It is a small group around a leader, conceived as the antithesis of a class under an instructor. It has been adopted in order to make pupils feel a sense of community with the leader, but at the same time to ensure that they turn to him as an infallible guide and interpreter. The word 'circle' has been construed literally. Classes are arranged in a circle, because it symbolizes equality and community. There is neither head nor tail and everybody sitting round appears to be of equal worth. Study circles are so organized as to obviate the necessity for teachers with specialized knowledge, depending instead on leaders trained to run discussions. Textbooks and course material are designed to that end. They provide the particular information required, leaving the circle leader to interpret and impart it. Circle leaders undergo periodical courses at ABF residential colleges, where they are taught the elements of dialectic and the methods of *guiding* discussions.

If the circle leader then does his work correctly, guiding discussions in the proper manner, he can persuade his listeners that they have all come to the required conclusions of their own volition, although they may in fact only be accepting what they have been told. By so doing, the experience of the ABF reveals, they acquire deep conviction and a desire to impart their convictions to others. They are infused with an evangelistic spirit, acting 'as unpaid party workers', in the words of an ABF leader. All this is the conscious aim of the organization.

Training in particular subjects, as distinct from general dialectic and teaching methods, was stopped after disastrous experiments. Leaders returned home from their courses to lord it over their fellows as approved authorities in various fields. This was undesirable, not so much because a few weeks' cramming does not make an expert, but because the rank and file resented arrogance and affectation in men whom they had been taught to regard as equals. In the long run, this could have been fatal for the hold which the Labour movement has on its members. *Community* and *Identity*,* the two qualities that the movement most desires, are eroded by crass authoritarian behaviour. Matters such as these are most carefully attended to, because the prime concern of the ABF is to maintain a hold on its public.

The system of avoiding specialist teachers allows the ABF great flexibility. Provided that the circle leaders are loyal to the organization (which they almost invariably are) they will impart exactly what they are told to. Where a conventional teacher will insist on maintaining what he himself has learnt, a circle leader will transmit without prejudice the material he is supplied with as if he were a wireless set or a TV receiver. For that reason, the leaders of the ABF can switch policy and change a syllabus with great rapidity, in the certain knowledge of being rigorously obeyed. It is a principle of the study circle system that textbooks must be uniform, and provided by the organization. All course material is prepared in Stockholm by a central office, and distributed by a central depot.

---

* The precise terms used by the ABF. It will be remembered that they are part of the motto on the Central London Hatchery and Conditioning Centre in *Brave New World*. Stability, the third word in that motto, also happens to be worshipped by Swedes at large, although it is not the immediate concern of the ABF.

Although local A B F branches enjoy a certain autonomy, they are submitted to central control by inspectors from headquarters in Stockholm. These inspectors correct teaching methods and adjust interpretation. Although there is no formal compulsion to accept their presence or their views, rejection is practically unknown. If for no other reason, subordinate functionaries accept central direction through an anxiety not to antagonize superiors in the hierarchy, conceivably jeopardizing a promising political career. Thus, by monopolizing textbooks and directing the individual study circle leaders the A B F headquarters exercise complete centralized control of everything that is taught in the organization all over the country. Ultimately, this means that the Labour movement leadership prescribes the exact curricula for political indoctrination and adult education for hundreds of thousands of Swedes. This centralization, coupled with the flexibility of teaching methods, ensures that training and propaganda follow changes of policy accurately, and that the requirements of the politicians are rapidly translated into action.

Recruiting participants for study circles is no problem, since night schools and adult education are a part of the Swedish way of life. Attending courses is a kind of status symbol. And if courses deal with the party, extra prestige and fuel for self-importance accrue.

Political study circles are aimed at members and sympathizers of the Labour movement. They imprint the party line, and are so cast as to provide arguments against the opposition parties. In the private discussions that precede an election and where, if Swedish politicians are to be believed, the outcome is decided, it is clearly a formidable advantage to have supporters instructed in the elements of successful argumentation. The party may be reasonably certain that their case is convincingly put whenever politics are discussed. But it is a privilege of the Labour movement; the opposition possesses nothing comparable.

In the 1970 General Election, for instance, the party chose to fight under the slogan 'More equality for a society with more justice'. For almost two years beforehand, the A B F had been preparing the ground by running study circles on the subject. They translated all issues into terms of 'equality' so that, by the time the final campaign opened, the word had been thoroughly established in the public consciousness.

Course material for this period had to convey an awkward set of ideas. On the one hand, it propagated the concept of 'more equality', which could be taken to mean more jam for everyone. On the other hand, the government was pressing for wage restraint and patience in the reduction of working hours, in order to halt inflation and maintain productivity. And on all sides rose the demands born of rising expectations. The A B F, executing the ideas of government strategists, reconciled the two demands by preaching increases for low wage earners and restraint for those with higher pay in the name of working-class solidarity – and equality. At the same time, the idea was hammered home that greater welfare was as valuable as more money, and therefore further marginal benefits ought to be accepted in place of wage increases. In this way, the rank and file were saved the puzzlement of reading one thing in the party manifesto and of seeing something quite different in reality. Under those conditions, the party would have damaged its credibility, almost certainly with disastrous results at the ballot boxes.

At the previous General Elections in 1968, denigration of the United States had proved an excellent vote catcher. The party decided to play on it again in 1970 (if not quite so violently), doubtless on the time-honoured principle that foreign affairs divert attention from domestic difficulties. What the regime was faced with was not so much embarrassing bread-and-butter issues as a nameless frustration mostly (but not entirely) found among youth. It was inherent in the restraints of Swedish society. When everything is too well organized, *ennui* is almost bound to appear. And there is in Sweden a taboo on the discussion of fundamental domestic issues, born out of a terrible fear of rocking the boat. Within Swedish society, there is no room for iconoclasm, indignation and the yearning for commitment. Unless suitably guided, feelings of this kind could be exceedingly dangerous for the government.

Mr Olof Palme, the Prime Minister, puts it thus: 'Of course people are dissatisfied. I tell them that they've got a right to be dissatisfied. I tell them that their enemy's reality, that they've got to fight it. Then we're all on the same side.' In both campaigns, Mr Palme vigorously attacked the thesis then fashionable that ideologies were dead, economics only remaining. 'Youth,' he said in the public speech, 'is idealistic. It sees on TV the horrors of the modern world. Of course it is indignant. Youth cares about what is going on in Africa and Indochina.' And, by concentrating on other people's iniquities, the Prime Minister deflected unrest that otherwise might have fallen to his lot.

It was not only the government that saw the necessity of such manoeuvres. A director of Bofors, the engineering and armaments combine, and certainly a man innocent of left-wing sympathies, said to an American journalist that, 'I can only say thank God for all this anti-Americanism and Vietnam protest. If there wasn't that outlet, d'you know what would happen? All these militant youngsters'd be attacking Swedish defence, or agitating for nationalization of firms like us. It'd make things very difficult, especially since the government's extremely vulnerable to pressure from youth. No, I'm not anti-American, but I'm very relieved that anti-Americanism has kept the heat off us. It's probably the only thing that could've done so.'

This, in so many words, was the attitude among the leaders of Swedish society. It undoubtedly explains why the Swedish government, despite its neutrality, adopted a militant anti-American pose over Vietnam. In the narrow field of electoral calculations, it brought younger voters into the party fold, and it helped to engage the loyalties of those approaching twenty, the age of suffrage. In taking sides against America, the government claimed to be reflecting public opinion. To a great extent, that was true. The mass media had long been hammering at anti-Americanism. And, through study circles in support of 'More Equality for a Society with More Justice', the ABF had been doing the same thing. The textbook for that course presented America as the villain of the piece, not only in Vietnam, but in all fields where a cathartic bogeyman was useful. Thus, Uncle Sam was linked with the non-socialist opposition parties by the insinuation that they existed only by courtesy of dollar-transfusions. Points were hammered home by a form of crude but effective cartoon which was clearly derived from Bolshevik propaganda art of Russia in the 1920s.

The efficacy of the ABF depends upon a reputation for infallibility. This may be a truism, but it happens to be very much the accepted aim of the Labour movement leaders. Mr Sven-Erik Stahre, Director of Studies at the ABF, has said that 'there is a certain reverence for the work done in a study circle'. To illustrate the point, he tells the following anecdote:

'At a certain trade-union branch meeting, a Communist speaker demanded a fifteen per cent pay rise, while the LO had said that five per cent would have to do. He was clearly trying to undermine the official union leadership, and there was a long silence after he had finished speaking. Finally, an obscure member of the audience, an ordinary worker, rose and, holding in his hand one of our study circle books, he went up to the podium.

'"I have been to a study circle," he said. "And I can see that five per cent is enough."

'And that finished the discussion. Because, you see, the Communist had not belonged to a study circle, and therefore, as far as the audience was concerned, no argument was possible.'

It may seem odd that a leader of the system should be so candid. But in the first place, to the Swede in authority, there is nothing consciously wrong in such a way of thinking. And secondly, it is the sort of thing that he would never openly discuss among his own kind. These explanations and such anecdotes are reserved for an outsider inquiring into the workings of Swedish institutions. Among Swedes, such subjects are taboo; they are thoroughly accepted, but to mention them explicitly would be to jeopardize the system. It is like a conjuring trick. If you explain how it is done, it loses its effect.

It is not enough for a government to be continuously returned to office; if it is to rule, it must be obeyed implicitly. That, of course, is one of the difficulties of constitutional democracy. The decisions of the legislature and the commands of the executive not infrequently founder on the rocks of popular opposition. The fate of the Labour government's wages and incomes policy in England is a case in point. It is the virtue of the Swedish system that such impediments to the efficient running of the State have been removed. In this work, the ABF has an important part to play. It not only works towards electoral victory, but it promotes the task of government. It does so by conditioning its members to obedience, and by palliating distasteful policies. This is well illustrated by application to the Labour Market.

The functioning of the Labour Market, and, indeed, the strength of the Labour movement, depend on an absolute respect for collective decisions. As the foundation of their political instruction, the ABF study circles promote the supremacy of the collective. Participants are taught that, once a decision has been made, *then all further discussion is necessarily at an end* and that, whatever their feelings might be, it is their duty to submit to the will of the group. But, as the study circle is designed to give received opinions the appearance of conclusions personally achieved, so is the individual persuaded to accept the will of the group as his own. Even if a person begins by opposing a majority opinion, he will purge himself of previous objections and adopt that opinion as his own as soon as it has been formally established. By a kind of conditioned reflex, this form of submissiveness is evoked beyond the study circle by this phrase: 'The decision has been made in a democratic manner, and accepted by the majority.' Quoted always in the identical wording, it has the force of the liturgical chants of the Buddhists' *O Mane Padme Hum;* it need not necessarily be understood to produce a certain state of mind. These are not ramblings from Utopia; they are the facts of Swedish life.

A particularly important application of this conditioning to the Labour Market is in respect of wage agreements. Indeed, the ABF go to a great deal of trouble to inculcate respect for such agreements, as a corollary of their general teaching on respect for the decisions of the group. Making unpalatable policies acceptable to the rank and file is vital in the labour field, since the economic health of the country often demands unwelcome wage restraint. Even if trade-union leaders accept this, they would be powerless without the agreement of their members. If nothing else, as exemplified in Mr Stahre's anecdote, it would give hostile agitators, mostly Communists and Syndicalists, a splendid opportunity to undermine union discipline. The ABF, therefore, preach constantly and with all their force the necessity of moderating wage claims and limiting increases. The usual line of attack is to explain that, unless pay is related to productivity, inflation climbs and buying power sinks, so that any increase will be eaten away by rising prices. So well do the ABF do their job that, on the whole, the Swedish working population have grasped this elementary economic truth. In good time, the ABF will be informed of the permissible wage increase, so that its teaching may be suitably tailored to the demands of the particular round of central bargaining.

If this work is successful – as it usually is – the LO is spared undue pressure from below. Consequently, it is more easily able to consider national interests, as opposed to the immediate concerns of its members, in the central wage negotiations. It is hard to exaggerate the services of the ABF in securing wage restraint without coercion; it is easy to show how disaster follows where the organization fails. For three months at the beginning of 1970, Sweden was entertained to a wildcat strike by 3,000 miners in the northern iron mines around the Lapland town of Kiruna. It was not the first illicit stoppage of work since the signing of the Saltsjöbaden agreement, but it was the largest and the most serious. Previous wildcat strikes had been small and sporadic, well within the limits of imperfection inherent in any institution born of Man. But the Kiruna discontent struck at the roots of the system, because union leadership had been repudiated wholesale. Understandably, the government was deeply perturbed. Had the infection spread, the economy would have been threatened by collapse. Both the State-owned iron mines and the LO agreed that the strike was due to a failure of trade-union discipline. This is the nightmare of the Labour movement, for upon that discipline depends not only the functioning of the Labour Market and the national economy, but the party vote. It is Social Democratic dogma that electoral support rests upon the psychological domination of the trade unions. If discipline were to wilt on the shop floor, it would do so at the ballot box as well.

For various reasons, the ABF had not been able to do its job properly at Kiruna. Local party and trade-union officials had been insufficiently trained and, furthermore, strong Communist influence had weakened the influence of the Labour movement. Consequently, the miners were not disposed to accept wage restraint. And, to cap it all, the miners' union had fallen into weak hands. The government realized that to interfere would be playing with fire, and left the affair to the trade unions. The LO started by replacing the unfortunate secretary of the miners' union with a temporary nominee of greater ability. Next, LO representatives experienced in shop-floor propaganda were sent to Kiruna as a kind of agitprop expeditionary force. Within a month or two, they had regained ascendancy, and re-established sufficient union discipline to bring the strike to an end. Subsequently, all that remained was to allow the strikers, or rather their leaders, a means of saving face. This was done by legalizing the strike committee, through turning it into a negotiating delegation infiltrated by official union representatives. The delegation then conducted peace talks with the employers, and gradually normalcy was reimposed.

But the damage had been done. At the General Election six months later, in September 1970, the Social Democrats lost many votes in northern Sweden to the Communists. Fundamentally, however, the Labour movement was sound. It had been badly frightened, but not shaken, and had the resilience to mend its own deficiencies.

In one sense, the Kiruna strike was the least unpleasant of the available alternatives, because it brought trouble into the open. The Swedish Labour movement has ever acutely feared the dangers of suppressed dissatisfaction, because it easily shows itself at the ballot box. The prevention of this is another duty of the ABF. It carries it out by encouraging people to express their dislikes, so that feelings may be innocuously relieved in words, before turning into actions inimical to the party. In the words of Mr Stahre: 'It is most essential to avoid inarticulate dissatisfaction, because that's very dangerous for political stability, and it threatens the sitting government.'

For that reason, one of the most important things that a study circle leader has to learn is how to listen. In this way, he can gauge his pupils' concerns and form an idea of what has earned their disapproval in party policy. His duty then is to coax them to put their criticism into words. At all costs, he must prevent the feelings from being bottled up. Among Swedes, this is often necessary and always difficult, because their nature is to brood, to nurse resentment and to have difficulty in rationalizing critical thoughts. The study circle enables critics to make their voices heard, so that, instead of joining the opposition, they can function inside the Labour movement. In this way, the A B F maintains a very necessary dialogue between leadership and members of the Labour movement.

The A B F is, in a word, concerned to avoid estrangement of the Labour movement and its members. In the formulation of policy, the study circle is of inestimable value. Through a system of contacts between the central management and A B F study circle leaders, there is a means of gauging both public opinion and the feelings of the Labour movement. The suitability of policies and reactions to new proposals may equally well be tested. In a sense, the A B F also serves as a refined vehicle for market research and the probing of public opinion.

Another duty imposed on the A B F has been to prepare the advance of technology by ensuring its acceptance by the ordinary working man. It has succeeded in preventing the rise of fears that new machines bring unemployment. At first, they had to deal with simple mechanization, but more recently with automation. Acceptance of automation was, indeed, one of the themes of the A B F course on 'More Equality for a Society with More Justice'. When automation is fully in command, according to the course book for 'More Equality . . .', work will take up little time, although most of it will probably turn out to be monotonous and uninteresting. What is the cure for this? 'A "dedramatizing" of the role of work in our existence. This evaluation of work is important. It will create the basis for political efforts to create society rich in leisure . . . we are to be compensated by a rich leisure.'

In this way, many of the strains of industrial society have

been obviated. Automation has met with no resistance worth the name. By and large, the Swedish workers have properly reacted to their instruction, and are prepared to see leisure as a form of bonus in kind. It is a question not only of quantity but quality. More leisure has been promised, through longer holidays and shorter working hours. But greater facilities have been offered as well, so that leisure becomes more valuable. More libraries, better sports stadia, State-owned country cottages at a low rent are in prospect. So-called municipal 'leisure consultants' have begun to make their appearance, with the duty of teaching people how to use their spare time. And the man in the street appreciates all this. He has learned that skyrocketing wages bring diminishing returns, and that a new municipal swimming pool, say, is as direct a reward for his work as a slightly fatter pay packet, and economically more defensible. Attitudes such as these prevent various strains and dissatisfaction; their encouragement makes economic and sociological sense. It is scarcely necessary to add that economists and sociologists have had a hand in their formulation.

If the ABF were restricted to members of the Labour movement, it would not have the tremendous power that it does. But, besides being the educational arm of the Labour movement, it also happens to be the dominant organ of adult education in the whole of Sweden. Two out of every three Swedes have had contact with the ABF at some time. They have thereby been brought into contact with the Labour movement, with incalculable benefit to party propaganda. The number of proselytes thereby garnered is difficult to assess, but there is no doubt that it has been the electoral lifeline of the Swedish Democrats on several occasions.

Adult education in Sweden has always been the concern of corporate organizations. The Centre party, the Liberals, the Temperance movement and half a dozen other interest

groups each have their own educational branches. But the
giant among them is the Labour movement, which was the
precursor of them all. In the last century, when the Labour
movement was reaching for strength and recognition, higher
education was the prerogative of the bourgeoisie. The trade
unions and the Social Democratic party then believed that
the only way to achieve political power was by redressing the
balance. 'Knowledge,' in the words of an early Social
Democratic slogan, 'is power.' The Labour movement set
out to provide its own education and, to this end, the ABF
was created in 1892.

In dingy halls, and in what there was of spare time, the
ABF educated the working class. They did not exactly have
to work from scratch. Illiteracy was unknown; compulsory
schooling has a long tradition in Sweden. Since the early
seventeenth century, the whole population had been taught
the three R's. But beyond that, there was nothing. The
ABF set out to fill the gaps, and did so successfully. Through
the Labour movement's night classes, the early trade unionists
acquired sufficient education to meet their employers more or
less as equals. To take a trivial example, one of the first things
a trade unionist was then (as he still is) taught was how to read
a balance sheet, so that he could refute employers' pleas that
they could not afford higher wages. By thus eradicating the
blind hatreds brought on by feelings of inferiority, the
ABF did much to avoid worse conflicts than the Swedes
had; perhaps they prevented revolution.

But as Swedish society developed and, in the 1930s, the
modern Welfare State began to emerge, adult education
became a national, rather than a partisan concern, and it
would be reasonable to suppose that the functions of the
sectarian organizations would have been taken over by the
public authorities. But the ABF fought tooth and nail
against handing over their non-political activities to the
municipalities. Mr Stahre, a Social Democratic veteran,

explains the opposition in these terms: 'The Labour movement tries to meet the needs of each group within the community, not only as party members, but as human beings.
Coming to us is like coming into a family; there is no need
to go outside. Because of our resources, many people outside
the Labour movement come to the ABF. They do this
because our resources and prestige combine to make us
almost a State institution. And we want to exploit ABF
goodwill for political purposes, by getting people interested
in the Labour movement through our contacts. It is the
contact, not the content, that matters. Although our courses
may be apparently non-political, they have a political effect.'

The ABF controls forty per cent of all adult education in
Sweden, the rest being shared between a dozen organizations.
In 1970, the ABF provided over 50,000 courses with 500,000
participants, in a total population of 8,000,000. These figures
mean that one in ten of all adult Swedes received instruction
of one kind or another from the ABF.

In the country, and in the smaller towns, the ABF is usually
the only source of adult education. It has come to symbolize
culture and the fulfilment of personal aspirations to most
Swedes. By association, it has thereby created a reservoir
of respect and goodwill for the Labour movement. This
has been translated into tangible profit at the ballot box.
More votes have been won at night classes than at political
meetings.

Local government, even if non-Socialist, will most often
confide adult education to the ABF, because of its size and
experience. In this context, the ABF is regarded by the
citizen, and treated by the authorities, not as a political
organization, but as a limb of the State. It is not, however,
required to forswear its politics in acting as a public educational body. The only official stipulation is that the central
directors of studies in particular subjects (adult education,
like political indoctrination, is rigidly centralized) must be

approved by the School Directorate, a precaution designed
to ensure a proper quality in teaching, and to prevent waste
of public money. This is reasonable enough, since a lot of
money is involved. Of the ABF's £7,000,000 annual expenditure, about £4,000,000 comes from public subsidies. The
content and selection of courses, however, is subject to no
public supervision, remaining solely the concern of the ABF.

The ABF has exerted great influence on government policy
in adult education. Its power in the Labour movement
brought privilege in the consultative process that preceded
legislation on the subject enacted in the 1950s. It not only
gave advice; it steered decisions. It lent officials to the Ministry
of Education, where they acted temporarily as civil servants
formulating policy and drafting laws. No other organizations
were so favoured. In reality, the ABF decreed, on its own,
the form that Swedish adult education has taken today.

The ABF is the most powerful, but it is not the only
instrument of agitprop available to the government. In all
fields where, for one reason or another, the ABF cannot work
effectively, some other body takes over. Not infrequently, a
special organization will be created for special purposes.
There was an example in the case of rents and motor cars.

Towards the end of the 1960s, the government was
bothered by high rents on the one hand, and excessive spending on motor cars on the other. The one aggravated the cost
of living; the other was a palpable encouragement to inflation.
In an ideal world, sumptuary laws would have been introduced
to prune luxuries, including motoring, while rents would have
been pared. But in Sweden, the population had to learn to
live with high rents and, if possible, be persuaded to renounce
the motor car. To this end, municipal and cooperative building concerns throughout the country established a central
propaganda office. To put this in the correct perspective, it is
important to note that all the organizations involved in the
campaign were part of the Labour movement, and that party

strategists had foreseen that high rents would be a grave
political liability. It is also worth remarking that the party
rarely conducts its own propaganda, except at elections,
preferring to allow other organizations to carry out that sort
of work. There is within the Labour movement a carefully
adjusted division of responsibilities.

The new organization launched an advertising campaign,
the burden of which was that, since a home was the fundamental commodity of a decent life, it had to be good, and
therefore expensive. It was pointed out that the cost of keeping
a car was roughly comparable to that of running a home.
Figures in a series of prominent newspaper advertisements
demonstrated that, compared to even the most expensive
flat, the car was decidedly the worse bargain. The public were
invited to consider that, by renouncing a motor car, the
burden of rent would fall away. Alternatively, it was not
rents that were exorbitantly high, but the added expense of
a car that made them seem so.*

Everywhere, the government is concerned to have channels
of indoctrination and propaganda. In the last analysis, the purpose of agitprop is that of Orwell's thought police or Huxley's
controllers: the control of minds. Under Swedish conditions,
absolute control is naturally unattainable, and indeed unnecessary. Only that degree of authority is required that will
persuade people to vote the right way and, equally desirable,
to follow without opposition the rescripts of the State. Self-
confessedly, the party dislikes the idea of people beyond its
influence, and it is concerned to have direct channels to all
categories of the population.

---

* Car-owning did not in fact fall, although people might marginally
have been reconciled to high rents. In 1970, 2,072,200 private motor
cars were registered in Sweden, 25 per 100 inhabitants. (America, with
about 46 per 100, leads this field.) It is an interesting comment on the
waning material privileges of Sweden that, in 1968, France overhauled
her in car-ownership, to take second place with 26 per 100 inhabitants.

The corporate nature of Sweden provides a most flexible and effective mechanism. There is, in the Labour movement, a politically oriented organization for all interests, so that it may gather converts to its fold and exercise corporate influence in all fields. To take two examples, pensioners and teetotallers each have their own Social Democratic organization. The party and the State are obsessed by the need for institutional links with the citizen because, apart from the corporate principles involved, they provide a form of intellectual control. Religion is no exception; the Church has been treated in exactly the same way.

Disestablishment of the Swedish State Church has been contemplated for some decades. Superficially, there ought to be no difficulty. On the showing of the party, only four per cent of Swedes are practising Christians. And the agnostic bias of the Social Democrats has, quite reasonably, given them a preference for not being involved in running an institution in whose tenets they do not believe. But disestablishment has been shelved, debated, shelved again and investigated by various commissions of inquiry; in short, subjected to the usual wiles of official procrastination. The national consensus of opinion was in favour of disestablishment. The clergy have certainly felt that separation of Church and State would give them more freedom. But that was precisely what the government did not want. Disestablishment would mean dismantling official supervision of a certain category of Swede, and therefore weakening the political influence of the party. It is the fear of losing a measure of ideological control over the population that has been uppermost in deciding government attitudes.

Mr Gunnar Gustavson, who was once leader of the Social Democratic majority in the Diet committee on disestablishment, had this to say: 'The Church is a kind of link between the individual and society, in the same way as the popular organizations. Separating Church and State could have political consequences. An independent Church might become politically active, and either form confessional parties, as in Germany, Italy and Austria, or become a pressure group. The Social Democratic Diet Group don't like the idea, and consider it a strong argument for keeping some kind of link.

'We've got to maintain a link, in order to keep religious people within society. The Swedish Church does this sort of thing for alien congregations, like Finns and Balts: it integrates them in Swedish society.

'There is also a danger that, if the Swedish Church is disestablished, the Catholic Church will become more militant and more active in missionary work. If the Church is disestablished, it would somehow weaken its hold on the people and, in turn, their sense of identification with Church and State. Disestablishment would weaken something and cut off certain links with the State.'

The Church in Sweden may have ceased to be of religious significance, but it has a residual political function. It takes its place alongside the A B F, the trade unions and all the other corporate bodies whose purpose it is to maintain a hold on the population. The A B F study circle and the Church service each perform the same function, on different people of differing tastes: keeping them attached to the State and, by inference, the party.

The Swedish Labour movement may seem unduly pre-occupied with the question of keeping the Swedes under control. But that is the natural consequence of having held power too long. After a certain time, a party, no matter what its political complexion is, loses its concern for ideology and becomes obsessed instead with the perpetuation of power for its own sake.

9. Economic Security and Political Servitude

If the propaganda of the Swedish Social Democrats has been so effective, it is because the recipients are so wilfully impressionable. Concerned only with economic security, the Swede is prepared to sacrifice most other things in life. For fear of quenching material progress by disturbing continuity of government, he has, with impressive regularity, returned the same party to office decade after decade; as the price of its maintenance, he has willingly surrendered to official regimentation. Whatever the moral arguments in favour of unseating a government too long in power, or of defending personal liberty against the advance of a technocratic State, economically there is none. Prosperity secured, the Swedes consider that they have fulfilled themselves, and they therefore see no reason to question or to doubt. In the country of the affluent, ideology is dead, and politics are a matter of economics alone.

But even if an affluent electorate may be lazy, contented and unadventurous, material prosperity by itself need not necessarily be a guarantee of power *ad infinitum*. When Harold Macmillan told the British public that they had never had it so good he was speaking no more than the literal truth. Yet, within a year or two, his party was tasting the bitter dregs of opposition. Less than a decade afterwards, Harold Wilson in his turn was summarily dismissed by an electorate that had never ceased to have it better still. Nor did a bulging economy save the German Christian Democrats in 1969.

The proper comparisons with Sweden lie, however, in her

Scandinavian neighbours, Norway and Denmark. In neither are there the political tensions and social discontent that Britain and Germany know, and that may obscure economic forces. In neither is there the poverty that is supposedly the spur to political action. And yet in both, during the 1960s, the electorate unseated socialist governments that, like their counterparts in Sweden, had held office since the 1930s, and whose rule coincided with the establishment of prosperity and the consolidation of social welfare. In both, non-Socialist coalitions of the right and centre were returned to power instead. The Swedish Social Democrats palpably had other advantages. They enjoyed, as it were, another dimension to security of office.

In both Norway and Denmark, there was no economic reason to turn out the sitting governments. Their fall was on truly political grounds. The Norwegian electorate voted as they did on a matter of principle. The government had been guilty of contempt of parliament. A Cabinet minister had concealed certain facts about the running of a State-owned mine. Economically, it counted for nothing, morally and constitutionally for a great deal. On several occasions the Swedes had been presented with issues of a similar complexion, of which the nationalization of the chemists is a good example. Yet the public scarcely reacted, because economically the consequences were negligible, and constitutional and moral considerations carried no weight.

To be fair, Norway, Denmark and Sweden are not strictly comparable. All are admittedly Welfare States, and the heartland of Social Democracy. But Norway and Denmark, having suffered Nazi occupation during the last war, learned that principles must sometimes be put above material comfort. The Swedes never learned that lesson. The concept of principle seems not to exist for the Swede: he sees the world in economic terms alone. In the late eighteenth century, when Catholicism and Judaism were prohibited in Sweden, a pamphleteer called Anders Chydenius proposed the admission of Catholics and Jews to the country on strictly utilitarian grounds. Sweden, poor and backward, needed capital and creative talent, and Chydenius suggested that, to remedy the deficiency, rich and clever men ought to be enticed from abroad. Assuming that the most desirable acquisitions would either be French, which meant Catholic, or Jews, he proposed that they ought to be permitted to retain their own forms of worship. His suggestion was accepted and foreigners settling in Sweden were allowed to practise a religion other than that of the State Church. Swedes themselves had to wait a century for the same privilege: Chydenius was interested in political economy, not toleration. By contrast Macaulay, the champion of Catholic and Jewish emancipation in England, was concerned solely for the well-being of his fellow-citizens. When in 1834 he helped to carry the removal of their civil disabilities (religious toleration was already old) in the House of Lords he spurned economics, and argued on moral principles alone.

Again, in 1864, the Swedish government refused to help the Danes in the war with Prussia over Schleswig-Holstein, although their king had promised to do so, on the grounds that it would imperil the economic development of Sweden.

For good or ill, then, the Swede recognizes none but economic motives. He accepts economic determinism as an article of faith. He has for centuries regarded the proper business of all human endeavour as the pursuit of economic goals alone. Today, he considers politics exclusively as a means to guarantee all forms of material security. Approximately the same might be said of many Western States. But the Swedish situation has lasted far longer. In other countries, the vestige of a politically directed past has survived to delay the advent of an economically motivated future. In Sweden, economics rule political institutions and form the national mentality with an absoluteness difficult to match elsewhere.

The Swede rarely talks about social welfare or the Welfare

State. The concept which obsesses him is something rather more profound. It is an extreme form of security in all its senses, expressed in an untranslatable native word, *trygghet*. It means both safety and security: the safety of a harbour in a storm, and the security of the womb. It implies the absence of all things unpleasant and uncomfortable, and always has a connotation of escape from danger or of a frightened child running to his mother. It is perhaps the most belaboured word in the Swedish political vocabulary; no orator will speak without mentioning it; all slogans must contain it.

In the political sense, *trygghet* means neutrality, the avoidance of war and insulation from the troubles of the outside world. At the same time, it conveys full employment and a certain comfort, and reassures the citizen that he is being looked after, and that the State has a paternalistic concern for his well-being. It is a highly emotive word. Many a careless politician has come to grief by accidentally threatening his voters' sense of *trygghet*. On the other hand, clever men have succeeded by bolstering it, and by playing on fears of its removal. It is one of the undertones of *trygghet* that it can be easily lost, and that without it there is nothing but the outer darkness.

All Swedish politicians have tried to play on this fear, but it is the Social Democrats who have appropriated it as their own particular weapon. In the grind of everyday politics, economic security is that particular branch of the all-embracing *trygghet* which is most easily exploited, because it is so tangible. The Social Democrats have imprinted on the electorate that economic security is the only issue to be considered at the polls. They have further impressed on them that its loss is the only evil, and that a change of government would bring about that loss. Absolute stability, a tinge of Nirvana, is another component of *trygghet*, and a view of change as a threat to that state is, so to speak, built into its definition. By exploiting this fear, the Social Democrats have induced the Swede to associate political change with economic decay. The fear of change, thus promoted to an *angst*, has ruled Swedish society for decades. It is this, more than anything else, that has enabled the Social Democrats to remain in office for almost forty years.

The concept of economic security has been extended with the rising of affluence. It no longer means exclusively the absence of need, but the maintenance of a particular degree of affluence. A pair of related concepts have been attached: prosperity and the standard of living. 'Prosperity' is a symbol for the corporate economic standing of society; 'standard of living' refers to the condition of the individual citizen. They have meant more things with the years: a wireless set, then T V, washing-up machine, then a motor car and so on. Although such things are the rewards of hard work and personal selection, general conditioning and political propaganda have presented them as the gifts of a paternalistic State. Equally important, from a political point of view, these possessions have been raised to the status of essentials. Prosperity and standard of living have become words of incantation to invoke the emotions of *trygghet*. By suitable manipulation, the government has associated a threat to the lesser concepts with danger to the greater one. In this way, the sensitivity of the electorate has been attuned to the advance of society. It would be futile to play on fears of the hungry 1920s and 1930s in order to affect the well-fed generations to whom these are but the blatherings of turgid folklore. The achievement has been to give to the dislike of losing a washing-up machine or T V set the same kind of *angst* which the fear of unemployment held in a harder decade.

Political change, in most constitutionally governed countries, appeals to the electorate at certain intervals as something desirable in principle. Where life is hard there is less to lose, and where there is conflict and political tension voters may take principle into account. In Sweden, however, change can only threaten material standard, and therefore, almost by definition, the desire of the opposition to unseat the ruling party repels the electorate and arouses their fears. Since material conditions have been consistently improving for years, the opposition has been unable to offer a convincing reason for a change of regime. Sometimes, they appear even unwilling to bring it about. Like their supporters, the politicians are afraid of change; they are also ordinary citizens, with the same hopes and fears.

The Swedish fear of change can take bizarre forms. After 1932, the first real chance of unseating the Social Democrats occurred in the 1968 General Election. A housing shortage had undermined the government's position, and there seemed to be a feeling that the well-being of democracy required a change at the top. Opinion polls suggested that the government could be defeated. The opposition parties had been bickering among themselves for over a generation and, on that account, had never been a convincing alternative government. Sniffing the prospect of power, they established a measure of cooperation for the election campaign, in order to convince the public that they were worthy of confidence. But at the last moment there was a stampede from the opposition, and the government won handsomely. Frightened at the prospect of change, the electorate drew back at the brink and rallied round the established power. And leaders of the opposition admitted afterwards that they had made the fateful mistake of convincing the electorate that a change of government was possible.

At the following General Election, in 1970, both the Centre and Liberal parties tried the opposite tack. They played down their prospects of assuming office. In their whole campaign, they never once mentioned change of government. They went to considerable pains to persuade the electorate that a vote for them was not a vote for change. Mr Gunnar Helén, the Liberal leader, said publicly that he expected the Social

Democrats to win the election. Mr Gunnar Hedlund, the leader of the Centre party, implied that, if necessary, he would enter a coalition with the Social Democrats to ensure continuity of regime. These tactics paid well. Discontented government supporters felt at liberty to register a protest without endangering their party. Mr Helén and Mr Hedlund made substantial gains, and the Social Democrats, although rapped across the knuckles, remained in office. And Mr Hedlund said publicly after it was all over that he was glad to 'escape being Prime Minister'. That may have been a confession of personal feelings; it was certainly uttered in order to help the Centre party at the next election.

The personal inhibitions against change are extraordinarily powerful. Take the case of a schoolteacher whose personal convictions, class, family and background persuade her to vote Conservative: 'My reason assures me that that is what I ought to do. But I have a struggle to follow my reason. I have a bad conscience, you see. I don't approve of what the government is doing – politically. They're destroying all the values I believe in. They're persecuting the individual and building up the collective. So I've got to vote against them. But then, as I say, my conscience tries to stop me. I feel that we have it so good, life is so easy, our standard of living is rising – I've got no right to vote against the government that's giving us all this. I feel that I'm betraying my fellow-citizens. I suppose, that's proof that I've been conditioned properly. Well, I vote the way I've reasoned, but I feel guilty every time I go to the voting booths.'

And here is a Conservative member of the Diet in a moment of private confession: 'I have a built-in emotional block against opposing vigorously. There are plenty of issues that make me want to get up in the Diet and protest. But only for a split second. Then I find plenty of excellent reasons for not doing so. My party, the electorate, my supporters, might disapprove. But, if I am to be honest with myself, I have to admit that this is only rationalizing an inhibition over which I have no control. It is an instinctive barrier, or should I say a conditioned reflex? It has got something to do with the way our rulers manipulate us. You see, they have discredited the principle of opposition, and made it difficult to exercise.

'Some of this – perhaps a lot more than I can grasp – has to do with the way they have debased the language. Often, there is no way of expressing oppositional thoughts. Let me give you an example. Obviously in a highly regulated country like Sweden, the classic antithesis of State–citizen and collective–individual ought to be a fundamental line of attack on the government. But you can't use it that way, because of the way the words are loaded. In Swedish, the words for individual always have derogatory connotations, and the collective can *only* be put in a good light.

'There is another psychological barrier with deep historical roots. It derives from our tradition of consensus.

'But I often wonder at the *general* reluctance to oppose, and at my own inhibitions.'

It is only fair to add that this man is an academic, and has travelled widely, lecturing for a time in America, so that he has standards of comparison and the necessary perspective to acquire personal insight. He exemplifies this curiosity of Swedish life, that criticism wholly from the inside is impossible, for the native tradition is conformist. All resistance demands a measure of alienation and the adoption of foreign models. This comes from being an outsider, like a Catholic, or from the cultivation of other people's political ideas. Amongst Liberals and Conservatives, this means the import of Anglo-Saxon concepts. On the left, it is acquired by identification with Mao, Castro and the rest. This puts the extreme left in Sweden in the same boat as the right. They are the only true opposition and both have had to import the intellectual wherewithal to oppose.

But, whether on the left or on the right, genuine dissidents are rare. The parliamentary opposition has agreed – or been forced – to remove controversy from politics, allowing consensus to rule the country. A Liberal politician has this to say: 'You ask me why we – the Liberals – don't oppose more vigorously. Because it's as much as our political life is worth to do so. It's walking a tight-rope every minute of the day. It's bad manners to break the consensus. If I attack the government too hard, I'll frighten the voters off. I've got to keep as close as possible to government policy, and manoeuvre in points of detail. I can't appear to criticize too harshly. I have to weigh every syllable I utter in public.'

Even the most obvious issues are denied the Swedish opposition. In most countries, taxes are felt to be unreasonable, and the promise of a reduction in the fiscal burden is often notably successful at the hustings. This is not the case in Sweden, despite the fact that it has the heaviest tax burden in the world.★ And a government administrative machine that persists in expanding year by year ought, on the face of it, to give the enterprising critic highly effective weapons in demanding less taxes and bureaucratic retrenchment. Only the Conservatives have dabbled thus, with electoral decimation as the invariable consequence.

To decry public expenditure of any kind in Sweden is breaking a taboo: a threat to taxes is a threat to feelings of security, and an invocation of *angst*. It is universally accepted that the State must constantly acquire greater wealth, otherwise social and economic security will necessarily disappear.

★ In 1968, total taxes were 40.6 per cent of the GNP; the figure for direct taxation was twenty per cent. In Britain the comparable figures were 28.6 and 10.7 per cent; in the US, 29.9 and 15.5 per cent. On an annual salary of 25,000 kronor (£2,000 or $4,800), that of an office worker, an unmarried person pays forty per cent income tax. At that level, any additional income is subject to supertax of sixty per cent. On an annual salary of 50,000 kronor (£4,000 or $9,600), earned by junior managerial staff, an unmarried person pays forty-six per cent. Supertax is sixty-eight per cent.

The Swede has not only been conditioned to regard the State as a paternalistic benefactor, but he identifies himself completely with it. To propose lowering taxes not only suggests to him that his guardian organization will be deprived of the wherewithal to care for him, but it is as if a vote of no confidence were being moved against himself. In the interests of *trygghet* he is prepared to pay yet heavier taxes and thank the government.

Even if money and taxes, those staples in the electoral armoury, are denied the opposition, there nevertheless remain issues that could, theoretically, be transmuted into political meat. There is the aggressive expansion of the administrative machine, the intrusion of officialdom into every corner of private life, and the contempt for parliamentary institutions evinced by party and Cabinet. Many Swedes are prepared, for the sake of argument, to concede that there may be dangers inherent in these developments. But few are willing to back their opinions at the ballot box. They are unable to swallow the notion that considerations of principle may take precedence over economic calculations.

By the acceptance of economic determinism, the Swede has somehow forsworn all other values. If the government proposes such and such a measure, however dubious, there will scarcely be any criticism as long as it is economically justified, because opposition would tend to defeat material progress.

In the autumn of 1970, a census of particular inquisitiveness was held in Sweden. Citizens were required to divulge information of a sensitive and personal nature. Some of the questions bordered on the inquisitorial: if, for example, a person was not gainfully employed, he was compelled to explain why. This might have been disturbing in its own right, but the nature of the census revealed that it was not a statistical investigation alone, but a thinly disguised registration of the individual citizen. A census usually guarantees anonymity, converting each person into unidentifiable figures. But in this case, every Swede, complete with intimate characteristics, was entered into a computer, carefully tagged for easy identification. At the same time, a central data processing system for the use of the police, credit investigation, banks and official institutions was being established, and it was quite clear that the census was being used to provide the necessary population register. Despite the prevailing submissiveness of the Swede, there was a certain amount of public distaste for the process. A few newspapers on the right attacked what the government was doing, because they thought they detected a threat to personal integrity and yet another addition to the power of the bureaucracy. Those who led the protest were admittedly almost exclusively of a small minority that has absorbed Anglo-Saxon ideas, but they carried with them enough of the country to cause the government some concern. The director-general of the Central Statistical Bureau (the government office in charge of the census) issued a statement explaining that 'the information is required in order to plan properly and *give the citizens better service*'*). The argument was sufficient to stop practically all criticism.

By the reduction of everything to economic terms, awkward issues may be disarmed or persuaded to vanish. Sometimes, a matter will be deliberately hammered into an economic shape; often a kind of auto-conditioning will do the job without prompting from above.

As a consequence of redevelopment in Stockholm, the only Catholic church was demolished. In recompense, the municipality offered a nearby site for a new church, on the stipulation that the specifications of the city plan were followed. This meant that, besides its religious function, the new building had to incorporate useful, commercial premises. If it was a device to engineer refusal, and thereby drive the church out

* Author's italic.

of the city, it failed. The clergy adopted a scheme combining room for bell, book and candle with offices and a car park. The town planning authorities approved the designs, the money was collected and all appeared to be settled. But, at the last moment, the Labour Market Directorate refused permission to start building, on the grounds of economic stringency. In the meanwhile, a levy of twenty-five per cent was imposed on all luxury construction, under which the proposed church was judged to fall, and the parish discovered that they did not, after all, have enough money.

It became clear that the refusal of building permission and the imposition of the levy had endangered the new church. Such obstacles invariably lead to long delays, and if the site were left undeveloped for longer than a certain time, for any cause whatsoever, planning permission would automatically expire, and the whole procedure would have to be started over again, with no guarantee that approval would be forthcoming a second time. What the authorities gave with one hand, they could take away with the other. To avoid the risk of the church failing to materialize by default, the Minister of Finance, Mr Gunnar Sträng, was approached with a request for a dispensation on the levy and the building ban. He refused, saying that the Catholic Church had no place in Sweden. In fact, at the time, all churches had been put on the list of inessential buildings whose construction was banned. 'We are,' to quote Mrs Alva Myrdal, the ecclesiastical minister at the time, 'dismantling the Church bit by bit. And where necessary we are using economic means to do so.'

I discussed the case with a man of no importance, an ordinary Swede holding no official position. He described himself as a liberal; he was not a government supporter. 'It's not a religious question,' he said, 'it's purely economic.'

'But,' I asked, 'is there not a case for making an exception for something that touches people deeply? After all, the

Catholic community is small, but devout, and to be deprived of their church is like taking a part of their life.'

'No,' he said, 'the country couldn't afford it. And everybody's got to accept economic circumstances, whether they're religious or not.'

'But,' said I, 'the effect is to impede people in the exercise of their religion.'

'Well, that can't be helped. We've got other handicapped people to look after; there are other cases of mental illness we can't deal with.'

'So, in fact, you approve of closing down churches?'

'Yes. But you must understand, it's not religious persecution, which is what you're getting at. It's a matter of simple economics.'

'From which I gather that you disapprove of directly prohibiting the erection of churches.'

'Yes. That wouldn't be democratic.'

'But you are prepared to approve the same result achieved by economic causes.'

'Yes, because that's equality. After all, we're only treating the Catholic community like everybody else.'

'From which one is forced to conclude that you are prepared to accept most developments, however undesirable, provided they are presented in economic terms.'

'I see nothing wrong with that. Well, look, I don't see what you're getting at. Economics is something natural, isn't it? You can't escape the consequences. And in this case, it's that the Catholics can't get their church. There's no *need* to go into politics or religion, because that'd be artificial.'

Favoured by this kind of mentality, that sees the world exclusively in economic terms, the authorities can avoid opposition, provided they use the correct presentation. They are further aided by a deep-rooted Swedish aversion to controversy. In the words of a quasi-proverbial saying, 'It is *ugly* to oppose'. To argue is to break the consensus, to rock the boat, and hence to jeopardize the balance of things. More than that, it is generally taken as a threat to feelings of security. Consensus, on the other hand, is worshipped as a guarantee of security, and confrontation is therefore regarded as suspect. A Social Democrat, a party intellectual, defines debate in this way: 'First you agree on your goals, and then you discuss the means. There's no other kind of discussion.' A leading publisher says much the same thing: 'We don't debate principles, because Swedes don't like intellectual games.'

In 1960, a new State pensions scheme was introduced. It took the form of a supplementary pension to provide on retirement the same material standards of a working life, for the old-age pension, while it prevented destitution, could not buy the comforts of an affluent society. The new pension is designed to provide two-thirds of a man's income averaged over the fifteen best paid years of his working life. Full benefit is conditional on the payment of contributions for at least thirty years. Socially, it was a great step forwards; politically and economically, the implications were less charitable. The pension is compulsory and financed entirely by the employers.* On actuarial principles, contributions ought to have been about three per cent of the national wage bill; in fact they were eleven per cent in 1970, and will rise to fifteen per cent by 1975. This means that capital is accumulating at a rate out of all proportion to that required by sound insurance practice, and the government has amassed a monstrosity of a surplus. It is in fact a kind of fiscal manipulation, in which a payroll tax designed for forced savings has been levied under the guise of social welfare. Contributions are paid into a special fund which, at the end of 1970, stood at 38,000,000,000 kronor (£3,200,000,000 or $7,300,000,000). At the same time,

---

* The old-age pension contributions are paid by the employee. They amount to five per cent of the taxable income, with a ceiling of 1,500 kronor (£120 or $290) per annum.

the total of all the outstanding bonds and debentures on the Swedish market was 81,000,000,000 kronor (£6,600,000,000 or $15,400,000,000), and the deposits in the commercial banks amounted in all to 43,000,000,000 kronor (£3,500,000,-000 or $8,300,000,000). In ten years, the fund had accumulated almost as much as the banks had done in 150 years. By the middle of the 1970s, the fund will provide the State with absolute possession of half the capital market. This represents enormous economic power which, the organization of the fund suggests, is exploited for political purposes.

To administer the money, a special State bank has been established. It has powers to make industrial investments, to help State industry and to make loans to public authorities. The interesting thing about all this is that the fund and the bank are beyond parliamentary control. Both, on the other hand, are firmly in the hands of the executive. They are run by boards on which the government is represented and, in deference to the corporate principles of Swedish society, the trade unions, the Social Democratic party and the LO as well. In practice, this means that it is the Labour movement *apparat* that rules the roost. It is certainly not the Diet. The consequence is that the party and the government are building up funds at their disposal, and acquiring an influence over the economy that gives them independence of the Diet. And that is erosion of the foundation of constitutional democracy, which is the power of parliament to refuse supply. While the executive has arrogated financial resources to itself, the legislature has been consigned to impotence.

At all events, the Swedish pensions fund has given the executive powers of a kind not usually found in Western countries. Perhaps it was not an issue to arouse the electorate: certainly the political implications were obscured by the social benefits. Not many politicians saw any constitutional threat in the scheme, and most of those who did wisely preferred to hold their tongues. A few conservative and liberal politicians who did in fact point out the dangers publicly were considered to be attacking the pension itself. Although this was not their intention, they rapidly desisted from their criticism in the interest of their parliamentary careers. The banks were understandably perturbed, but refused to voice their reservations in public. Thus a banker, in a moment of confidence: 'The fund is the ultimate deterrent. It forces us to do what the government wants. It is an instrument of manipulation. Of course, businessmen saw the dangers. But they were afraid to oppose the government. And they compelled the opposition politicians not to do so. The political climate was such that the banks felt that they had to act with restraint. The country doesn't like opposition.'

He is undoubtedly right. Swedes, of high or low degree, are obsessed with smooth functioning, whether it be of their lives, their work or their society. Their attitudes are exclusively utilitarian. They can afford to ignore all considerations but the grossly material, since they are so truly materialistic. With astonishingly few exceptions they admit of nothing that cannot be seen, measured and priced. Their test of validity is uniquely that of material advancement.

While Swedish debates leave no corner of material progress unilluminated, other values are almost completely ignored. The question of the liberty of the individual is rarely touched on, mainly because it is vaguely suspected as a disturbance of a properly functioning social machine and hence a threat to economic security. Discussion of the advance of the administrative juggernaut is actually taboo, for the same reason. It is not uncommon to hear (as I have heard) that 'to be concerned about liberty is pathological'. What the Swedes require therefore is prosperity alone. They have been conditioned to believe that their material security is the gift of the State. They regard political servitude as a necessary condition and a fair price for its continuation.

10. Welfare as an Instrument of Control

Even if material security has been essential to the generation of political compliance, it has limitations as a medium of control. Principally, it suffers from the defect that, since it is demonstrably the result of work, the notion of personal initiative is never entirely absent. It will do for the cruder types of political manipulation, but not for the subtler forms of conditioning that lead to changes of mentality, and a supine frame of mind. Something more vigorous and profound is called for for that. In the hands of the Swedes, social welfare has proved an appropriate instrument.

This has nothing to do with the once propounded tendency of welfare to dull the will to work. That hypothesis has surely been discredited sufficiently by now; but if yet more evidence is wanted, Swedish experience provides it. In Sweden, social security is not only deeply entrenched, but full employment has been a part of life for so long that anything else lies only in the memories of the middle-aged. The country, therefore, is deprived of those time-honoured gadflies, fear of starvation and the threat of unemployment. Yet the Swedes work, and work so hard that, if medical opinion is to be believed, their health is impaired.★

The phenomenon of rising expectations has seen to that. Or, to use unfashionable concepts, the vices of greed, ambi-

★ Doctors frequently give warnings of the rise of stress diseases. Heart trouble has been increasing, as it has elsewhere among highly industrialized nations. Insomnia and mental strain attributable to pressure of work have also increased.

tion and vanity override that of sloth with ease, at least where the Puritan ethos prevails. What was luxury yesterday is essential today and, although it may perhaps be trite to observe, attitudes shift correspondingly. The *angst* once concentrated on having enough to eat is transferred to maintaining a share of prosperity. Keeping up with the Joneses will do very nicely as a substitute for keeping the wolf from the door; social insecurity is quite as tyrannous a master as physical survival. And, if this were not enough, official propaganda is there to help, with its insistent message that the rise in the standard of living is the most important thing in the world, and its fall the worst conceivable disaster.

In short, the Swede has no lack of goads. And his social benefits are so constructed as not to undermine their strength. Social security will guarantee bread and butter, but you must earn the jam yourself. The old-age pension comes to conscientious worker and drone alike. Starvation is impossible. But, as explained in the last chapter, the total pension is related to earnings and arranged in such a way that it is necessary to work hard for some years to ensure retirement in the comfort to which the average man has become accustomed. Likewise, sickness compensation, while proportionate to wages, is always less, so that while ill health does not mean destitution, malingering does not pay. The purpose of social security is to dispel need without crossing the threshold of prosperity.

If, in its Swedish form, social welfare does not substantiate allegations of necessarily inducing laziness, it nevertheless has displayed other and more insidious capacities. Provided it is extended so far that it appears to wrap the citizen like a protective garment, it may be used in order to create a feeling of absolute dependence on the State.

In Sweden, welfare has become the fount of security in all forms. 'The Swede,' to quote Mr Bertil Wennergren,* the

* From a private conversation.

assistant Ombudsman, 'does not, let's face it, have much respect for the law. Why? Well, all people want security. Now you in England, in America, and I might say in most Western countries, get your feeling of personal security from the rule of law. But the Swedes get it entirely from social welfare. So that our people regard welfare as you regard the law.'

Starting, then, with the elementary concept of personal integrity as it is understood in constitutional States, the Swede ascribes all security to social welfare. He has the sensation of being looked after in all ways. He feels protected from all the dangers of the world. He is mortally afraid of being deprived of the embrace of omnipresent security. He is like a determinedly unborn baby clinging to the womb, fearful of birth and the unknown outside.

This is not inescapably a consequence of social welfare. It is the result of the particular use to which it is put. In the form that welfare has taken in the enlightened countries of Western Europe, social security exists as a public service without overtones of conditioning. It is a neutral medium, to be used or neglected like the railways, the telephones or the post office. English social welfare is really an extension of charity. It means giving help to the citizen; giving is the operative word. Welfare in this sense has no direct political aims (although it may have political consequences for those who seem to threaten it), and it neither binds the citizen to a party nor tethers him to the State. Although the Labour party founded the modern Welfare State in England, that did not prevent their ejection from office as the benefits started to flow.

In Sweden, however, social welfare has had the effect, and has been exploited with the intention, of creating in the citizen a sense of obligation. The Englishman, by and large, regards his social security as a right for which he need make no return; the Swede considers it a privilege for which he must perpetually thank its creators, party and State.

Although Sweden is generally imagined the most advanced of Welfare States, in fundamental social security it is not particularly far ahead of other industrialized Western countries. In some ways it is behind. Family allowances are more comprehensive in France. Dentistry is free in England, where it is not in Sweden. West Germany and Switzerland offer cheaper medical insurance and better attention. The superiority of the Swedish organization lies mainly in higher pensions, and a flexible system of specialized assistance that enables pockets of deprivation to be cleared.* But that is a matter of degree only. The advanced countries of Western Europe provide their citizens with roughly the same amount of social security, and it is possible to argue that welfare is not so much a socialist invention as one of the characteristics of

* For example, families with children at home, and earning a gross income of less than 18,000 kronor (£1,460 or $3,470) annually, receive a rent allowance of up to 780 kronor (£63 or $140) annually plus 330 kronor (£26 or $63) annually for each child. Needy housewives are provided with cheap holidays. Newly married couples or unmarried parents (no distinction is made between those who are wedded and others) with children who are minors (the age of majority is eighteen) are eligible for an interest-free loan to furnish their home up to 5,000 kronor (£400 or $960) repayable over eight years or longer. Disabled people over sixteen are entitled to an early old-age pension. Industrial injuries are compensated by annuities financed by employers. Cripples, mentally retarded people and, indeed, the handicapped of all descriptions are schooled, cared for and helped free of charge. Those able to care for themselves qualify for a grant of up to 15,000 kronor (£1,220 or $2,900) for special household equipment. Old-age pensioners are also eligible for this help. When these and other specified benefits are exhausted, there remains extra blanket assistance which is unlimited in form and amount and which is at the discretion of local welfare offices. It may take the form of an immediate cash grant to avert pressing need, or an advance against other benefits which take time to acquire. In cases of threatened destitution, substantial monthly allowances may be granted. This does not pretend to be an exhaustive list of all the benefits available, but it covers the main points. It requires considerable ingenuity to escape social welfare.

modern societies. Neither Bismarck's Prussia nor de Gaulle's France could be described as either socialist or egalitarian, yet both in their own age advanced the cause of social security. Paternalism among the rulers, whether of the right or the left, is the necessary condition, and modern governments, whatever their political complexion, display that quality to a greater or lesser degree.

Where Sweden diverges sharply from other countries is not in the nature of social security, but in its use. The Swedish government has consciously exploited welfare to control the population. It has learned how to bind its citizens by playing on a sense of obligation. In Switzerland, social security is treated as insurance provided by a company, the citizen seeing himself as a customer, and hence the master, patronizing a service. In Sweden, the position is reversed. The citizen has been taught, or chosen to believe, that he is the servant, humbly suing for favours from his master, the State. It is a kind of serf mentality, constantly imprinted, and not only in the sphere of social welfare. In education, for example, the universities (like the schools) are free, and State aid to cover living costs is freely available, without a means or ability test. But there is a certain refinement. Only a bare minimum, 2,500 kronor,* is provided as a grant. This barely covers textbooks and a fraction of the rent. More is required for survival. This too is provided, but as a loan. It is repayable, at the rate of 120 kronor† monthly, from the third year after graduation. This commitment may follow the graduate until his fiftieth year. Combined with the other pressures in the same direction, its main effect is to remind the citizen of his *obligation* to the State.

Welfare in Sweden has taken a militant form, used in order to exert a kind of tyranny by insistent benevolence, to make the State appear all-seeing and all-caring. It has been employed

* About £200 or $480.
† About £10 or $24.

to forestall political change. In its most advanced, and yet experimental forms, it will possess the capacity to strangle social and personal conflicts at birth, and to condition people to their environment. 'Round pegs in square holes,' to quote Huxley again, 'tend to have dangerous thoughts about the social system and to infect others with their discontents.'*

Of course, all governments play on welfare for political gain. By associating themselves with social security, they hope to glean some profit at the polls. But this is generally crude campaigning, no different in essence from any other social or economic advances that may occur during their rule. There is no fundamental difference between, say, ten per cent on children's allowance and a ten per cent increase in industrial growth. It is the figures that count. But in the case of Sweden, social welfare has been converted into a specialized instrument of manipulation. Western countries have nothing comparable to offer. Their politicians have not yet grasped the true potential for ruling and indoctrination in everyday institutions.

Welfare in Sweden has for many years embraced more than its counterpart elsewhere in the West, and it therefore offers greater scope for manipulation. It has not only been concerned with the relief of material need and the provision of medical attention, but also with the social guidance of the citizen. In Swedish, the word 'welfare' not only means physical benefits, but supervision of behaviour. This is the sense in which it is administered, and the sense in which it is understood. Its power of legal restraint over drinking habits is a case in point.

There is in each locality a so-called temperance board, whose purpose is to supervise the behaviour of the citizen. It is an administrative body, with considerable powers of coercion. By law, it is empowered to recommend for compulsory treatment in a State institution any person who

* Preface to *Brave New World* (1948 edition).

'regularly uses alcohol to the detriment of himself and others'. The provincial administrative boards issue the necessary orders, generally following the advice of the temperance boards. There is no appeal against an order. Where necessary, the police use force to impose it. It is important to note that this is a case in which the citizen may be deprived of his liberty by an administrative order without due process of law.

The influence of the temperance board extends beyond the custody of heavy drinkers. The police are required by law to report to the board every arrest, prosecution or contact in which drunkenness is involved. That information is used to compile a list of citizens who drink. About 200,000 entries are made annually. Recurrent 'black marks' bring the attention of the committee, with investigators entering the home and the threat of commitment to an alcoholics' institution. In 1967, the temperance boards investigated 36,429 cases of alcoholic abuse, about 0.5 per cent of the population. Of these, 7,064 were committed for treatment (about 1 per 1,000 of the total population): the hard core of alcoholism.

The Swedes are undoubtedly hard drinkers, but they are distinguished more for their hysteria and obsessions when it comes to alcohol, than for what they actually imbibe. Figures are not particularly sensational. In annual consumption Sweden is twenty-third, with 8.4 pints (9.2 US pints) of pure alcohol per inhabitant, behind both Britain, eighteenth with 9.8 pints, and the United States, fifteenth with 10.8 pints. France lies first with 31.8 pints. In the consumption of spirits, Sweden lies fourth, with an annual figure of 4.6 pints of pure alcohol per inhabitant. Spain, with 5.6 pints, and Poland and Yugoslavia, both 4.9 pints, are ahead. As far as alcoholism is concerned, Sweden is not particularly remarkable. France, with about 1,000,000 alcoholics (about three per cent of the population) is in a worse situation. Sweden has about 50,000, less than one per cent of the population.

Habits, however, say more than statistics. Whereas the

Frenchman or the Spaniard drinks as a daily custom, spreading his intake evenly, the Swede concentrates his drinking in Dionysian bouts. The drunkards littering the centre of any Swedish town on a Saturday night tell the tale of men who drink to get drunk. *Aquavit*, the native eau-de-vie distilled from potatoes, being an effective means to do so, is the usual medium. But anything will do. An eloquent figure in an official survey says that fifty-five per cent of the Swedish population regard beer as something to get drunk on.

If a man is considered by the local temperance board to be incapable of coping with drink, he will be legally debarred from purchasing alcoholic refreshment. It is an indictable crime to supply him, or to act as an intermediary in circumventing the disability. He need not necessarily be a dipsomaniac; if he is tippling more than a social worker thinks suitable, he may still find himself under interdict. Orders are strictly enforced because, in Sweden, the sale of wines and spirits is confined to a State monopoly which by law is required to cooperate in the control of drinking. Once branded by a temperance board, a man is entered on an official black list, a matter of administrative decision against which there is no appeal. The list is circulated to all branches of the State alcohol monopoly, and any customer suspected of being on it is required by law to identify himself before being allowed to make his purchase. Malefactor and innocent alike accept this system; the one evading, the other in support. If asked to show his identity card, the unlisted customer will do so without demur. 'It doesn't bother me,' in the words of an elderly journalist, 'because I'm not an alcoholic. But others have to be stopped for their own good. I don't mind showing my identity card. Why should I? I've nothing to fear. It's only a formality. And think of the good it does.' An advertising designer puts it this way: 'A man can't be allowed to drink as much as he wants. It can hurt him, and hurt society. He's got to be saved from himself.' No member of the temperance lobby, he was an enthusiastic wine drinker.

Welfare has long been taken for granted in the rest of Scandinavia, in England and elsewhere. But in Sweden, after decades of existence, social security remains an issue constantly praised and held up for public worship. It is the subject of obeisance by politicians, it is celebrated without end in the mass media as if it were some hallowed religious dogma that it was vital to assimilate for peace of mind. It is taught at school like a religion. Above all, it is presented as a vital possession that, ever threatened, must constantly be defended, for its loss is the worst of all possible dangers. 'We must rally round our social benefits' is a cliché amongst speakers of all political camps.

If Sweden is more susceptible than other countries to this particular type of manipulation, it is largely because of her long neutrality. Having been sheltered from wars, insurrections, and other ills for a century and a half, the Swede is afraid of any trouble. He is like a man who, never having stood against a blizzard, hides from a flurry of snow. A person of this background is patently open to intimidation, of which the Swedish leaders are acutely aware, and which they never cease to exploit.

In all elections, the government party accuses the opposition of threatening social security. Social security was successfully invoked by the Social Democrats to discredit the Common Market on the grounds that bringing Sweden into Europe would entail submission to arrangements designed by inferior States. By playing on such carefully nourished fears it is possible to frighten people into certain general patterns of behaviour and thought.

Coupled with the adoration of material security, and the exclusively economic interpretation of the world, social welfare has become the ultimate tool for avoiding political change and subjecting the citizen to the State. It has debilitated the population by depriving them of independence. That, at least, is the way reactionary politicians, frustrated by the limits imposed on their campaigning, will sometimes express it in very private moments. The government side puts the same thing in different words. Professor Bror Rexed,* the director general of the Directorate of Social Affairs, expresses the situation thus: 'Social welfare limits political action, because nobody will tolerate a threat to their benefits and the power of the Welfare State.'

Seen in this way, welfare is one of the pillars of the sitting government. Because political change has been associated with the decay of material standards, so it has been made to seem a threat to social security. And social security, having been turned into a component of the collective and individual personality, is a channel of subconscious manipulation. It has become to the modern State what hellfire and damnation were to the medieval priest. Just as the threat of hell could assure obedience to the Church, so the vision of lost security keeps the Swede under control.

The fear of change has led to a distaste for alteration in the outer framework of the administrative structure and political institutions, since that might suggest a threat to social security. A consequent reluctance to change governments has been

---

* All quotations from Professor Rexed in this chapter are from a private conversation that I had with him. It may be wondered why he spoke with such candour. Part of the answer is that most Swedes see nothing abnormal in the way they are moulding their society, and they feel a touching urge to dispel the ignorance of the foreigner. On the other hand, I believe that there is also an undercurrent of doubt, per- haps of remorse, or of bad conscience plaguing them, so that they seize the opportunity to make their confession. Certainly I have had the feeling, in talking to important Swedes, of playing confessor to their penitent. I have the necessary qualifications: I am an outsider, I am not involved in their politics and, as far as they can see, I am ideologically detached. It only remains to add that the professor is a most important Swede. He is a Social Democratic doxologist, and he has been put where he is in order to effect the party's intentions.

deeply embedded in the public consciousness. On the other hand, internal changes, that is to say those that leave the political stage scenery untouched, are perfectly acceptable, provided they are understood to promote the Welfare State. As a result, profound reforms are easily and rapidly carried out, the only condition being that they guarantee political continuity and stability.

By and large, the Swedes had been conditioned by the late 1940s to the meek acceptance of official edicts, because questioning had been associated with arousing fears of jeopardizing security. But the breath of wind brought by the intrusion of Anglo-Saxon thought induced a certain restlessness, particularly among the young generation, and, by the late 1960s, it became apparent to the authorities that the word 'welfare' had begun to assume undesirable associations.

'It suggested an hierarchical organization, from which we felt that people were shying away,' Professor Rexed has said. 'I don't think it was a fear of "Big Brother", but there might have been a fear of intrusion. We wanted to avoid antagonism on the part of the public. The term "social welfare" produced a sense of humiliation, in asking for help. We wanted to eradicate this, and make people regard it as their right. To correct the situation, the word "service" was substituted for "social welfare". "Service" is a neutral concept, free of undesirable associations. The word welfare was eradicated from our terminology.'

In the official analysis, the development of Swedish social welfare is classified into three stages. The first, during the 1930s, saw the provision of basic material help, given when asked. The second, thirty years later, was to impress the citizen that social welfare was his by right, and that aid would come automatically. This means that case workers, instead of waiting to be approached, had to go out and find people who needed help. In the words of Professor Rexed, this was to show 'that we are all clients of the State'. The third stage, taking shape at the beginning of the 1970s, is the most advanced of all. It sees help being taken to people before they need it. In this form, it will become preventive, where before it had only been curative.

Unlike England, Sweden has never considered selective benefits nor the question of economizing on social services. On the contrary, the great concern of the Swedish authorities has been to sweep away all distaste for asking for help, and to bring everybody, willy-nilly, into the system. Whatever else might suffer financial cuts, the welfare services never do in Sweden. Even education has to allow them precedence. Reluctance to ask for public assistance is considered subversive by the social welfare authorities. 'It shows,' to quote a social worker in a newspaper interview, 'pride. And pride is stupid. You must learn that, whenever something goes wrong, you must run to the State.'

It might be argued that the Swedes need no such urging. There are admittedly pockets of resistance. Old country people may sometimes nurse a pride in managing on their own, and a suspicion of charity. Occasionally somebody from the middle classes will consider the acceptance of welfare degrading. The numbers are, however, insignificant. But the Swedish authorities are obsessed with the necessity of bringing everybody into their system, and consequently worried by any group, however small, which remains outside. Reluctance to disestablish the Church for fear of losing control over the residue of practising Christians is one example. Another is the case of older people who, with the obstinacy of a peasant upbringing, prefer to manage on their own, and refuse to accept public assistance. The social welfare authorities have sought these out, persuading them to renounce their prejudice, and bringing them aid.

The Directorate of Social Affairs, the agency in charge of all health and welfare matters, ranges over all fields concerning the well-being of the citizen, from pre-natal care to criminal psychiatry. It interlocks with two agencies that are considered as falling within the domain of welfare: the Directorate of Industrial Safety and the Directorate of Criminological Care.

This last includes the running of the prisons. But, as its title implies, it is concerned not with punishment but with treatment. It has been decided by expert debate, and accepted by public opinion, that crime is a sickness. This is connected with another debate, that on free will against determinism which, in Sweden, took the form of personal responsibility against environment. This has been settled in favour of environment, and the general conclusion is that all crime is not only a form of mental disease, but the product of un-favourable circumstances. It is one of the virtues of a mono-lithic State of the Swedish type that theories rapidly become consensus, and consensus policy, so that this view of crime has for some time been officially adopted. Lawbreakers in Sweden are, therefore, in theory, not punished for an evil act, but treated for a disease. Their care is considered to belong to the domain of social welfare, rather than criminal law. The rigid demarcation between legal and social spheres has been deliberately softened.

It has become the presumption in Swedish law that crime is not the action of a man in full possession of his faculties, but a symptom of mental derangement and, in the last resort, a product of environment. With any offence that carries a sentence of one year's imprisonment or more, a psychiatric investigation of the accused is compulsory. It may also be invoked where terms down to six months are concerned. This procedure is undertaken before sentence is passed; sometimes before court proceedings begin. Besides the psychiatric examination, there is also a so-called 'investigation of the person' which is an inquiry into the circumstances under which the accused has been living, and the company he keeps. If it can be shown that he is unbalanced, or the victim of a bad environment, he will be recommended for psychiatric treatment. This may take the place of a prison sentence, either in a closed institution or as an out-patient, living at home, but on probation.

It is one of the official dogmas, frequently expressed, that crime is not a matter of personal responsibility but of social influences. This view has not remained the prerogative of criminologists and social workers, but has been accepted by the country at large. When the newspapers report a major crime, they ask, almost without exception, why the man acted as he did. They assume that it was the fault of his family, his friends, his class, his environment, and that if only the circumstances of his life had been correctly adjusted he would have behaved in the right manner.

There was an example of this line of thought in the well-known case of Colonel Stig Wennerström. Colonel Wennerström, a Swedish air force officer, was convicted in 1964 of spying for Soviet Russia and sentenced to life imprisonment. But he was also given a psychiatric investigation of unusual thoroughness. It took almost a year, where the usual time is about a month. No mental derangement could be diagnosed that would save him from conviction as a sane man in possession of his faculties, but the psychiatric board pronounced that he suffered from megalomania, emotional frigidity and asociality which, while not being legally extenuating, *were an explanation of why he acted as he did*. This was included in the official psychiatric report and, as it is the Swedish legal practice, became a part of the judgement.

This was a famous example of a form of conditioning and suggestion. The Swedes have been taught for a decade that crime is a form of disease. More than that, they have been taught to regard it as a form of asociality. Indeed, in Swedish law, as it was beginning to take shape at the end of the 1960s, crime is defined not in terms of moral depravity or ethical wrong but purely and simply as asociality. It is not the act, but its asociality that is the crime. It is not a long step to the belief that asociality *by itself* is a crime, and therefore a kind of mental illness. As a result, the man in the street has come to believe that to break the laws of society necessarily implies insanity. But, as he is in logic bound, he has also come to consider all dissidence as a form of mental derangement, or at least the product of an undesirable environment. It is an analogue of criminological theory; the result is that difference can be explained away and, in the long run, the rebel will be impossible by definition.

It has become common in Sweden to discredit an opponent by suggesting mental disease or an unbecoming background. It is, of course, impossible to say dogmatically that this has been ordained by the rulers of the country, but it happens that the trend has advanced with the propagation of the official views that personal responsibility is at a discount and that it is environment alone that counts in human behaviour. Not only has what might be termed a behaviourist view of opposition become prevalent among the general public, but it dominates intellectual debate and the mass media. If somebody departs from the fashion of the day, he will not be given the credit of his opinions, but explained away as the product of an unfortunate environment. This is particularly true in book reviews. The tendency is to dismiss the rebel in psychiatric terms, with the implication that sanity is equated with conformity.

The power of this kind of thinking is reinforced by the working of the law. In criminal practice, a man may not refuse to be treated as a psychiatric case. The authorities, and the authorities alone, decide. To do them credit, most criminals accept without demur. Major trials usually result in conviction, but with the rider of psychological disturbance. Seen with English eyes, this provides the interesting situation of a man being judged fit to plead, but not responsible for his actions. But the Swedish public thereby receives the impression that crime necessarily implies diminished responsibility.

Very occasionally somebody protests. One convict in an open prison expressed himself thus in a newspaper interview: 'Why do they have to treat you as a mental case? Look, I did what I did. I chose my path, and I've paid for it. Now I want to get on with building up a new life. So why don't they give you credit for having been a bad boy, and treat you as a human being, instead of a mental case?' He had not been convicted of a crime of violence, but of defalcation.

Through the admixture of law and psychiatry, the concept of social welfare in Sweden has been extended to mean the care of the whole man, body and soul (even usurping the functions normally exercised by the law in Western society). The theoreticians of the Social Democratic party and the administrators of the Directorate of Social Affairs see welfare going far beyond the archaic concept of the relief of material distress. They consider that welfare encompasses the care of both the citizen and his relations with society. They see mental health as a vital field, because it can help to produce socially well adjusted people.

An interesting experiment was carried out at the end of the 1960s. With the approval of the trade unions, the employers and an insurance company owned by the Labour movement, a mental health campaign was launched among factory workers. It set out to detect stress and eliminate it by group therapy. In other words, it was an attempt to adjust or condition people to an uncomfortable environment. The curious thing about this was that almost nobody in any political camp saw anything wrong. It was rational and, therefore, to the Swedish mind, acceptable. It was left to a few extreme left-wing members of the medical profession and intellectuals to protest. The burden of their complaint was that the experiment was a form of brain-washing.

The third stage of social welfare, now being evolved, is the most ambitious of all. From a passive element originally designed to correct deficiencies in a society shaped by other forces, it is turning into one of those forces itself. It is to control the planning of society. 'The whole environment,' says Professor Rexed, 'has to be arranged to bring people into the Welfare State.'

Town planning is already largely determined by maxims of social welfare. The new Swedish suburbs are based on the principle that everybody within them must be physically arranged within the orbit of the welfare authorities. The density of population and the placing of buildings are so ordered as to exploit welfare services economically. The guiding principle is that welfare agents, operating from one or two central posts, must be able to reach everybody within their care with no more than a few minutes' travelling. To put it another way, the configuration of the Swedish cities is being decided by the radius of action of social workers.

As part of this grand scheme of total welfare now unfolding, the medical profession is being reorganized. The aim of the reform is to change the nature of medicine from the treatment of the patient as an individual to that of the patient as a member of society. It will convert the medical profession to the practice of social medicine.

Eventually, it will be impossible to consult an individual doctor. Instead, a patient will enter a local health centre which will span the whole gamut of treatment from medicine to psychiatry. The theory behind this is that many physical disturbances may have psychosomatic or social roots, and that the whole man must therefore be treated, not a part. Anybody asking for medical attention will stand the chance of undergoing psychiatric treatment, *nolens volens*. He may also be given group therapy in order to iron out conflicts of personality.

The foundation of this system lies in absolute obedience on the part of the patient, so that he will accept the kinds of treatment allotted by the supervisors. 'Our aim,' says Professor Rexed, 'is to change the nature of the doctor–patient relationship. We are breaking down the simple authority of the doctors, and substituting more of a Freudian influence. In this way, a doctor will appear to be more on a level with the patient, instead of someone above, and he will thereby exert a greater hold. Every doctor will have to be something of a psycho-analyst.'

Obviously a system such as this will make extremely efficient use of the medical profession. It is clearly irrational and a waste of time and resources if patients insist on seeing particular doctors; it makes far better sense to move between practitioners as his needs require, and as vacancies occur. On the other hand, the nature of the system will give the medical profession, and therefore the State, a psychological grip on the population. They will doubtless be well equipped to cope with psychosomatic illness. They will also be able to eradicate personal conflicts before they become socially dangerous, and thus, by extension, disarm opposition.

This is not entirely idle speculation. A senior official of the Directorate of Social Affairs has publicly admitted that the system, as being put into practice, would give an opportunity of treating rebels as mental cases, thus avoiding potential rebellion in society by psychiatry licensed for brain-washing. He further admits that the health centres, by turning over the peculiar power of a doctor to an organization, would give the State tremendous possibilities for exercising authority over the population. He claims, however, that there will eventually be safeguards without specifying their nature.

To carry through a reform of such a profound and complex nature requires a compliant and tightly organized medical profession. The first stages have been designed to bring all doctors into public service. The Swedish national health service was originally conceived as a system of public insurance, with doctors in private practice, and patients recovering fees from the State. This has gradually been changed, so that most practitioners have become publicly employed. Then, by a reform introduced in 1970, doctors employed in hospitals were prohibited from attending private patients. Furthermore, the system of health service reimbursement was changed so that, financially, private practice would become unattractive, and young doctors would be forced into public employment.

Professor Rexed has said that he 'has nothing against private practice, provided doctors accept our ideas'. He wants private doctors to go into group practice, working in health centres. In this way, they will in fact be complying with the new system, and only their system of payment would differ. Their manner of working and, presumably, their way of thinking would be the same as those of the public health service.

Professor Rexed considers that his main obstacle lies in the reluctance of the profession to follow the new precepts. However, he finds that such opposition lies mainly with the older doctors. 'The younger doctors, who are products of our new school system, think the way we want them to.' And it is undoubtedly true that very many young graduates have radical attitudes, and a commitment to social medicine. Furthermore, not a few of the older practitioners, between thirty and forty years of age, also have leanings that way.

Now, interest in social medicine and rejection of traditional attitudes are not peculiarly Swedish attributes. The conflict is to be found wherever medicine is practised. What is original is that the debate has been settled, and one view has triumphed so rapidly. The radical line of social medicine has been given official approval, and the medical profession, by and large, has made its submission. This is an example of the Swedish idea of consensus; once the aims have been decided, further discussion is out of bounds. And again, the monolithic structure of the institutions of Swedish society ensure compliance with the new doctrine. Perhaps more important, it allows doctrine to be promulgated. Once the pronouncement has been made, it is largely accepted. In this case, it is the Directorate of Social Affairs that decides. So far as the formation of the profession is concerned, the privilege of the State in appointing all professors ensures that the medical schools teach the requisite opinions. And the gradual elimination of the private practitioner in the classical sense means that dissidence will be pared to the bone. 'Of course, we will always have a few people practising on their own,' in the words of Professor Rexed, 'but that will be negligible, and they won't affect the way we run our organization.'

If people wanted to escape this degree of organization and control, the system would be seriously undermined. But it is one of the great advantages of the Welfare State that it has lent itself to the prevention of this undesirable state of affairs. In the first place, the Swede has been taught that nowhere else can he obtain the security to which he has grown accustomed at home. This means that he is, in general, afraid of moving away because he has been led to believe that beyond the frontier there is no security at all.

This, understandably, is the message of government politicians; it is also the test of most education in this sphere, and of the mass media. Newspaper articles about foreign countries rarely fail to point the moral that social security abroad is non-existent, or inferior to that of Sweden. When Swedes are abroad on holiday, they are officially reminded that they can take their welfare with them. If a Swedish mother happens to be away from Sweden while her children's allowance falls due, she will receive a notice from the Social Security office which says, 'Don't forget that, even if you are abroad, you can still enjoy your social benefits. Fill in the enclosed form, and we will send your children's allowance to you wherever you may be.' The arm of the Welfare State, this seems to say, is long.

Understandably, there are many Swedes amongst the professional and moneyed classes who find the maternal solicitude of their government stifling, and who will often talk, and occasionally do something, about emigrating. Perhaps the most celebrated example was Professor Hannes Alfén, a nuclear physicist, who moved to California. He is the titular head of a small, but select and highly qualified brain drain, mostly to America. In the welter of statistical information with which the Swedes provide themselves, emigration must take an extremely modest place. Yet it is impossible even to obtain figures. They do not appear in the official statistics, and emigration is scarcely ever mentioned in the press. Government departments parry inquiries on the subject, and may even deny its existence. In short, the brain drain is taboo.

This is understandable. To acknowledge that the country's gifted citizens prefer to try their luck elsewhere is to admit a blemish on the State. And this would vitiate one of the central tenets of Swedish social welfare: that it is a guarantee of perfection. In all seriousness, Mr Bertil Ohlsson, director general of the Labour Market Directorate, once said in a newspaper interview that, 'There is no Heaven on earth, but Sweden is the nearest approach'. To admit the existence of a brain drain would also jeopardize another mechanism of indoctrination through welfare, that the citizen is automatically grateful to the State for favours received; to admit the existence of ingrates would be straining credibility too far.

Even among candidates for emigration, there nags a feeling of forced gratitude and guilt. I met one man, a photographer, who, after working abroad for some time, found on his return to Sweden that Swedish society somehow shackled him. 'But,' he said, 'I can't bring myself to think seriously of emigrating. You see, this country has educated me, and given me so much security that it would be ungrateful of me to leave.'

It is quite common to hear talk of emigration but, apart from the fear of losing the Swedish level of social security, the most powerful inhibitions seem to be connected with deep guilt feelings. Traditionally, Sweden has been a country of emigration, and the authorities have worked hard over the past three or four decades to counteract its legacy. The trend has been to explain away the mass emigation of the nineteenth century in any convenient way: at one point it was by talking about the exactions of the capitalist class. As far as the present is concerned, social security is projected as a gift bestowed by an all-caring society, so that the citizen has something tremendous to be grateful for, and rejection is felt as ingratitude so black as to be equated with immorality.

It is observable from early schooldays onwards. So deep does the suggestion go that guilt feelings sit securely on anything related to renunciation of the established order. This applies particularly to emigration: it has helped greatly to stem the brain drain. In More's *Utopia*, the only crime was to want to leave. In Sweden, social welfare has been used to make it the only sin.

11. Education in the Service of Conditioning

Social and economic security have been essential to the control of the populace. But they have never been considered ends in themselves. They were to prepare the ground for social engineers, giving them malleable human material with which to work. The ultimate aim is to create the new man for the new society and, among the agents of its achievement, education is obviously of crucial importance.

All education is a form of moulding the young according to the ideas of their elders. The character of the age, the nature of society and the ambitions of its rulers will naturally affect the specifications set forth. 'The study of liberal arts and of the philosophic sciences avail much in Christendom,' writes Humbert de Romans,* the medieval Dominican. 'It avails for the defence of the faith . . . it avails to the honour of the Church.' For Victorian England, Dr Arnold gave his celebrated definition of schooling as the production of 'a Christian, a gentleman and a scholar in that order'. Turning to Sweden in the last third of the twentieth century, we learn from Mr Olof Palme, the Prime Minister (and sometime Minister of Education), that, 'You don't go to school to achieve anything personally, but to learn how to function as members of a group'.†

For their intended society, the Swedish planners require a type of person that, thinking collectively, and suppressing

* Humbert de Romans (1194–1277) was the fifth Master-General of the Dominican Order.
† From an address to schoolchildren.

his individuality in favour of the group, is technologically orientated, and socially well adjusted. To this end, the educational system was profoundly altered during the 1950s and 1960s. From imparting knowledge, its aim was changed to that of guiding social behaviour.

In Western countries, the very intimation of educational reform, even without ideological undertones, usually arouses ferocious opposition, and authority does not always get its way. But in Sweden it took less than five years from the adoption of policy to the recasting of schools and universities, new textbooks and all. There was some public discussion, but no substantial opposition. In Sweden, all education is rigidly centralized under government direction. It is a long tradition and a legacy of the Reformation.

Perhaps the most important change brought by the Swedish Reformation was in the educational system. In order to enforce Lutheran doctrine, and tear out Catholicism by the roots, teaching was minutely supervised. It was a means of controlling what was put into the minds of the population – and what was kept out. The original purpose has faded away, but the mechanism remains. It has really come into its own in the twentieth century, and only now is Sweden fully reaping the benefit.

During the Reformation, the schools were turned into a monopoly of the Church. Similar arrangements have existed elsewhere, but usually in a form that ensured independence of the State. But in Sweden the clergy were the State. And centralization of a kind rare in contemporary Europe was enforced. The schools were removed from the jurisdiction of the local parishes and placed directly under the orders of the national ecclesiastical authorities in Stockholm. Curricula for the whole country were decided by a government committee; schoolmasters could only be appointed or dismissed by the central authorities in Stockholm. Since the Reformation, local divergences have been impossible, there has been uniformity throughout the land, and the State has prescribed exactly what every schoolchild was taught.

This system has been preserved down the centuries. When the Social Democrats decided to change the school system, they had the apparatus waiting. They were not obliged to fight local authorities; they did not have to indulge in the irksome task of imposing the writ of the central government. All education below university level was now directly and rigidly controlled by an elaborate central State institution, the Directorate of Schools in Stockholm, that had developed out of the uncomplicated old government committees to keep pace with the advancing complexity of modern administration and modern education. It was sufficient to make out the necessary administrative orders to impose the reform. The creation of the seventeenth century had stood the test of time.

The universities* were also rigorously subjected by the Reformers to the central authority. Like the schools, they were a Church monopoly. Academic freedom was never known in Sweden; the independence of universities was unwanted, because it would have impeded the control of thought. From the start, professors have been appointed directly by the government; curricula and even the detailed content of individual lectures were decided by ecclesiastical functionaries and State officials. This arrangement was never disturbed; in modern times, the only change has been the elimination of the Church as intermediary, and the substitution of direct State rule. Outside the dictatorships, there are few countries in the world, and certainly none in Western Europe (not excepting even France), in which education is so uniform and so thoroughly subject to government control.

The Swedish school reform took the outward shape of a

* Until the middle of the seventeenth century, there was only one university at Uppsala. In 1669, the second Swedish university was established at Lund, in the south. Its chief purpose was to make good Swedes of the provinces then captured from Denmark.

device to promote egalitarian principles. The old order divided children at an early age according to intelligence, ambition and, some would say, class. After six years of compulsory primary schooling, common to all, pupils were streamed. On the one hand were vocational training schools, on the other, the secondary schools which, being exclusively academic, had the greater prestige. Within the secondary school a distinction was further drawn between the three-year *real* division for those who did not propose to study further and, the apex of the whole system, the six-year gymnasium leading to matriculation and university. Entry to secondary school was selective. Children had to make their choice between the ages of eleven and thirteen.

Under the new system, all children stay together for nine years in the same basic school. Choice of subjects is allowed after seven years, when there is streaming into practical and theoretical lines. But this now takes place within the same school where it used to involve moving into separate institutions. Whereas before, children were separated at twelve or thirteen, social mixing is now guaranteed until sixteen, at least on paper. At the same time, the school-leaving age has been raised from fifteen to sixteen. After the basic school, there are vocational training institutes, and a new version of the gymnasium, leading to university. These are voluntary.

The new Swedish school has been derived from the American system, and resembles the comprehensive schools in England. The change was radical, abandoning as it did a time-honoured selective principle. It was defended by an official argument on the following lines. By putting all children into the same schools, the opportunities for everyone are increased, and nobody is penalized for making the wrong choice, or for failing to pass a selective examination at an early age. This explanation has been accepted by most Swedes, and the new school has therefore come into being with little resistance.

There are two sides to every argument, and there is therefore a case to be made against the new system, at least in the case of bright children. It is reasonable to suggest that a selective school, ensuring a minimum level of attainment, will attract good teachers, providing a better environment and higher standards than one indiscriminately open to all. Parents may regard a new educational theory as not proven until it has stood the test of time. They may even be reluctant to let their children act as guinea pigs.

This has not been the case in Sweden. The ease of reform and the lack of resistance are in no small measure due to an almost complete lack of competition from private schools, and an absolute lack of alternatives. Private schools, all originating towards the end of the last century, are few, and will gradually be eliminated. But they never attempted to compete with the State system, only to provide the same teaching in more exclusive social surroundings. They *wanted* to follow the edicts of the State, the Church and the establishment. This is rather different from the English public schools which generally arose out of a determination not to submit to ecclesiastical monopoly.

Perhaps the chief advantage of the new Swedish system lies in the way teaching resources are fully exploited. The reform involves concentration into fewer and larger units. One large school can provide more facilities, and use money more efficiently, than several smaller ones. It can maintain laboratories and libraries of a size and quality difficult to justify in lesser institutions. With more pupils to choose from, it can offer a wider choice of subjects, and provide instruction in some that, for want of numbers or goodwill, might be denied elsewhere. In a school of 500 perhaps only half a dozen might want to study Russian, clearly too few to warrant classes. But among 1,500, the number would be rather higher, justifying instruction. Moreover, and this is a particularly important consideration in a small country like

Sweden, where manpower of all kinds is at a premium, the system uses teachers more intensively, and therefore exploits them more economically.

Administratively, the new school system is also advantageous. In a large, sparsely populated country, such as Sweden, it has been irksome to service and supervise many small and scattered units. The village school, while the stuff of praise from nostalgic sentimentalists, is clearly indefensible in any other terms. By replacing a number of such schools with a single one, administration is simplified because it is concentrated. It is much easier to deal with a few large institutions than with many small ones. In Lapland, where population is five to the square mile, school inspectors and other administrators are saved a great deal of travel.

It is not only in the countryside that the comprehensive system offers such advantages. Even in the towns, by streamlining organization and, above all, by eliminating choice of school, it makes administration far easier. The reform, by promoting centralization, has followed official policy in other fields, particularly the reorganization of local government. It is part of a far-sighted plan to consolidate the powers of the central authorities and make their work easier.

So much for the practical aspects of the school reform. But that reform is, as it were, the forging or refurbishing of a tool. The purposes for which it is to be used are another matter entirely. From the mid nineteenth century until the early 1960s the Swedish school system was modelled on Imperial Germany. Its purpose was to turn out good civil servants devoted to the interests of the State. It set out to inculcate solid bourgeois attitudes and respect for a kind of stable hierarchical and authoritarian society whose form (but not nature) was inimical to the aims of the Social Democrats. Change was not only inevitable; it was politically necessary.

The most obvious requirement was to break down the old class structure in the name of equality and to attack bourgeois values. A neatly symbolic reform was the abolition of the so-called *student* examination, or matriculation. This was not so much an academic attainment as a mark of social class. Upon passing his examinations, the matriculant was entitled to wear a little white peaked cap, similar to the distinguishing headgear of members of the Imperial German student corps. Since higher education in Sweden used to be a privilege, the student cap became the symbol of the bourgeois and the official classes. With the spread of learning and the cultivation of the proletarian mystique, it was treated by men of the left as the hated badge of a despised class. A writer well known among the Swedes, Vilhelm Moberg, made his protest by refusing to don his cap. Others have done likewise. The last student caps were awarded in 1968. Their disappearance was widely billed as a blow for equality and a herald of change.

But these are clearly superficial messages. What are the underlying aims of the new Swedish schools system? Let one of its architects, Mr Sven Moberg,★ deputy Minister of Education, explain: 'Education is one of the most important agents for changing society. It has been integrated into our scheme for changing society, and its purpose is to turn out the correct kind of person for the new society.

'The new school rejects individuality, and teaches children to collaborate with others. It rejects competition, and teaches cooperation. Children are taught to work in groups. They solve problems together; not alone. The basic idea is that they are considered primarily as members of society, and individuality is discouraged. We want to produce individuals who are integrated into society.'

This is how the Minister of Education, Mr Ingvar Carlsson, defines the purpose of schooling: 'It is to produce a well

★ Quotations from Mr Moberg in this chapter, together with those of his superior, Mr Carlsson, are from private conversation. Where this is not the case, the source is given.

adjusted, good member of society. It teaches people to respect the consensus, and not sabotage it.'

In the schools, the emphasis lies heavily on the collective and on the necessity of subjecting personalities to the demands of the group. Society is seen, not as a collection of individuals, but as a union of corporate organizations. One of the subjects taught in the upper classes of the secondary school is entitled 'popular organizations', explaining how they function and how to work within them. These organizations are presented as equal to the Diet, and as a branch of the State. 'Popular organizations' is a loaded term. It has come to mean 'Labour movement', and therefore schoolchildren have been induced to consider the movement as synonymous with the State. Comparisons with Soviet Russia, Mussolini's Italy or Falangist Spain are superfluous.

It is a truism that to change people it is desirable to cut off the past. In the Swedish schools, the study of history has been truncated and the emphasis laid on the development of the Swedish Labour movement. The French Revolution is seen as the beginning of things. Otherwise, the European heritage and the classical background have been dismissed, and an atmosphere created in which only recent decades appear to count. 'Nothing matters before 1932'* cries a student of political economy at Lund University. 'The young economists,' says Professor Gunnar Myrdal, 'don't know anything about history, and they don't care.' Of course, the anti-historical bias of younger intellectuals is a universal phenomenon, at least in the West. What is distinctive about Sweden is that this bias is, if not exactly shared, at least encouraged and exploited by authority.

It is, naturally enough, a Social Democratic aim to steer Sweden to the left. This is expressed in educational bias. A guide for teachers in the higher classes issued by the Schools Directorate suggests how social development may be

* The year in which the Social Democrats came to power.

illuminated by the consideration of authors during the past century. Those recommended are Michael Sholokov, Émile Zola, Richard Wright and militant American negro authors, and in Sweden 'the socially committed writers . . . Vilhelm Moberg, Harry Martinson and Ivar Lo-Johansson'. These last are the proletarian Swedish authors, all Social Democrats. The implication of the phrase 'the socially committed writers' is that only among the Social Democrats is social conscience to be found. To propose Sholokov, Zola and Wright as exclusive, and, by implication, approved examples of Russian, French and American literature, is to intimate a socialist interpretation of history. It is, of course, a perfectly valid one; under the Swedish system, it appears as the *only* valid one.

The power exercised by the central authority is profound and detailed, so that the State directs all education. The individual teacher has no independence, and is bound in his methods of instruction and the contents of his lessons by the exhaustive ukases of the Schools Directorate. Headmasters are, scholastically, supercargoes. They have no say over the conduct of teaching within their domain; that is decided in Stockholm. Their function is administrative; they are the agents of the Directorate, enforcing its orders.

Since the educational system is monolithic, control from the top is effortless. A small group of planners in the Directorate establish ideology and methods to be adopted by all teachers. The centre of power is therefore compact and easily controlled. And the teachers, for their part, follow their orders with little protest.

By ensuring that the leadership of the Schools Directorate is in their hands, the party has imposed its own ideas, without the approval of the Diet. The director-general at the time of the school reform, Mr Hans Löwbeer, was a militant Social Democratic ideologist; his successor was also a Social Democrat. In this way, party programmes and party slogans have rapidly been brought to the classroom, and incorporated into the body of established truth. Textbooks are severely controlled. They must be approved by a State commission, subordinate to the Directorate, and they may not be used without approval. The power of the Commission is absolute, and, in consequence, not only teachers, but their textbooks are also directed by the State. Official influence is secured even further by the practice of issuing authors with instructions to avoid criticism and rejection. It is known that approval will be almost certain if this guidance is followed, and to avoid discussion and change, publishers see that authors comply. In this way, the State ensures that schoolbooks are constructed to its specifications.

Centralized control of textbooks has been an invaluable aid to the enforcement of official policy and the undermining of incipient criticism. At one point, the Schools Directorate decided, against the wishes of many teachers and, indeed, the advice of some of their educational advisers, that language teaching should take place by the so-called 'direct method', that is, without translations, and solely through the medium of the foreign tongue concerned. To enforce the rescript, only those textbooks were approved that followed the system.

The attitude of the government to textbook control was illustrated by Mr Palme, the Prime Minister, at the 1969 party congress. In a speech touching on the importance of ideology in education, and the necessity of eradicating reactionary tendencies from the schools, he quoted a passage from a certain textbook that displayed a non-socialist viewpoint. 'That book,' he said, 'had not been investigated by the textbooks commission',* implying, justifiably, that if it had it would not have passed.

---

* At the time, the jurisdiction of the commission was confined to the nine-year basic school, and certain subjects in the gymnasium. It did not yet include political economy in the latter, whence the example was taken.

It is party policy, and the urgent wish of Social Democratic ideologists, to make school textbooks a State monopoly. The reason given is that society has the sole right to decide what is taught to children, and that 'bourgeois' evaluations must be eliminated. Only by eliminating private interests can this be achieved. By 1970, the State had gone some way towards the realization of this ideal by nationalizing certain publishers, so that it controls about a third of the market at school, and a half at university level. Furthermore, a State publishing house was established, with the ultimate aim of dominating the field. The Minister of Education, in 1969, applied pressure on university staff and schoolteachers to write for the official publishers only.

By the definition of its creators, the new Swedish school system is strictly utilitarian. It suggests the abandonment of the concept of education as something that makes the complete man and develops the individual. It appears to have the aim of producing, not independent citizens, but cogs in the society-machine. This is how Mrs Maj Bossom-Nordboe, a departmental chief at the Directorate of Schools, expresses it: 'Everything in our school system is practical. History has been cut down, because subjects of practical application, and especially those dealing with communication, are more important. Classical studies have been abolished, because they are unpractical and therefore unnecessary.'

A comment of some interest on this development was published by a Mr Sven Delblanc in a Stockholm newspaper. The importance of Mr Delblanc is that, besides being a lecturer in the University of Lund in the history of literature, he is also a left-wing writer, and can therefore scarcely be accused of being a reactionary. Besides, he has held lecturing posts at American universities, and therefore brings something of the eye of an outsider.

'The literature of the Roman Golden Age,' writes Mr Delblanc, 'is interesting in many ways. For example, it illustrates how different poetic temperaments react to the State's demand that poetry shall have a certain political and propagandistic content. Nobody can possibly deny that such a phenomenon is devoid of topicality and interest. But in my teaching at university, I cannot expect my students to have more than the vaguest and dimmest ideas of who Augustus was and what he wanted.

'In the European political and cultural debate, the history of Rome from republic via military dictatorship to the Empire has been a classical paradigm. It has not only taught us something about the relation of the writer to the State, but also demonstrated economic and political patterns of development. It has even provided us with a terminology. Our youth are obviously to be prevented from learning where and how concepts like proletariat, imperialism and plebeian arose. Why? Is that knowledge politically dangerous?

'Scrapping historical knowledge deprives pupils of the instrument for criticizing society here and now. And perhaps that is the intended effect.'

Mrs Nordboe again: 'Perhaps something can be learned from the ancients. But it's not important. We've got to concentrate on society today, with the accent on practical matters such as sex, narcotics and poisons. This has a pedagogic effect of relating what we teach to reality: children learn in that way about their environment.

'Our school has to produce people predisposed to change. If they were not, they would be unhappy.

'It's the same with the question of the individual. It's useless to build up individuality, because unless people learned to adapt themselves to society, they would be unhappy. Liberty is *not* emphasized. Instead, we talk about the freedom to give up freedom. The accent is on the *social* function of children, and I will not deny that we emphasize the collective.'

The traditional class, with pupils working individually, has been largely replaced by group work. The purpose behind this, according to the official directions to teachers, is to teach children how to adapt to the collective and to show that an individual cannot accomplish much on his own. 'By assigning a project to a group,' according to these directions, 'and requiring pupils to divide the task among themselves, they can be taught the satisfaction of bringing their contributions to the collective, and grow used to the conditions they will meet when they go to work.'

Reflection of life outside, school is obsessed with the question of eliminating the non-conformist and the man away from the crowd. To remain outside the group, is the sin against the Holy Ghost, and immense pains are taken to round up the independent and the unwilling. Personal initiative is not encouraged, unless it benefits the collective. Individualism is not admired. 'It may happen that the occasional pupil will want to withdraw from the group and work on his own,' says the preamble to the curriculum for the higher classes of the Swedish schools, 'This may naturally be allowed. But it is often possible to make the individual's task part of the group's project.'

In a junior civics course, there are two sections entitled 'People who are Different' and 'To Nurse and to Help'. They are not, as their titles might imply, designed to encourage admiration for individualists, or to teach personal charity (in the Greek sense), but to point out the necessity of togetherness as the only tenable way of life, and to hold up the State as the omniscient provider. Distress, children are taught, is relieved by the authorities, and social welfare looks after anybody in trouble. It is only necessary to call on some official agency, and the need of the moment will be dealt with. You are not your brother's keeper, the message seems to be, but the State is.

Individual attainment is disparaged; it is proficiency within the group that is favoured. The Swedish schools aim at producing citizens who will devote their talents to the service of the collective. The attributes officially honoured are not a sharp wit or scholastic ability, but a will to cooperate and adapt to a group. Competition has been abolished. The wish to excel is considered undesirable and asocial. This is, of course, in stark contrast to, say, the English public school system, where the team spirit is supposed to be drummed in on the playing fields, but suspended in the classroom. The fact that the swot has been despised in England (or grind in America) has never vitiated official approval of the good scholar and the scholarship boy. And, at a totally different point of the compass, competition reigns mercilessly. A Russian educational official on tour in Sweden was shocked at the Swedish system, and lectured schoolchildren in Stockholm on the necessity of contest in learning as the only way to efficiency.

There is general antipathy towards the individual in educational work, although it may be concealed in words suggesting the opposite. Instructions issued by the Directorate of Schools declare that teaching must be adjusted to the individual, but not so much for the sake of his personal development as to absorb him more efficiently into the collective. Put another way, individualized teaching is suggested as a device to encourage group thinking in the most efficient manner. Rigid teaching, assuming that all pupils are exactly the same in all respects, defeats its own purpose by creating outsiders and, what is worse, rebels. Adaptation of methods, say the educational authorities, can bring everybody, or nearly everybody, into the collective.

In one sense, the school system has not changed; it has only done old things better. Uniformity of opinion has ever been the achievement of Swedish education; it is simply that the identity of that opinion has changed. In the late 1950s, conventional nationalism, with a tinge of nostalgia for the age when Sweden was a great power, was still the lesson imparted to schoolchildren. A decade later, this had swung over to a guided internationalism, expressed as solidarity with the underdeveloped countries. It is an illustration of the powers held by the central authorities in directing what is to be taught. The Directorate of Schools decreed this particular ideological shift, and it was obediently enforced. School-children and school-leavers all over the country displayed the same homogeneity of opinion as they had always done, and it was at the bidding of the State.

It was also at the bidding of the party. At the time, the Social Democratic party had decided that interest in the under-developed countries and support through technical assistance were politically profitable. The interval between their adoption as party policy and their enforcement in the school curricula was a few months. This was easily done, since the Directorate of Schools was run by Social Democrats and, because it is completely independent of parliamentary control, the party could have its say unobstructed. It is only one of many instances in which items on the party programme have rapidly become educational policy.

By the late 1960s, most teenagers (and younger voters) supported aid to the underdeveloped countries,★ as they had been taught at school. This makes an interesting comparison with England or America, where attitudes among corres-ponding groups are generally those of indifference with minority groups that are fiercely hostile or in favour. But the younger Swedes are uniformly and overwhelmingly in favour of overseas technical aid, with a degree of emotionalism that may surprise the outsider. This is closely related to neutrality. 'Neutrality,' says a professor at Uppsala University, 'is like cutting off a piece of the personality, and to make up for it we have to find some ways of extending our feelings of responsibility – it's an urge peculiar to Sweden. That explains the obsession with the underdeveloped countries.

★ In 1970–71, Sweden spent 800,000,000 kronor (£65,000,000 or $154,000,000), 0.41 per cent of the Gross National Product, on aid.

It is an approach to the world outside. By identifying ourselves with a unit larger than Sweden, we can satisfy a need for significance.'

It is probably correct to say that Sweden has been dechristianized more efficiently than any other country, Russia not excepted. Among non-communist countries, Sweden is unique in deliberately encouraging the process. It has been accomplished by a form of instruction, labelled 'religious' but which is in fact anti-religious. The course, which starts in the upper forms of the secondary school, sets out to review the different forms of religion in the world, and places Christianity on a level with all other faiths, and with no faith at all. Religion, in this course, is presented as an escape from reality.

'Marxism's criticism of religion, based on Feuerbach,' says the syllabus for religious knowledge in the gymnasium, 'ought also to be treated. In order to make Marx's views comprehensible his dialectic view of evolution, as it appears in the materialistic interpretation of history, must be clarified. If possible, texts from modern Marxism–Leninism ought to be analysed.

'It is also desirable to touch on psychology's view of religion as a compulsive neurosis with infantile characteristics. The relationship between the Marxist and psycho-analytical viewpoints can thereby be illustrated.'

In a sense, this is probably more efficient than the Russians' concentrated attack on religion which can more easily be shown up as propaganda. By reducing the importance of Christianity, but still teaching it, no question of prejudice arises, and the appearance of 'objectivity', one of the tenets of the new school, is maintained. In this way, Christianity is taught not as a faith, but as a phenomenon, and the idea of religious experience and religious emotion may be dismissed.

Since this course is compulsory, with the only exception made for Jews in the part concerning Christianity, the school has a means of counteracting religious instruction in the home. Those leaving school at the end of the 1960s were predominantly anti-Christian, considering religion as indefensible and ridiculous. The concept of religion as a form of mental illness was prevalent. Since the instruction had largely been given in the form of discussions so guided that the pupils felt that they had themselves arrived at the conclusions, conviction was deep. It is interesting to note the similarity between this and the study circle ABF; and, indeed, the architects of the new school system freely admit that they have been influenced by the methods of the Labour movement.

While most Swedes are indifferent to Christianity, it is doubtful whether a Diet majority could have been mustered in support of anti-religious teaching of this kind. It is not at all certain that the Social Democratic party was wholly in favour. But it so happened that the party leaders and ideologists had decided and were able to influence the Directorate of Schools accordingly.

If religion has been reduced to political theory, political concepts have been elevated to religious rank. In the senior course in 'Religious knowledge', there is a section on 'Ethical and moral questions'. 'Instruction in moral questions is intended to give pupils insight and understanding of the place and function of morality in the life of the individual and society,' says the syllabus issued by the Directorate of Schools. 'Suitable areas to deal with are the ethics of home and work.

'When the ethics of employment are dealt with, one can take up questions which, on the one hand, affect the relations between workmates and, on the other, between employers and employees. In the case of the former, there is, for example, the question of taking work and earning at the cost of your workmates against the possibility of sharing opportunities; further, the advisability of belonging to a trade union. The morality that has been developed in our country through the regulation of relations between employers and employees also belongs here. For example, there is the LO's principle of solidarity between high and low paid groups, solidarity with the country's economic situation in wage demands, and respect for wage agreements.'

This is an illustration of the way in which political slogans are turned into classroom dogma. What are basically Labour movement, or at least trade-union, concepts, are taught as if they were received truths. The Swedish Labour Market is here given the same treatment as the Song of Songs and the Sermon on the Mount. Ideologically loaded words, with a partisan impact, are present on a level with the Gospel. Party catchwords, by being presented as 'religious knowledge', are given an authoritative touch. 'The advisability of belonging to trade unions' is a precept of the Labour movement and, by teaching it at school as the Eleventh Commandment, the idea of the closed shop is given the sanction of moral compulsion. 'Solidarity' was a slogan of the Labour movement, and by no stretch of the imagination could it be associated with any other political camp. 'Solidarity between high and low paid groups' was at the time a Social Democratic electoral slogan, not a principle enforced by national consensus, and of doubtful success into the bargain. Likewise, 'Equality' was uniquely the clarion call of the Social Democrats. But both it and the word 'solidarity' occur liberally in textbooks and teachers' manuals. 'Equality and solidarity are important goals,' says the official syllabus for the senior classes of the Swedish schools, 'and ought to be imprinted, *inter alia*, by school activities.'

Similarly, equality of the sexes, once it had been adopted as party policy by the Social Democrats, was placed on the school curriculum. This helped in no small measure to secure rapid and national acceptance for the idea. At an early age, conventional ideas of male and female roles were broken down. Boys were taught to sew, and girls to wield hammer and chisel. Equality was taken to its logical conclusion. It was pointed out that there is no reason why a father cannot stay at home to look after the family while the mother goes out to work. At all events, children were persuaded that both can and must work. This was to eradicate the traditional attitude of women that their business was to catch a breadwinner and avoid gainful employment. It was also to destroy the customary belief that a woman's place is looking after a family and substitute the idea that her proper duty is by the man's side, in office and factory.

Schoolwork was reinforced by radio and T v. What was dubbed 'sex-role discrimination' was officially banned from children's programmes; instead, the message of absolute equality (apart, naturally, from the purely anatomical) was enforced. The press loyally followed suit, so that the adult population was also informed. The interval between the adoption of equality of the sexes on the party programme and its enforcement in the school curriculum and the mass media was about three months.

One of the purposes in predisposing women to go to work was plainly economic. 'It is being an enemy of society, to have a training and not to work,' declared a lady from the Labour Market Directorate. 'All those in production have to pay for it. Sweden is a little country, and needs all its labour force out in production. Women can't expect to be privileged by staying at home.'

Economic common sense suggests that as many women as possible must go to work. But there are other reasons as well. Educational theorists want to get both parents out of the home, so that children are forced out as well. The family bond is to be weakened, and children brought up in crèches and day nurseries. Compulsory pre-school training will be established by the middle of the 1970s.

Mr Ingvar Carlsson, the Social Democratic Minister of Education, has said that pre-school training is essential to 'eliminate the social heritage'. By this, he means that progress at school depended on home influence and that, by eradicating it, everybody would have an equal start, and could be guided into the appropriate occupations required by society. It would utilize national talent more efficiently, by bringing out abilities obscured by unfavourable home environment. What he was particularly thinking of was the anti-intellectual bias of working-class homes, which deprived many educational institutions of people who had the necessary abilities.

But the main function of pre-school training was social. 'It is necessary to socialize children at an early age,' says Mr Carlsson. 'In pre-school play groups of the future, children must be taken outside the home to learn how society works. They will develop the social function of human beings, and teach children how to be together. They have to learn solidarity with each other, and how to cooperate, not compete with each other.'

Ideally, the Swedish government would have liked to introduce compulsory pre-school training from the age of three years, following the discovery of a commission of inquiry that it was easiest to influence behaviour at that age. This could not, however, be realized immediately, since it was considered that the economy would be over-strained by so explosive an expansion of the educational system. A starting age of five was therefore accepted as a temporary expedient. In 1970, the training of kindergarten teachers and play leaders was augmented so that their supply will be guaranteed when the scheme is introduced by about 1975. Research was being conducted by State institutions to devise teaching methods that would best accomplish the goals adumbrated by Mr Carlsson.

The school age in Sweden remains at seven years. Pre-school training is to concentrate on the formation of social behaviour, so that the correct attitudes will have been imprinted before the child begins his scholastic education. In a word, the aim is to produce socially well-adjusted people, with a collective mentality. Uniformity will be guaranteed by making pre-school training a State monopoly. It has been officially announced that no private institutions will be tolerated. By the middle of the 1980s, it is expected that compulsory pre-schooling will have been extended to three-year-olds.

These are radical plans being speedily effected. It might be supposed that, as in all matters of educational reform, opposition and debate would have arisen. But, by and large, Sweden has accepted the development. Most parents now earnestly believe that their children must be 'socialized' early. Again, they think in the way they have been told to, even the middle classes, and particularly the intellectuals. A journalist (politically in the centre) says in deadly earnest: 'Of course, I want my children to go to properly organized play groups. They've got to learn to become part of the collective. Individualism is unhealthy, isn't it?' And this is what a manufacturer, a man who had built up his own firm, an old-fashioned kind of entrepreneur, had to say:

'Of course, the trend of Swedish education is to break down individuality and promote the collective. I suppose I should be sorry. You can't build up a company as I have done without being an individual. But that's all over and done with now. I don't want my children and grandchildren to be taught to be individuals. They'd only be unhappy. So, I say, let the rising generation be trained for the collective. They'll be much happier. So, when one of my sons complained about the collective, and talked about being an individual, I slapped him down, and sided with the school. And I hope that the new kindergarten will do their job properly with my grand-children. Sweden is a collective society, and there's no place for the individual. Much better for all concerned if we bring up citizens adjusted from childhood to the collective.'

The intellectual purpose of education, in the definition of the Swedish school system, is to 'develop an independent and critical way of thinking'. In fact, this is Newspeak for group thought. And it must be the correct group, with approved ideas. Pupils are not taught to maintain their personal opinions, but to stick to a consensus. The words 'independent' and 'critical' turn out to mean not what they appear to mean, but a shift from older accepted views to new ones. It is connected with another aim of the new Swedish school, which is defined by the curriculum as the eradication of authoritarian attitudes.

At first glance, this is flying in the face of everything upon which Swedish society is founded. The stability of the Labour Market is built on absolute obedience to trade-union leaders. This has been made possible by a school system which, in imitation of Imperial Germany, has inculcated respect for superiors and acceptance of hierarchical structure. The disappearance of these attitudes might be expected to cause unrest.

The situation is not what it appears to be. Behind the terminology of egalitarianism and advanced educational theory, the authorities were concerned to maintain old discipline in new forms. They had understood that traditional ideas were not only useless, but productive of rebellion in the new ideological climate. The 1968 students' revolt in France proved them right; by party foresight, Sweden escaped virtually scot-free from that contagion. What unrest there was, was turned by the government to their own advantage. Let Mr Carlsson explain it in his own words:

'The purpose of the new school is to break down respect for authority and build a sense of cooperation. The old system would have broken down anyway and a substitute had to be found. This meant that we had to encourage collective attitudes.

'The new school has been based on lessons learned from the trade unions. They have built up a system which depended on information and respect for your negotiating partners. This meant that you had to respect your employer and talk to him, using rational arguments.

'Now, this is mirrored in the schools, and therefore their products would fit very well into the trade unions. Of course, the development of the schools is going to affect industry. Influence in running the schools would result in demands for more say in the running of factories.'

A leader of the LO thought that the new school system would help his organization: 'It will encourage the pursuit of more democracy in industry. It will produce dissatisfaction with authoritarian forms of management.'

When schoolchildren are taught to question 'authority', the word is equated with teachers, employers and parents. They are asked to reject the old masters of society and respect new ones instead. Going out to work, young people have attitudes tailormade for the Labour Market: antipathy towards their employers, and respect for union leaders. They have been conditioned to resent a certain form of authority, but not to question authority *per se*.

As part of their 'independent and critical thinking', schoolchildren must learn how to resist 'propaganda' and 'the mass media'. But this resistance, it turns out, is rather selective. Advertising, public relations and the newspapers are taught as the principal objects of scepticism and inquiry; the businessman and the *private* communicator are held up for suspicion. The institutions of the State and the corporate organizations, however, are honourably excepted. The business executive is made suspect, but not the bureaucrat. The official communicators are left unquestioned. In this way, there is a form of conditioning in which children are led to question private advertising, but to accept State propaganda. Indoctrination pivots on the concept of society. As long as something is presented under the label of 'society', it is good; if not, it is bad.

Schooling, in the words of a frequently quoted Swedish

cliché, has to teach people 'to function in their environment'. This means that the average pupil and the dullard have to be pushed and pulled a little in order to fit in. *Mutatis mutandis,* the brainy and ambitious ones tend to want to influence the environment, and the schools therefore have started turning out people predominantly disposed to social engineering. The wish to be a planner of some kind, a sociologist or an economist, has become increasingly common.

The Swedish schools are therefore turning out two kinds of person. There is the submissive average man, who has learned to accept his circumstances, motivated by a kind of fatalism, in a world arranged by economic determinism. On the other hand, there is the *élite,* ambitious of commanding its subordinates and of deliberately manipulating the environment in which they live. Both believe in the supremacy of the group, and both are animated by a collective mentality. Neither gives promise of individual thought or action.

The new curriculum has, on the admission of its designers, departed from the idea of imparting fundamental knowledge. Its purpose is not to develop the intellectual faculties, but to create desirable social attitudes. In the senior classes leading to higher education, the academic virtues have been self-confessedly abandoned, and the emphasis laid on political and civic instruction. The study of grammar has been abandoned, for example, but a subject termed 'welfare theory', which is an ideological justification of the Welfare State, has been given considerable prominence. There is a heavy sociological bias throughout: it is the practical subjects of use to society that are in favour.

University teachers complain of a drop in academic standards. Returning to Mr Delblanc: 'It is an illusion,' he writes, 'to believe that one can expect a university student to meet the elementary requirements of reading foreign texts. It is possible that those leaving the new school can, as package tourists, converse with waiters and hall porters. But, further than that, their knowledge of languages is practically invisible. Put simply, they know neither German nor French. They think that they can speak English, but in reality they cannot even do that.'

So far, this sort of reproach is to be heard in most countries in most ages. Academics are prone to bewail the decadence of their students. Sweden, however, has been distinguished by a sudden change of undergraduate mentality. Mr Delblanc again:

'What then has the new gymnasium given instead? The only advance I can detect is a new mentality. It is a useful impertinence, wish to debate and mistrust of authorities. Unfortunately, this new liberation is expressed more often in the form of watching over their own interests as a student body, a kind of trade-union mentality, than in a broad criticism of society and its established institutions. Student criticism is directed towards the form of education, the form of lessons and examinations, but further than this it rarely gets. Shining exceptions confirm the rule; the much vaunted anti-authoritarian teaching creates, not critics of society, but coming trade-union bosses.'

Anti-authoritarianism, in the Swedish educationists' sense of the word, means a rejection of the individual leader, but submission to the dictates of the group. It produces, as Mr Delblanc suggests, the perfect corporate man in his various manifestations, and the mentality of the *apparatchik*. As all those concerned with education admit, these achievements demonstrably accompanied the denigration of the individual and the glorification of the collective imprinted by the Swedish school system. It is quite conceivable that the educational theorists who originally propounded the scheme had other ends in mind, but, as it turns out, the results achieved serve the intentions of the managers of Swedish society very well.

Corporate man may be desirable, but he must possess the

correct tendencies if he is to be of use to his society. A conservative is clearly unwanted in the Swedish world. So, indeed, is anybody with a particular creed and independent and steadfast views, be he of the right or the left. What is required, as the architects and administrators of Swedish education so ingenuously announce, is people predisposed to change. Not change of a particular nature, but change for its own sake.

In the attainment of these goals, great care has been devoted to severing intellectual roots. The general curtailment of history has been one method. Within this, there has been included the more refined concept of cutting Swedish links with Western Europe. Whatever the public justifications for such a step, the consequence has turned out to be a cultural vacuum, and it is in such a state that mass conditioning is really effective. It may be said to be a necessary requirement. To achieve this end, a kind of perverted Toynbeeism has been invoked.

Arnold Toynbee's *A Study of History* has been one of the great tracts for our times, at least in the English-speaking world. Its message – that the West ought to renounce egocentricity and, by paying more attention to other cultures, put itself in perspective – appeals to the age of uncertainty. But Toynbee speaks as a man of the West. Admittedly he betrays a whiff of ambivalence, but the sense of his life's work is that he wants to provide a cure for the ills of the civilization into which he was born. There lurks behind his writing a pride in the power and achievement of the West; he has been one of the articulate few to praise the European bourgeoisie, 'the most powerful and inventive class that the world has ever seen'. To use him, as many do, in order to discredit the West is scarcely defensible. He wanted the West to imbibe a sense of proportion; from that to the repudiation of Western culture is a long step. Unfortunately, what Toynbee presented as critical analysis has been interpreted as abuse, and it is this misconception that has been widely adopted as the message.

Toynbee, like Savonarola, searched for a regeneration, but his name has too often come to stand for an anathema, of a society. If true Toynbeeism is an appeal for a soul-searching of the West, the false kind preaches its rejection. It is in this perverted form that Toynbeeism has taken root in Sweden.

'In teaching,' says the preamble to the curriculum for the Swedish school system, 'it is desirable to desert a Western European perspective.' This applies to all possible subjects, but to current affairs and history particularly. In the public justification, this has the laudable aim of eradicating nationalism and encouraging global solidarity. But the effect is to generate a kind of inverted chauvinism. Africa and Asia appear as more important than the West. Western values, even the admirable ones, are disparaged. Mrs Camilla Odhnoff, Minister of Family Affairs, replies, on being asked whether she is a European: 'How can I associate myself with the West, when children are being murdered in Vietnam'? Mr Olof Palme answers the same question by saying, 'I don't see anything special about Florence, or Paris or Rome. I feel more at home in Prague and Warsaw and Sofia; they're just as important. The Renaissance So-called? Western culture? What does it mean to us?' The voice of a liberal publisher: 'I don't feel anything in common with Western Europe. But I do feel a deep sympathy with Russia. Russian literature tells you why. Authors like Chekhov and Tolstoy write about the same thing that we (Swedes) are concerned with. It is the problem of a man fitting into the world.' A conservative university professor says that, although he likes visiting the Continent, it is to him very foreign, and he is glad to return home.

By and large, the educated older Swedes passively regard Western Europe as something alien, to which a small number may regretfully wish they belonged; younger people display an actively hostile attitude. This has largely been achieved by school instruction that the only European accomplishment has been to exploit other continents, so that the sins of the West have been visited on its virtues. By association, all Western European values have been made suspect, and what otherwise would be a politically awkward heritage has been discredited. Of this, the most vital are the questioning of fundamentals, the concern for the individual and the genuine suspicion of authority as an institution.

The attack on the West has been supported by the mass media, most particularly school radio and TV. As mentioned before, it has been made respectable in the interests of international equity, and the atonement for European sins. But it has not widened Swedish horizons, it has merely shifted them. By diverting attention to other quarters of the globe, and inducing a specious glow of solidarity with faraway peoples, it has deepened Swedish isolationism by cutting links with Continental neighbours. Trade and economics have been no antidote. The expansion of Swedish trade with Western Europe, and a resultant commercial interdependence, have not been accompanied by an intellectual approach to the Continent; but rather the reverse. These developments have not gone unnoticed by the outside world. A French diplomat taunted a Swede in Brussels when Sweden made her half-hearted approach to the Common Market, by saying: 'You would make such good Asians or Africans. Why are you such bad Europeans?'

In reality, the Swedes are merely reverting to type. It was not much more than a hundred years ago that European culture was introduced into the broad stream of Swedish education. And Strindberg was the first exponent of that culture. He remained the only one. After a short honeymoon with the West, Swedish writers turned their backs on it, and pursued a path of national introspection leavened with some mimicry of Russian and American models. By cutting adrift from Western Europe, the Swedish rulers are not so much making a bold step into the future, as fathering a relapse into their past.

Nevertheless, it may be asked why the change occurred so swiftly and painlessly. Toynbeeism, it may be argued, while by now a perfectly respectable creed, has nevertheless not triumphed elsewhere in the West, and is still the subject of controversy. It has not yet informed a whole educational system in other countries. But in Sweden it has (albeit in a twisted form) conquered without hindrance. There has, after all, been considerable admiration of the various forms of Western culture among Swedes. Old gentlemen display yet misty eyes at the thought of Goethe, Schiller and Heine; Balzac and Victor Hugo have their distinguished worshippers among academics. Less than fifteen years ago, it was assumed and taught that Sweden was an adjunct of the West, and that the West was the best of all possible worlds. All that is now past. Pseudo Toynbeeism has triumphed, and a nation appears to have turned a collective mental somersault at the crack of some intellectual whip.

But it was only to be expected. The change came because it was decreed. Once the educational leaders had decided that Toynbeeism was to be adopted, it was. The few teachers who had doubts remained silent. But most genuinely accepted the new consensus. It would have been a social solecism and personal betrayal not to have done so.

With this in mind, it appears superfluous of Mrs Alva Myrdal to say that 'We won't get our new school until the old generation of teachers disappears, and the new one takes over.' At all events, student teachers at the end of the 1960s after the new school had been in action for five years, had the required attitudes. They conformed, with few exceptions, to what the school authorities required. Moreover, the academic staff of the various institutes of education had also conformed to the new order of things, the government's wishes were being carried out, and there was little criticism and no departure from the line of accepted truth. It had become virtually impossible to obtain an appointment in the training of teachers, without, if not the correct party membership card, at least the correct opinions. As Mr Ingvar Carlsson said on one occasion:* 'School is the spearhead of Socialism.' One need not take the ideological noun too seriously. He was only saying the obvious: that in Sweden the teaching profession is, as it has always been, wholly in the service of the State, not merely in its pay.

Enclosed in their isolation, plunged into an intellectual vacuum, the younger Swedes have begun to show all the signs of indoctrination, or at least new patterns of behaviour. Among the products of the new school, fantasy has declined. This is on the admission of officials: some of them welcome the development, because they see fantasy as subversive and undesirable. 'We must avoid the encouragement,' says an official teaching guide, 'of young people's imagination.' Scientific research has suffered; originality has been suppressed. The head of a chemical research institution in Stockholm says that his younger workers seem devoid of personal initiative. They are afraid of rising above the level of the group. If somebody produces a new result, he appears unwilling to proceed on his own. He will ask his chief for directions as to what to do next. And the work is generally poor and unimaginative.

In other words, the same effects have appeared in Sweden as in Soviet Russia and the kibbutzes of Israel. It is perfectly feasible to mould children into socially well adjusted creatures, and good members of the collective, but at the cost of originality and initiative. This has already begun to perturb Soviet educationists and to exercise public debate because, if engineers are deficient in inventiveness, then economic progress is threatened. It has become apparent in the Soviet Union that, in the final analysis, it is not the number of technological

* In a speech to schoolchildren.

graduates that counts, nor even the quality of their degrees, but the nature of their mental processes. The Swedes appear neither to have considered this eventuality themselves, nor to have concerned themselves with the examples just quoted. Their general view is well stated by Mr Åke Isling, who is the director of education of the TCO and a member of the ruling cadres of the Labour movement.

'We haven't considered the question,' he says, 'because it's hypothetical. I'm quite prepared to admit that there may be something in it, but it doesn't concern Sweden, at least not in its present stage of development. We are not interested in inventions, we want application. The great original advances are made abroad, and we need to be able to exploit them. We want technologists, and we want them in certain numbers. Provided we expand our educational facilities enough, we will get what we need. We need technologists, not original scientists. We've got to have people who can give society what it orders.'

The last sentence expresses another aim of Swedish education. Taking the more precise definition of Mr Moberg, it is 'to supply the Labour Market with what it requires'. That, and the avowed wish to mould a new kind of person are the twin goals of the system, school and university alike.

A select government committee has been working since early 1971 to make all education exclusively vocational. The Schools Directorate, the universities, and the Labour Market Directorate were represented. There was no clash of interests; all three agreed on the aim. They were not, however, concerned with implementing general policy (which had already been imposed), but rather with the eradication of troublesome details. For example, there was felt to be an irregularity in the continued existence at the universities of what were termed 'luxury subjects'. They were those with no obviously vocational connotation, such as certain courses on philosophy, history of art and classical languages and literature. These were pruned, in the face of an existing demand, in the pursuit of a strictly utilitarian goal. It was the removal of blemishes from the system.

The Swedish method is a refinement of an exclusively vocational approach to education. One way of preventing the disqualification of school leavers from earning a living is to provide vocational training more or less haphazardly, in the hope that, given the supply, there will always, somehow, be an answering demand. Optimism of that kind lies not in the nature of the Swede. The educational system is being so adapted that the supply of various accomplishments can be varied according to future demand. Of course, the success of this aim depends on reliable crystal-gazing and an acceptable method of guiding vocational choice. As far as the first condition is concerned, Sweden is well provided with economic forecasting institutions and the planning powers of the government (sometimes) ensure that their prophecies are fulfilled. And in the second place, the centralized direction of all education allows for co-ordinated guidance of vocational choice.

It is in vocational matters that the comprehensive system has been found to be so efficient. With their children of each district gathered into one single establishment it is easy to guide and choose. A child is not condemned at an early stage to this or that form of education. It gives opportunity to all, and makes efficient use of educational raw material. Vocational guidance is mandatory, and there are specialists in most schools. The top of the tree is the academic secondary school, leading to university. In Sweden it is voluntary and selective. Entry is granted on a system of points, decided by examinations at the previous level. The necessary points are varied from year to year, according to the supply of places. When vacancies are too few, the points go up, and conversely. These points are relative; that is to say, they represent the standing of pupils in relation to their class. By adjusting the minimum values for entry to the gymnasium, the successful proportion of applicants can be nationally established, and the number of entrants adjusted. Two aspects of this system are worth noticing. In the first place, there is no longer any question of passing or failing an exam. What used to be called a pass is no guarantee of matriculation; with the stigma of failing removed, what remains are low points. As long as the examination is completed, a pupil is deemed to have completed his studies. Secondly, to get into a higher school, he must rise above a certain level of attainment. But, since the measure is relative, it is advantageous to be in a class with a poor average ability, because it is the hindmost pupils, whatever their ability, who are discarded. Those who do not make the grade are shunted off to vocational training, if they had not beforehand been persuaded to move over of their own free will. Thus, the comprehensive school, in the right hands, can be an efficient and relatively painless mechanism for sorting the young and making the best use of the available raw material.

As with the schools, so with the universities. Entry into the most desirable, and therefore restricted, professional faculties, such as medicine, engineering and psychology, is regulated in much the same way as that to the gymnasium. And, in higher education, an implacable centralized administration exists as well.

The Swedish universities are ruled by a centralized government office, the Office of the University Chancellor. It has absolute power over the universities, and academic independence is unknown. The universities are run directly by the State: it is the way that the politicians want it. 'Academic independence,' says Mr Moberg, 'is incompatible with a modern educational system. The aims of the universities are set by society and, since society produces the economic support, it has the right and duty to direct their activities. Universities must fit into their allotted place in the general educational system.'

There is a radical difference between the treatment of the faculties in Western universities, and in Sweden. In the former, the academic staff is the ruler, and the administration (theoretically at all events) is their servant. But in the Swedish system, the administration is considered the ruler, and the professorial staff its subordinates. The administration is not, as in an English or American university, an organization running an independent body, but a branch of the civil service.

Professors are directly appointed by the government, and their own universities have no say in their selection. The Chancellor's Office in Stockholm prepares the nominations, and the Cabinet confirms the choice. The Chancellor, a high civil servant equivalent in rank and power to a director general, is the ruler of the Swedish universities. His is a political appointment, ensuring that in its own turn the professorial incumbents possess views consistent with those of the government. This is vital in those chairs concerned with the formation and direction of society, notably education, economics, sociology and political science. It is interesting to observe that those reaching the top in these faculties all possess, or at least profess, a uniform *weltanschauung*, compatible with that of the Labour movement.

Lacking all autonomy, the universities are thoroughly subject to the State. Professors alone are chosen by the government, but lecturers are in the gift of the University Chancellor's Office. That office, indeed, arranges, as of right, the detailed running of all universities. Direction is not confined to staff appointments. Budgets, grants and the steering of research lie within the absolute jurisdiction of the office. All curricula, examinations and the very content of lectures are decided there.

Central direction is obviously conducive to efficiency. In the view of Swedish educational officials, it is clearly a waste of resources for different universities to teach the same subjects in different ways. This would mean, they say, that students might prefer one university to the other, simply because of a particularly academic style, whereas it is much more rational to ensure that courses in the same subject are identical in content and approach, so that entrants could be distributed among the various establishments without prejudice. Ideally, it ought to be possible to transfer from one university to the other without noticing the difference. In practice, this may not yet be literally true, but the authorities are pursuing the goal with great tenacity.

All institutions of higher learning in Sweden are no more than branches of a single establishment, directed from outside. This applies no less to the ancient universities of Uppsala and Lund, than to the modern institutions in Stockholm, Gothenburg and Umeå. The Chancellor's Office has enforced uniformity of curricula and teaching. 'It would be foolish,' says Mr Hans Löwbeer, the University Chancellor at the time of the reforms at the end of the 1960s, 'to allow any variation. Because what would happen if you had two graduates, let us say from Gothenburg and Stockholm, who had had such different teaching that they had no common ground? How could they talk to each other? And that is the situation on the Labour Market.'

The most serious objection to the independence of the universities in the Swedish view is that it allows them to decide what to teach. Instruction has been designed to produce graduates in the image of the system. Economics, to take one example, is so taught as to present the Swedish mixed economy as the only acceptable norm. In the 1960s, as official doctrine moved towards greater State control, so did university teaching follow. It is interesting to observe that the Swedish system was presented as lying before a watershed, on the other side of which lay the capitalist world. There seemed less difference, in this presentation, between Sweden and the Communist countries than between Sweden and the West.

Teaching acquired a distinct Marxist colouring. There was a good example in the first-year economics course at Stockholm University for the academic year 1970–71. The part on the United States prescribed as textbook, *The Age of Imperialism*, by the Marxist author, Harry Magdorff. The course was clearly tendentious, aimed at denigrating the whole American system. To a lesser degree, the rest of the Western world was similarly treated. But the main object was to present dollar imperialism as the gravest of contemporary dangers, which happened to be party, and to a certain extent government opinion as well.

The conversion of Swedish education to an exclusively vocational system guided by the State has necessitated thorough-going and complicated changes in the universities. A technological society requires not only technologists. As the Swedes discovered a long time ago, these are not even necessarily in the majority for the proper functioning of a modern State. Equally necessary are teachers, economists, administrators, sociologists, planners; in short, all the social engineers without whom a modern society cannot be directed. In the middle of the 1960s, then, the Swedish university system was reformed in order to supply the specialists required.

The faculty of Arts, which in. Sweden includes all subjects not taught at technical universities, and which in the past was a school for bureaucrats, used to allow considerable variation in studying. As is the case with most universities in the West, one proceeded from the general to the particular: in other words, the freshman started off by embracing a number of subjects, and specialized as he approached graduation. The Swedes have turned this scheme on its head. Swedish students now have to specialize in their first year in order to prepare themselves for a profession recognized by the Labour Market Directorate.

It would be too much to suppose that even the meticulous

Swedes could match every occupation with a university course. Apart from anything else, this would have extended the choice, instead of narrowing it, which was the object of the reform. Instead, the recognized occupations were arranged in the seventeen main groups of the official Labour Market Directorate system of classification, corresponding to which there were seventeen permissible combinations of courses. Studies are what is known as goal-directed; that is, they are chosen not to satisfy the desires of the student, but to fulfil the requirements of some more or less realistic end. To take a few examples. Studying history in the first year necessarily implies that teaching has been chosen as a profession; no other possibility is admitted, because the Chancellor's Office and the Labour Market have decided that no other occupation needs that subject. Subsequent years' curricula are automatically adjusted to that assumption. Or, consider the course designated in all Swedish universities as No. 6 (uniformity extends to the minutest details). It starts with Economics, Law and Statistics, and produces two specialists much required by the State for Swedish society: the economist and the community planner.

Ideally, students would be deprived of their freedom of choice, and so distributed, after suitable testing, among the courses of study, that the supply of occupations was adjusted to the demand. In practice, the Swedish authorities have gone some way to achieving the same ends by a system of pressures without overt compulsion. In the first place, the pattern of the courses itself makes automatically for a general channelling from beginning to end. In the nature of things, interests generally narrow with time, even in the compressed space of the average university sojourn. Normally, if a student shows a disposition to shift studies, he does so in his early terms, concentrating later on something that absorbs his interest, or that is forced upon him by the necessity of satisfying the examiners. If he is compelled to specialize as a freshman, he will tend to continue in the groove thus allotted, for the narrowing tendency will apply in his case as well. Moreover, a student forced to select his studies according to a closely defined future profession will feel constricted and even fearful as a result of the act of commitment. He is unlikely to spread his interests as he advances in his university career, even though the authorities do permit greater choice in later terms.

But other, more obvious, pressures have been added to the system. Since Swedish universities have become rigorously and exclusively vocational, it is logical that vocational guidance has in turn been made compulsory. It is, in fact, combined with study guidance, but the dividing line is obscure. All students must have their courses approved by a director of studies, without whose permission a change of course is impossible. Since that approval is not lightly given, a first-year choice is almost certainly irrevocable. By tuning such persuasions to the suggestions of the Labour Market Director-ate, national planning is helped. Intimate consultation between the Directorate and the universities ensures that guidance conforms to State policy.

The concept of education as a civilizing influence has been dropped. It is now considered exclusively as a practical device in the service of a technologically dominated society. The authorities openly, and indeed with some pride, admit that their institutions of learning are to be considered as educa-tional factories. Production is their only concern, and quantity their only standard of judgement. Quoting Mr Moberg again: 'Our concern is to promote economic efficiency.' And it is in this way that resources are being exploited from kindergarten up. 'We have to spread education,' says Mr Moberg. 'We used to favour the clever children, and gave too little stimulus to the average. Consequently, there has been a wastage, which we now have to rectify.'

It has become official policy that encouragement of extra-ordinary talent is wasteful, since it concentrates too much

effort on too few people. The energy spent on helping one
bright child has less effect, economically, than if it were
distributed among several average pupils. The approved aim
is to extract the untouched reservoirs of ability among the
ordinary mass of schoolchildren. In practice, teachers neglect
brighter children, to concentrate on the less gifted. And there
is a school of thought in the Schools Directorate that has
canvassed the idea of actively handicapping the talented
pupils in the interests of equality. It is generally conceded by
teachers and educational officials alike that the Swedish
system is devised for the child of average ability, and the
clever one is penalized. 'A clever child will always manage on
its own' is the usual justifying formula.

This would be verging on the suicidal for any society
which set store by originality. But it is perfectly understandable in a society, like that of Sweden, where it is the obedient
administrator and interpreter of other men's discoveries who
is required. In the terminology of *Brave New World*, it is
the Beta Pluses, possibly the Alphas, that are wanted, but
decidedly not the Alpha Pluses.

Besides the sheer economic reasons for the university
reform and the limitation of courses, there were equally
important social ones. Mr Moberg again: 'The expansion of
education, and the rising demand for graduates was certain
to bring to the universities a new kind of student. He would
come from the lower middle classes, with a new social
background, and without a tradition of study at home. Left
to himself, he would be likely to become confused and
frustrated, and liable to revolt.'

This shows some foresight. Mr Moberg is describing here
the very private reasoning of the Swedish educational reformers when they were formulating their plans in the late
1940s and 1950s. It was almost two decades before the epi-
demic of student unrest and the French 'events' of May 1968.
That was a time, it will be recalled, when undergraduates

were a singularly docile body, intent only on taking degrees, and letting off steam, when necessary, by the politically innocuous methods of womanizing or drinking.

By being forced to specialize early, students would then be spared the primary confusion of uncertainty and the necessity of making up their minds themselves. Moreover, it was supposed that, by an insistence on the vocational nature of university, and by playing on the obsession with security, or rather fears of its future loss, the new students would be more amenable to guidance and direction. And so they were.

This was one reason why, during the troubles of 1968, the Swedish universities got off so lightly. There was some unrest among sociology students in Stockholm, but this must be attributable, not so much to indigenous motivation, as to mimicry of foreign models. On one occasion, the Swedish TV broadcast a lengthy and romanticized programme on the day's rioting among students in Paris. Approximately two hours later, students were on the rampage in the streets of Stockholm with war cries and hastily contrived banners that were obviously copied from the sounds and images they had absorbed from the little screen so short a time before.

There has been no lasting unrest, with the exception perhaps of consistent new left agitation in sociology and education faculties. Starting with a militant core in 1968, sociology students at Stockholm University were converted wholesale to a neo-Marxist way of thought. Marxists acquired control of the student representative bodies. It became necessary to toe the party line in order to avoid unpleasantness. Anybody who elected to ignore the Castroesque style of dress accepted as the norm at the sociology institute was boycotted as an undesirable and a reactionary. The atmosphere was so strained that students with moderate tastes in dress (and opinions) felt obliged to leave for other lines of study.

Perhaps unrest is an inappropriate description of what happened. The new left did not want disruption so much as change. They were supported by most of the academic staff, for the emergence of a radical student body coincided with a change of generation among their teachers that brought Marxism in its train. The agitation caused (or accompanied) the abandonment of the orthodox American sociology previously imported, and the rejection of what was termed 'official Western' teaching. Instead, a more radical learning was embraced, and extreme left-wing textbooks dominated. It is unclear how far all this is heretical, and how far approved by the authorities. At least it is not inconsistent with Social Democratic aims of moving to the left. And, by desisting from suppression of the movement, the government confirmed a policy of exploiting radical student activities for its own ends.

In research, control of the universities and the institution of rigorous financial measures have given the State a well-nigh absolute hold on all activities. A small committee, reporting directly to the Prime Minister, decides on research policy in all fields, and related agencies, notably the University Chancellor's Office, administer it in detail. Each single project must be centrally approved before it can be started in a public institution, and all financial grants are likewise centrally made. Small schemes are discouraged, and large ones favoured, the effect, if not the intention, being to simplify management by reducing numbers. This promotes the governmental direction of virtually all research. So urgent is this power considered to be that university research workers have been required to reject all foreign grants for activities within Sweden, in order to close loopholes in supervision. Under certain conditions exceptions may be made, but only with the permission of the central authorities.

This very possibly sounds like news from Utopia. One of the problems in the complex labyrinth of modern research is how to distribute resources and exploit facilities. Duplication is only the most obvious waste that can be avoided by centralized direction. And the Swedes have truly managed to realize at least that Utopian goal. Their State directs all research of any significance. Private institutes are non-existent, and private industry, concerned mainly with the improvement of production, does not compete. But even there, communications with the government are such that official desires are generally honoured.

Since the government is in complete control, the shape of Swedish research suggests something of government intentions. To start with, pure research has been all but eliminated, the applied kind being the only variety approved. This holds both for the natural and for the political sciences. Work concerned with the advance of technology has been restricted in favour of sociological and educational research, which deals with the control of people. This is perfectly sensible. Technology has run away from human institutions, and to make proper use of what we have requires a compensating advance in the latter. It is not new technological discoveries that are wanted, but new sociological ones. New ways of running a population are required, in order to apply the benefits of science and industry.

Scientific prediction is a field which the prudent ruler ought to control. It is manifestly awkward if expert opinion contradicts official policy, for that casts doubt upon governmental credibility. Conversely, convenient oracles confer the added force of doing something so that, in the biblical phrase, 'it may be fulfilled'. Not surprisingly, therefore, the Swedish government has taken steps to harness futurology. When the Swedish Academy of Engineering proposed to establish a futurological institute, the government demurred, because that would have meant the appearance of an independent body. Instead, an official commission of inquiry was appointed in 1971 to study the development of futurology in Sweden. Its terms of reference suggested that State direction was the ultimate goal.

A comment on the commission by Mr Olof Palme indicates that the Swedish government regards futurology not so much as prediction as manipulation. 'Foreign projects,' he said when the commission on futurology was established, 'are directed by military and industrial interests.* It is quite natural, therefore, that studies of the future are influenced by the special wishes of those who give the orders.' Mr Palme was not interested in doing away with direction, but with seeing that it was in the right hands. He wanted neither foreign influence in Swedish futurology, nor domestic competition, but State control. Indeed, it has for some time been a Social Democratic dictum that research of all kind must be subordinated to the political goals established by the government. Exactly the same thing was propounded by Mr Leonid Brezhnev, secretary of the Russian Communist party, at the 24th Party Congress in 1971.

It may seem odd that a democratically elected Swedish government should share with a despotic Russian regime the aim of curtailing the independence of scientists. What is even odder, is that there has been virtually no public protest. Scientists may occasionally murmur in private, but they prefer not to voice their reservations publicly. The little criticism that makes its way into the open comes from the left, and is concerned, not with intellectual independence, but with the identity of the commissars. From that point of view, what is wrong in Sweden is not that research is directed, but that it is the capitalists, rather than the people, who do the directing. One is left with the impression that intellectual independence is not quite understood. Indeed, the lack of public outcry against the constraints upon research in Sweden

---

* Referring to American institutions, notably 'think tanks' on the lines of the Rand corporation. This was not spelled out, however. Innuendo plays an important part in the Swedish political armoury, and rightly so; it can be much more powerful, by appealing to the faculty of suggestion, than saying things directly.

is reminiscent of the Spanish Inquisition. During the almost four centuries that that peculiar institution existed, virtually no native criticism appeared, clandestinely or otherwise, to the discomfort of those who have tried to prove that it did not enjoy overwhelming popular support.

A pattern discernible in Swedish economic, political and sociological research suggests that only those projects are permitted that further the aims of the government and the programme of the party. Pedagogical research concentrates on the conditioning of children to act and think collectively; a great deal of work has been carried out in preparation for compulsory pre-school training. Sociological research tends towards a Pavlovian behaviourism and, in general, the means of altering people by the use of environment.

Someone engaged in criminological research once proposed – and came within a hair's breadth of having accepted – an experiment in brain-washing. Selected prisoners would be kept on short rations, always fed by a particular warder, in order to establish an intimate contact. Then, by increasing meals, a kind of dependence would be built up, giving the warder a mental hold on the prisoner, and rehabilitation carried out by suggestion. The point about this is that the director of the State prisons approved the experiment, but it was stopped at the last moment for fear of the immediate *political* consequences. There were no ethical reservations; it was assumed that, when public opinion was ripe, the attempt would be made.

Sometimes research, or at least scholarship, may be used for relatively crude political purposes. In the middle of the 1960s, it became imperative for the Swedish government, then exploiting anti-Americanism, to dissociate itself from, or explain away, subservience to American pressures during the Cold War, notably in following export embargoes to the Communist bloc. A well-known party intellectual, Dr Gunnar Adler-Karlsson, was, therefore, permitted to do a doctoral thesis on the ineffectuality of economic embargoes in general, and this one in particular. He was given a State grant to do so and, furthermore, was patently given access to State papers and Cabinet minutes not available to the public. In his dissertation, he proved, on his own evidence, that the Swedish government had been subject to American pressure, which seemed to exonerate Sweden. By presenting the case in the form of an academic thesis, the credibility of an official State Paper was achieved, without the necessity of having to take official responsibility. There is some evidence that Adler-Karlsson's work had the desired public effect.

Education and research, then, have been harnessed to the needs of the State and the party. In the overwhelming majority of cases, people accept the system. Students follow vocational direction and submit to the regimentation of the universities. Admittedly, the vision of the planner sometimes falters. Too many students fail because of defective schooling; the production of graduates acquires an unintentional lopsidedness so that, for instance, there was a threat of a glut of teachers at the end of the 1960s. The important thing is, however, that most academics have made their submission. Some may grumble; others may busy themselves along the path of the *apparatchik*; a few pretend to the correct political opinions in the furtherance of their career. There is acquiescence all along the line.

Education and research in Sweden, then, are consistent to a remarkable degree. They show that when government and party say that education is to be used to change society, it is no idle chatter. To sum up, the Swedish educational system has been recast to serve the new society. It discounts individuality and seeks to produce socially well adjusted people with a collective way of thinking. It has broken up old patterns of loyalty and, instead of accepting teachers, parents and the old ruling class of individual rich men and industrialists, the new Swede submits to a collective ruled by autocratic cliques. It discourages originality and independence, and encourages a willingness to serve the interests of the State. Students allow themselves to be streamed and classified, to staff occupations prescribed by authority. Not the advancement of knowledge, but the manipulation of society is the highest of aims. Not the technological, but the social engineer has become the most desirable of occupations. And above all, it is society, the group, the collective that holds sway.

'Technology,' says Mr Moberg, 'demands the collective. People feel that they lose too much if they develop their own individuality.' There is no reason to doubt his words, at least in Sweden. But education is only one means of conditioning to the collective: we now turn to another, and equally persuasive instrument.

12. The Environmental Mill

It requires no special philosophy to recognize that men are affected by their surroundings. But only a confirmed behaviourist would deliberately seek to modulate personality by varying the human habitat. The Russians, naturally, have done so. Since the Revolution they have put all their urban and many of their rural citizens in large blocks of flats, not only because it facilitates spying and control, but because that form of living may be used to encourage a collective way of thought. Conversely, private houses (despite *dachas* for the privileged) have been banned because they might encourage bourgeois individualism. Of itself, of course, flat living is not necessarily a medium of regimentation. It is doubtful whether the favoured tenants of Sloane Square or Fifth Avenue are made any the more amenable to State domination because their residences happen to be piled one on top of the other, rather than being spaced out along the ground. To become an instrument of manipulation, living conditions must be consciously exploited. They must form part of a general pattern of social engineering. But, given that, architecture and town planning are among the most subtle and powerful agents of conditioning.

It is only to be expected that the Soviet Union would recognize the potential of indoctrination by environment. What is perhaps not so obvious is that a country outside the Communist bloc would pay it so much attention. But the Swedes have pursued broadly the same aims as the Russians: the creation of the new man for the new society, the restraint of individuality, the generation of a collective mentality and the advancement of central direction. What is more, Sweden even seems to have outstripped the Soviet Union. Other considerations aside, this is probably because she has better engineers and administrators, and because Swedish architects have willingly become servants of ideology. When the Swedes change ideas, they do it to the full, leaving no room for criticism or reservation. The country lacks intellectual defences; anything new will conquer without resistance being offered.

The Swedish landscape suggests at first glance the hand of a master planner and the shovelling of people into new patterns of habitation. Although there is plenty of land, with a density of population often verging on the semi-desert, yet round every town there are clusters of young skyscrapers. Vast stretches of unpeopled forest or undulating farmland are periodically broken by concrete turrets crushed up against each other. Outside Stockholm, whole suburbs have been poured into a single building. Everything – at least around the towns – seems new. It is so, and it has to be. For Sweden since the 1930s has been a planners' dream. In the four crowded decades since then, industrialization has been consummated with a vengeance. The country has been urbanized, people have been forced into the cities from the country. So, with people uprooted and moving, it was the ideal situation for those who wished to create a new environment.

Successive legislation regulated all building in Sweden, and gave it into the power of the public administration. Local authorities have a legally entrenched monopoly of all town planning and property development. This does not mean that private contractors are proscribed, but that municipalities, besides having the duty of approving and the right of altering plans, also have the prerogative of deciding who will build and what is to be erected. In practice, about eighty-five per cent of all new building belongs to the public sector of the economy. This means municipalities and cooperative housing societies which, by their financing and political connections, may be considered as subsidiaries of the State. Of the construction itself, about half is carried out by private contractors; the rest by various public concerns, or organizations related to the government through some corporative body. The best example of this is the *Riksbyggen*, owned by the trade unions and generally led by a politically appointed managing director, sometimes an ex-Cabinet minister. It is, in fact, a part of government or, at least, party patronage.

Theoretically at least, local government is supposed to enjoy great autonomy in Sweden. But various financial and administrative devices in fact give the central government all the coercive power it needs, so that local matters are to all intents and purposes under its control. In town planning, imposts are used to curtail unwanted building. Furthermore, municipalities are subject to constant government direction through the credit market. The municipalities, when they borrow money to build, do so through both private banks and government credit institutions. Either way, they are subject to the will of the State. In the first case, the central bank decides how credits are to be apportioned; in the second, the State says directly how and when the money is available. Furthermore, loans and mortgages can be so restricted as to decide the kind of building permitted. Money for small houses, to take one example, can be made so expensive that, even if a municipality wanted to favour the owner-occupier, it would be financially impossible to do so.

Besides financial instruments, the State also has administrative devices to supervise local government. The country is so administered as to match local government with central agency branches. Sweden is divided into twenty-seven provinces, within each of which there is a dual authority. First of all, there is a provincial Council (*Landsting*), elected by the inhabitants, and forming the body superior to the municipality. It would, in England, be roughly equivalent to the County Councils; in the United States, to the State Government. But within each province, parallel to the local administration, there is a regional agent of the central government. This, in fact, although not in theory, keeps the local authorities in line. In planning, it sees that municipalities do not diverge too far from the policies enunciated by the State. Theoretically, its powers may be restricted; but in practice, the Swedish system of government gives it considerable strength. Behind the scenes, along the 'contact network', the State representatives can make their wishes known, and avoid most public controversy. And since the bureaucratic establishment, at whatever level, wants to avoid any breath of scandal, a form of natural conspiracy makes the system work. To take a concrete example; if, despite all State directives, a municipality persists in building small houses rather than flats, then a discreet hint from the central government regional office that the requisite credits will not be forthcoming will induce the necessary change of mind.

The government has a central agency to enforce land policy. This is the Directorate of National Planning, a body that supervises the municipalities and plans the use of all land in the country. This board has decided how every square inch of territory is to be used, and reconciles municipal schemes with each other, so that there are no conflicts, overlaps or inconsistencies.

By the use of planning legislation and financial power, the State can then enforce central planning and a uniform building policy. A small centralized administration can shape the country, unencumbered by private resistance or municipal obstruction.

Planning is no empty letter, because of public powers in the vital business of acquiring land. Expropriation in Sweden is easy. It requires a simple administrative order against which there is no appeal. In practice, expropriation is a matter of routine, subject to little delay, and the authorities acquire land as they wish, since their decisions are incontestable. Since the whole matter is confined to administrative procedure, courts and all, it confirms the hold that the bureaucracy has on the citizen. To an Anglo-Saxon it might appear iniquitous; but to the Swede it is normal, and only rarely are there any protests.

The State can decide, without hindrance, how the citizen is to live. In consequence, it is not so much to architects and town planners to whom one must turn in Sweden for the elucidation of the aims of architecture and town planning, but to politicians and bureaucrats. The State holds unchallenged powers to change the face of the land: what does it want, and what are its motives?

The purpose of architecture and town planning, as it is defined by Social Democratic ideologists, is to change society in the direction established by the party. Put at its simplest, and taking the most explicit of aims, this means the promotion of 'equality'. The first aim must be to mix the population, to destroy class differences, and it is here that the first objections to small houses begin to appear. Mr Lennart Holm, the director general of the Directorate of National Planning, says: 'Estates of small houses are bad. They encourage social stratification, and this is what we want to avoid.' Another authority, Mr Rune Johansson, Minister of Industry, puts it in these words: 'Suburbs of private houses mean social segregation. Ordinary workers can't afford to live there.'

'We cannot allow this to continue,' Mr Holm says. 'We cannot allow people to preserve their differences. People will have to give up the right to choose their own neighbours.'

In fact, there are very few such suburbs. In the surrounds of Stockholm there are only two, called Bromma and Djursholm. Both are products of the 1930s, and imitations of the English garden suburb idea. But in 1970, the city planners expected them to disappear within a decade or two. Re-development of Stockholm would involve their demolition and conversion to a form of habitation more in keeping with the times. Disapproval of these suburbs is not confined to a few planning mandarins. When they speak, they speak for public opinion which, in turn, has been moulded by incessant propaganda.

What distinguishes the homes in these few suburbs from other Swedish homes is that they stand in their own grounds. They therefore provide a way of life that is different in kind from that of most urban Swedes. Whether he lives in a flat (the most likely case), a terraced or detached house, the average Swede finds himself in an atmosphere of togetherness, with no closed-off garden into which he can retreat. But those in the few garden suburbs have this privilege. *Dagens Nyheter*, a leading Liberal national daily newspaper, once published an aerial photograph to show the space taken up by this kind of living. It was wrong, said the newspaper, because it was a privilege, and because it encouraged selfishness. Those who live in these suburbs are of the upper or professional classes, and people who hanker after a different style of living. They can well afford their choice; they know that they are denying nobody a reasonable standard of living by their privilege, and yet they feel beleaguered and ill at ease. A publisher living in this manner puts it in these words: 'There is a pressure on environments that are different. It's not a matter of expense. There are in fact plenty of suburbs more expensive than Djursholm, but they are of an approved kind of living: thats to say, blocks of flats, terraced houses or detached houses crammed together. But if you live in a villa standing in its own grounds, that's different. Every day there are attempts to discredit it and destroy it. The inhabitants are accused of being "reactionary", but that's only an excuse. It's not the tenants, but the environment they're after. After all, many people of extremely radical views like myself, for example, live in this way. But we are different, and want a "different" way of living. And that's resented. You are expected to live in the approved pattern. I can feel a "pressure" on Djursholm, "they" want to destroy it.'

Thus one of the ruled. Here is the opinion of one of the rulers, Professor Bror Rexed, a man of influence in town planning: 'Our educational system is socializing people at a much earlier age, and young people dislike the idea of private houses away from the centre. They have learned that isolation is not good, and they will want to move away, into the centre. Consequently, places like Djursholm will disappear naturally. It will not be necessary to abolish them.'

If this is a case of the wish being father to the thought it is none the less of interest. Professor Rexed, director general of the Directorate of Social Affairs, is a Social Democrat, and his party has shown fundamental disapproval of one-family houses and private ownership. But it is not simply a matter of political bias. The same opinions exist among Liberals, and certainly among the bureaucrats engaged in planning, whatever their party affiliations.

The most serious objection to the self-contained house and the owner-occupier is that they interfere with the mechanism of planning. The man with a house will clearly stand up to officialdom in a way that a tenant won't. Inhabitants of the northern Swedish provinces had diligently saved and worked to build their own homes, only to find when they settled in that there was no more work to be had and 'there they were stuck, with homes and no jobs', to quote a housing official. Obviously a house-owner will not lightly move, even when unemployed. The owner-occupier, therefore, with a stake in his native patch of soil, will resist blandishments to migrate. This does not suit the government's book because they avowedly want mobility of labour.

It is deliberate policy to depopulate the country and concentrate the inhabitants in the towns. Compulsory migration is unenforceable, and economic and social pressures are used instead. The districts to be so treated are starved of finance and transport. Country schools are being closed, and the fact that the children then have to travel perhaps twenty miles each day to the nearest towns for education becomes a strong inducement to move.

Financially the pressures are aggravating the economic plight of small farming and encouraging the drift from the land. The government wants a large urban population concentrated around the main industries in southern Sweden, and a small number of large highly mechanized farms. It is urbanization encouraged by the State.

The government wants mobility and, as planning officials frankly admit, ownership is an impediment. There was during the 1960s a celebrated illustration of this point at a place called Båtskärsnäs in northern Sweden. This was a sawmill *bruk* at the head of the Gulf of Bothnia. It was of double significance, being not only a subject of rural depopulation, but a State enterprise as well. The sawmill was closed in 1966, ostensibly because of sustained losses. The government offered all manner of inducement to move, providing work elsewhere, preferably somewhere down south. But instead of liquidating a rural district, the State found itself with a problem on its hands. Most of the workmen had acquired their own houses and refused to budge. They lived on social security, they badgered the government for a reopening of the mill, they tried (unsuccessfully) on their own initiative to attract new industry. The exceptions were those few who happened not to own their own homes, but to rent accommodation. They moved with little persuasion, if deep regrets.

That tale pointed a useful moral. Recognizing that home-ownership constitutes an anchor, the State prefers not to encourage it. Even if the detached house cannot always be avoided, it is policy to discourage ownership. Housing authorities prefer letting because the sense of possession is absent, private savings are not sunk in fixed property and ties to a particular locality are minimized. This reasoning applies to the country and cities. The planners see before them a society of change and mobility; factories will come and go, and the citizen must be prepared to move with his work. Permanence is not to be encouraged.

On all counts, living in blocks of flats is favoured by authority. Figures show that the authorities have their way. Of all new building, about one third is in houses, the rest in flats. Around the cities, the proportion is under fifteen per cent of houses to over eight-five per cent flats. Yet the Swedes, a nation of peasants, surely might be expected to want their own homes. Conversation suggests this to be true: the standard Swedish dream is 'a little red house in the country'. (The colour is traditional: Swedish houses, always wooden, have for centuries been painted a bright maroon, made of a copper salt.) Figures confirm it. Opinion polls show that two-thirds of all Swedes now living in flats would prefer small houses. The space in their country would make this possible. Yet they have been persuaded to deny their own desires, and to adopt an alien way of life. Protest has been absent and complaint rare. A housing shortage has provided the necessary coercion.

Since the last war, a housing shortage has been endemic to Sweden. Whether or not it has been deliberately fostered, it has been extremely convenient. Swedes, denied alternatives and forced to take what they can get, have been compelled to live in the way that the planning authorities have decreed. The older Swede has forgotten what choice of housing means: over half the population has never known it. Two generations have grown up convinced that this is the only conceivable state of affairs. Most Swedes refuse to credit that in other countries it is possible to pick and choose: in their own country even the wealthy are unable to do so.

A Swedish housing shortage is hard to understand. Neutral and unmolested, Sweden escaped devastation in both world wars, and was therefore spared the burden of rebuilding. Other countries, less fortunate, have still contrived to overcome their difficulties. Finland, poorer and smaller than Sweden, with a population of 4,500,000, fought Russia between 1939 and 1944, ceding, as a result, one fifth of her territory, and having to absorb 450,000 refugees, besides sustaining the destruction of 100,000 homes. Yet by 1956 the Finns had made good their losses, since when housing difficulties have ceased to exist. The Swedes excuse themselves by claiming that finance had to be diverted to industry for expansion. But the Finns were in far worse straits. Sweden had kept her factories working during the war, enjoying an uninterrupted boom and unimpeded investment. Finnish industry, on the other hand, was decimated and, in addition to post-war reconstruction, steel and shipbuilding had to be expanded in order to pay heavy reparations. It is possible to argue that the Finns recovered rapidly because they abolished rent controls, thus giving market forces their head. It would follow from this that, by insisting on government interference, the Swedes created a shortage.

This may or may not be. But at least it is a controlled shortage. If choice is non-existent, at least abject hardship has been rare. By law, all urban housing must be negotiated through municipal agencies, where waiting lists are permanent and long. Families in the big cities might be allotted a flat after a few years' delay, but a single person in Stockholm has to wait up to fifteen years. The public have patiently accepted this state of affairs, and in election after election the government was returned, without suffering from the issue. It was yet another product of economic fatalism. Building proceeded – a landscape ever dotted with bulldozers and cranes proved that – and, if it was insufficient, economic duress was officially invoked in repetitive explanation. And, since they believe in economic forces as something irresistible and quasi-divine, the Swedes accepted the situation passively.

Painful shortages and distress exist only in the cities. In smaller towns, and in the country, supply usually meets demand, but the nature of the housing is rigidly determined by the mechanism of town planning. A most extreme example is to be found in Lapland, where peasants and hunters, used to independence and freedom in the wilderness, have been forced into an urban pattern of living. At Svappavaara, a straggling village in the northern Swedish tundra, open-cast iron-mining was begun in the late 1950s. It gave employment to a depressed population of small peasant farmers. They owned land in the vicinity, and what they wanted (and could well afford) was to build their own homes. They were perfectly willing to live far out and travel to work each day in order to preserve their old way of life. But they were not allowed to do so.

Although Svappavaara lies in semi-wilderness, it was placed under town planning orders and subjected to the rule of another mining town, Kiruna, twenty-five miles away. Despite the open tundra, the replica of a suburb in an over-crowded country was built at Svappavaara. Its centrepiece was a rambling block of flats, four storeys high and almost 200 yards from end to end. It was scornfully dubbed 'the long serpent'. Crammed up against it were several hundred houses, some terraced, others detached, but mostly wall to wall. The occupants were almost universally miserable. They had been used to living with plenty of space around them, preferably out of sight of the smoke from their neighbours' chimneys. Even if economics now forced them to the mines, they still wanted homes of their own, with generous grounds, so as to preserve some contact with their former life. Physically, there was nothing to prevent this. That area of Sweden is one of the most desolate parts of Europe. A stretch of tundra, mountain and thin pine forest as big as Scotland and Wales together, its average population is one per square mile. The population of Svappavaara in 1965, when the new town opened, was 600: it is unlikely to exceed 2,000 in the future. By no stretch of imagination was the countryside at risk, or urban sprawl a possibility. There was space for houses, gardens and estates, without encroaching on the emptiness. But the unhappy occupants were crowded together as if they lived on the edge of a sick city gasping for breath.

Prosperity was there for all to see. The miners were all moderately affluent; they had TV, good furniture, they were well dressed. They possessed motor cars, washing machines, boats on the nearby river and hunting cabins out in the forest. But they were prohibited from owning their own homes.

The Svappavaara pattern suggests a deliberate concentration of the population that is politically motivated. In terms of building economics the advantages are doubtful. Controversy over the relative costs of flats and houses is inconclusive. The authorities claim that flats are cheaper; housebuilders say otherwise. There is a breath of suspicion that official costing methods were manipulated to prove the economy of flats and to forestall criticism. Comparison with Norway tells another tale. In that country, although the Welfare State has advanced as far, social engineering lags behind, and individuality, historically more pronounced than in Sweden, has held its ground. Small houses dominate. Over seventy per cent of all new building is in the form of semi-detached or free-standing houses. Size for size, they cost the same as flats, and often somewhat less.

But the Swedes have deliberately tried to turn their population into clients of the State. Town planning authorities will admit reluctantly, when pressed in private, that there is plenty of land for a nation of home-owners while yet preserving the environment. Green belts could be secured around the cities, and open spaces guaranteed, with national parks and

mountains and deserts in the north. Even the highest conceivable increase of population will leave them with a density
more suitable to some frontier territory in a far continent,
than a modern State on the edge of Europe. Quite other reasons
are adduced for the patterns of building actually enforced.

The density of building is decided not by considerations of
architecture or landscaping, but by the demands of ideology
and administration. Planning in Sweden does not simply
imply the physical arrangement of buildings in the landscape,
but the total control of the environment. This means that the
design of a new community is conditioned by the mechanics
of providing public services. Where building is spread out,
the provision of public services becomes too expensive and,
conversely, an economic supply requires a minimum density
of population. It is on this principle that Swedish town
planning is based.

By public services, the Swedes understand everything
required by society. This means not only the utilities, such as
water, power, telephones and roads, but education, social
welfare and public administration. As far as the utilities are
concerned, it is freely conceded that the extra expense caused
by scattered habitation can be recouped through taxes.
Social welfare is the vital criterion.

Professor Rexed defines it in this way: 'The whole environment has to be rearranged to bring the community into the
Welfare State.' In practice, this has meant that housing has
been built within immediate reach of social welfare and
medical centres. The principle has been that the periphery
must be within walking distance of the centre. Although this
ostensibly benefits the individual, it is also geared to the
organization of welfare. Social welfare workers and doctors
function more efficiently in a dense area than a thinly populated one. For this reason, then, the new cities, suburbs and
housing estates of Sweden, wherever they may be, are constructed to a density determined not by public taste or indivi-

dual wishes, but as an acceptable ratio of population:welfare resources. On this principle, a housing estate of small homes alone is considered too thinly spread. Instead, communities are built with tower blocks of flats at the centre, surrounded by lower blocks of flats (about four storeys high), with terraced houses, and a few free-standing houses on the periphery.

The appearance of the satellite towns around Stockholm is almost medieval in the way that habitation clusters round a power centre. But whereas, in the medieval city, the power was symbolized by a castle, in the contemporary Swedish suburb it is hidden in some bland offices housing official agencies in a corner of a building virtually indistinguishable from its neighbours. The intent of the town planner is, cutting through the jargon, to discourage independence, and bring the citizen within the control of the central administration and within the orbit of the collective.

Some administrators are prepared to admit this in so many words. Mrs Ingrid Jussil, a Social Democratic ideologist and a town planning expert in the Ministry of the Interior, said this: 'Town planning must emphasize the collective. We can achieve this by breaking down barriers, and forcing people into contact with each other. In that way, we can, for example, socialize children early. Society has got to decide how people are going to live.'

But the Swedish planners, behaviourists though they may be, do not expect the environment to work unaided. They acknowledge that the mentality of the citizen needs to be primed, and it is in this field that the different agents of the State are so profitably dovetailed. Where the attitudes for new surroundings are required, education may be allied to town planning. Professor Rexed again: 'Our schools promote social thinking and new evaluations of society. They promote a social revolution within society, a revolution that the teachers have accepted as well. The general ideas of our younger people have been levelled out and, broadly speaking, the new school system is producing people who accept the same evaluations of ideas and society. And the main body of the people accept them as well.'

To a great degree, he is right. The inhabitants of the new suburbs at least profess a certain consensus which accepts the planned community as the norm. There is a compact resentment of anybody who admits to a preference for a distinctive style of living that suits his individuality because it implies rejection of the approved viewpoint.

Commonly in the press, the house-owner will be presented as anti-social, one of the worst of accusations in Sweden. Politicians, on the other hand, cannot openly attack private houses, because a substantial minority of the Swedish population (about thirty per cent) still live in them. Nor, however, is it policy to support them. That would antagonize a public that has accepted the doctrine of collective living or alternatively, in a peculiarly Swedish way, is uniformly jealous of anybody different or better off.* 'You can praise the owner-occupier,' a leading Liberal politician has said, 'but not too loudly.'

Although the Swedes have been persuaded to accept urban and collective styles of living, it is against their traditional habits. At heart, the Swedes are still northern peasants. What they want is a little house in the forest; what they get is a flat in the suburbs. Paradox and conflict – yet their lot is not unbearable. If, as is most likely, the flat is high rise, at least it will be separated from the next block by a properly landscaped space, and the whole will be surrounded by a green belt, most often in the form of untouched forest. Yet, there is always a kind of insidious suffocation in these surroundings which, expressed as *ennui*, isolation, brooding, juvenile delinquency and inchoate resentment, settles upon the

* 'The Royal Swedish Jealousy' is a proverbial saying among the Swedes.

inhabitants. This is particularly true of the showpieces, like Vällingby, Farsta and Skärholmen, outside Stockholm. Thus, although urban concentration is planned to reinforce the welfare system, it also aggravates the strains of urbanization.

People are oppressed by the sensation of transience. Their flat is not their home, and they often look for the compensation of a cottage in the country. The standard explanation of this instinct is that it is a form of nature worship. More properly, it is a search for relief from an alien pattern of habitation. Without the institution of the country cottage, the splendid new suburbs of Sweden would long ago have turned into expensive lunatic asylums. Since the country cottages are generally purchased outright, they confer the sense of ownership which is so conspicuously absent from everyday housing. So it is that the Swede sees his real home in his country cottage, a necessary outlet for care and feeling, while his workaday dwelling appears only a temporary shelter. And yet, every year, he will spend no more than a summer month or so in his cottage.

Ostensibly, the authorities view the possession of a cottage in the country benevolently, because it is a sign of affluence. But in fact it is a cause for concern, because house-ownership is an escape from centralized authority. The flight to the country cottage not only evades administrative control, it is also a sign of failure in town planning. It is perfectly true that shovelling the population into unaccustomed housing estates has confirmed their passivity and vindicated the effectiveness of government propaganda and control, but it has also entailed strain on the individual. A sense of grievous isolation has become the accepted price of living in the new towns, and children growing up in them display the classic symptoms of lassitude and aggression.

The authorities have not ignored this. The rulers of Sweden are morbidly anxious to avoid any disaffection, because they know that an irritated person has a propensity for turning against his masters. For this reason, each new housing development is anxiously watched for signs of discontent. Staffs of sociologists are set to watch the inhabitants and report on their collective behaviour. Upon their reports depend the changes in future planning and the attempts to marry environment to social reactions more closely.

It is important to realize that the public remains completely passive in this process. The housing shortage alone has eradicated initiative. Most people are glad to take anything allotted them. The house-hunter, deprived of choice, can no longer influence design. Because the mechanism of the free market has been eradicated, the forces of supply and demand no longer operate. Private building is restricted, and private planning outlawed, so that competing forces have been banished, and the central authorities hold undisputed sway. The State has a monopoly of planning, and a stranglehold on architectural design. It is therefore able to specify without obstruction how its citizens are to live. In turn, this means that a technocratic *élite* controls the shaping of the environment; unquestioned, unrestricted and unchallenged. As a result, the Swedes, with some infrequent exceptions, live more or less how and where they are told.

Nevertheless, the desirability of avoiding undue strain upon the inhabitants has led to the reconsideration of some planning. It is no longer sufficient to produce housing estates that arrange people in predetermined patterns of density, but it is necessary to create surroundings in which fretting and alienation may be reduced. It has been necessary to coin a term for this concept. In Swedish it is *trivselsamhälle*, roughly 'the congenial society'. It was launched towards the end of the 1960s *as a promise for the future*: the implication, of course, is that society, as hitherto formed, was notably uncongenial.

In thinking up their 'congenial society', the Swedish

planners have acknowledged that the urge to own a country cottage derives from a legitimate wish to escape from dehumanized living conditions. The National Plan for the 1970s, which specifies the use to which every square yard of Sweden may be put, has been so conceived as to regularize what the Swedes call duplicate dwelling. Henceforth, retreat to the country is to be considered too important for the individual to deal with alone. Municipal 'leisure villages' are being introduced to replace the private cottages. These consist of small, mass-produced wooden bungalows, placed closely together, and let, not sold. Mr Rune Johansson defines the aims of leisure planning in these words: 'Leisure villages are more economical, because they permit four or five families to use each cottage during the year, instead of, as under private ownership, each family using one house for about a month each year. The advantages to the national economy are obvious.'

But the government has proceeded slowly. To have banned private cottages abruptly would have alienated a dangerous number of voters of the middle ground. Moreover, until 1970, about fifteen per cent of the Swedish population owned their own cottage, and this was not confined to the upper classes. Working men often have a cottage in the country, since the peasant nature of the Swedish population means that many urban inhabitants are of farming stock, possessing a little rural property. But, as earnings rise and leisure extends, the ability to purchase a cottage will spread, and a situation might arise in which most of the population would thus be able to escape community control. The government has acted to forestall this. Gradually, as planning zones are fixed, it is becoming correspondingly more difficult to find plots for private building, while municipalities have started to erect their 'leisure villages'.

But this is only regulating the escape valve. Ideally, the Swedish rulers would like to eradicate the desire for a country cottage by obviating the need for escape. They have sought to improve everyday living conditions in the cities, and in the late 1960s an attempt in that direction was made by changing architecture in order to establish contact with the soil, which environmental planners then saw as the key to the problem. Sociologists had discovered that the chief defect of living in tower blocks of flats was that it produced a feeling of suspension in mid-air, out of contact with the earth. They decided that this contact was vital if tenants were to cultivate a rudimentary sense of being at home. The architects were therefore instructed by the environmental planners to stop concentrating on tower blocks, and to turn to lower structures instead. It had been discovered that four storeys was the limit beyond which the sense of contact with the soil disappeared.

But this did not go far enough. The planning authorities accepted a rising demand for a house of one's own as urbanization proceeded and country dwellers moved to the cities. If it could not reasonably be eradicated immediately, at least it could be brought under control. 'It has been managed,' says Mrs Jussil (the town planning official mentioned above), 'by building two-storey blocks of flats *which are indistinguishable from terraced houses.*'

'They give some of the advantages of small houses,' to quote Mrs Jussil again, 'and about half the flats have gardens. But they are to let.'

In all probability, this deceit has worked up to a point. Sociological studies have found that blatant juvenile delinquency, while most prevalent in tower blocks, is considerably reduced in terraced houses and their simulations.

Towards the end of the 1960s, a form of town planning had been worked out which will probably be definitive for the next decade or so. This consists of a central core of high-rise flats, surrounded by lower blocks and terraced houses and, on the outskirts, a few detached, but crowded houses.

Apart from the requirement, already mentioned, that town planning must bring the citizen within reach of the authorities, the thoughts behind such distribution are these: Most people, when they start their working lives, are either single or live as childless couples. In which case, they want a small flat. They also have to commute, therefore it is most efficient to live in one of the central tower blocks close to underground station, suburban train or bus stop. Then, when they start raising a family, they will want more space close to the ground, so that the children can play outside without being out of sight and earshot. So comes the move to the lower habitations farther out. For those who absolutely require it, and are willing to pay with a higher rent and extra travel to the centre of the suburb, there are the detached houses on the periphery. Then, as the children move away from home (so this official reasoning goes), and the necessity of space departs with them, so can the parents, now middle-aged, return to the modest kind of quarters in which they started. 'A young mother can look out of her window,' to quote a town planner, 'and see the skyscrapers, and she will have the security of knowing that there, within reach, is a small flat for her to move into when the time comes. So she feels secure. She won't have to keep a larger place on. Also, when the children move away, they will have bachelor flats to move into, in the same suburb. You can see the solutions to all your housing needs around you.'

But what of those who eschew being patterned and organized and prefer another way of life? There would be no ban on them. 'But,' quoting Mrs Jussil again, 'if you are able to get a house, you will have to accept a longer journey to work.' This will eventually mean two or three hours by car or train. Clearly, the exigencies of transport will add another pressure to keep town dwellers to the officially approved suburbs.

It is a maxim of Swedish planners that they must identify

public need, as distinct from public demand. The one is 'objective', and therefore measurable and acceptable; the other 'subjective', hence beyond mensuration, and consequently lacking in reality. Needs, being definable, can be directly formulated by an outsider; demand is a matter of individual taste and requires more elaborate forms of influence. In the official Swedish dialectic, demand is further divided into what people really want and what they think they want. The former is considered meaningless, and the latter the only reality. This is natural for behaviourists, since their principles entitle them to reason that a man's requirements are not a matter of free choice, but a product of environment and conditioning. Those dealing with consumer affairs, and most particularly housing, define their task as that of discovering what people think they want, *and then persuading them to want the correct thing*.

This is merely another version of the advertising man's work of creating demand. It is the same type of manipulation but, instead of being in private hands, it is employed by the State. Given this, the value of a segment of Swedish educational policy becomes apparent. Schoolchildren are taught to be on their guard against private manipulators, but not against public ones. The State consequently has an unchallenged line to the citizen's subconscious, or whatever mechanism it is that determines his reactions.

It has not, therefore, required the arcane skills of sophisticated propagandists to tailor the wants of the Swedes to the requirements of their rulers. Quite ordinary and uncomplicated methods of suggestion have been perfectly adequate: the relatively straightforward A B F propaganda has been remarkably effective. In the case of housing, the average Swede has been more than half persuaded that his desire for a small house of his own is illusory; that what he really wants is a flat in a rigidly controlled environment. In various ways, a kind of indoctrination against small houses has for long been undertaken. In a particular ABF course-book on housing, aimed at minor party and trade-union officials, virtually all the material was concentrated on flats. Only a single, small section on houses was included. It was so phrased as to cast doubt on that form of living. 'Live in a house?' was the title. 'Houses have been ascribed great advantages in comparison with blocks of flats. Is it simply romanticism, or is there any realism in such a line of thought?' Various reasons were then advanced, in the subdued manner of somebody acting as devil's advocate, as to why houses might be wanted. One of them was that there 'is ground for belief that many people consider that the spread of motoring will make it possible to live in small houses farther out in spite of worse communications than in the more central living areas'.

'But on the other hand,' the course goes on to say, 'we can find other reasons against small houses. The drift from the country to the towns, especially the medium-sized concentrations, continues. This means that more people are moving to places where the way of living is, by tradition, less in houses than is the case in the country, and in small villages.'

This is not strictly true, but it is persuasive: even in a forward-looking society, tradition is a powerful justification. Flats are traditional in all towns; houses are not; the public accepts that, and adjusts its tastes accordingly. Town planning may concentrate on flats, in the knowledge that resistance has been undermined beforehand. The ABF course betrays, in passing, yet another means of discouraging small houses. By starving such developments of public transport, their attractions are reduced. There are small housing estates in the environs of Stockholm, for example, which are practically devoid of public transport. In a few cases, existing railway services have been left to decay. On the other hand, the new approved suburbs have been well provided with underground railways and rapid bus services.

Most building in Sweden is highly industrialized. Prefabrication is the rule. Long production runs are common. In consequence, uniformity is guaranteed. Over large areas, thousands of flats are identical, and it is possible to visit homes in widely separated parts of the country and yet have the impression of staying in one place. In one way, this serves the purpose of regimentation. People all live in more or less the same kind of flat, and the thought of asking for distinctive architecture as a contribution to identity is rare. A schoolteacher put it this way: 'All rooms have four walls and a ceiling. So what's the difference?'

To the average Swede, a house, in the words of Le Corbusier, is 'a machine for living in', although not perhaps in quite the sense that he meant it. Standards are uniformly high. Construction is solid, workmanship impeccable and jerry building unknown. Refrigerators and deep freezers are always provided: kitchens come fully equipped. Bathrooms are superb and plumbing faultless. Walls are insulated, and central heating universal. Windows are large, and rooms are light, although often in a clinical way. Functionally, a modern Swedish flat could hardly be improved on. Rooms are admittedly small and ceilings low, but since tenants appear not to mind, that can scarcely be labelled a serious defect.

The ABF housing course mentioned above asks: 'How far can one standardize in order to keep prices down? Are the fears that simplification can go too far, justified? Standardization, after all, is a link in efforts to economize, i.e. to husband the limited resources we have. If we can do that, we can create the resources for a higher housing standard, or lower housing costs: the housing consumer gets more for his money.

'It is the function of the architect to provide a neutral frame for those who live there. In this way, individuals have greater possibilities to create an environment according to their own personal evaluations. Furniture, textiles and other decorative objects are an expression of personal taste,⋆ which comes out far more clearly within a neutral framework.'

That proposition is an exercise in triteness and sophistry. It is merely an argument for anonymous architecture, dressed up in respectable clothes. Nevertheless, it has been generally accepted.

To achieve this steering of architecture, architects must of necessity be the servants of politicians and planners. Alternatively, they have to subordinate their originality to the exigencies of policy. The architect is customarily a man of independence, with certain aesthetic and social ideas which he wishes to embody in a building. This is not so in Sweden. Architecture, with the acquiescence of the architects, has become the servant of the State and the agent of its ideology. The function of the Swedish architect is officially defined as that of changing society. Architects, turned by their commissions into irregular civil servants, have identified themselves with the State, and helped to realize its aims. And this has been compounded by a singular development in professional ideas.

For the modern Swedish architect, aesthetics do not exist. This is only a local application of a general trend. Beauty has been denied validity, because it cannot be defined; for the same reason, ugliness is said to have no meaning. It is nihilism dignified by professional acceptance and supported by philosophy. 'Value nihilism', which denies the existence of values that cannot be exactly measured, is the accepted Swedish

⋆ The late industrialization of the Swedes has happily left them with roots in their traditional peasant culture. This has meant that they have preserved a sense of colour, pattern and texture which makes the average person an accomplished interior decorator. The connection with the Scandinavian countryside can be seen in the constant use of the forest colours; the muted pink and grey of granite outcrop, the sombre greens of the conifers, and the hot ochres and viridian of the lichens. Such subtle elements are handled with dexterity: rarely in a Swedish home is there visual disharmony.

creed. It is a comforting doctrine. It dismisses metaphysics. Applied to architecture, it means that function alone counts. The architect is no longer concerned with designing a beautiful building, but only with the production of rigidly specified structures.

These specifications are social, economic and technical, in that order. The social requirements have primacy, and determine the nature of the others. Broadly speaking, their aim, like that of education, is to change men in the way demanded by the new society. And as the schools imprint, to use official catchwords, equality and community so is architecture expected to do the same things.

Equality is a word of many meanings, particularly in Swedish. In the strict sense of social levelling, the environment is used for its consummation by mixing classes. The municipal housing offices try to distribute tenants in the new suburbs so that there is no separation of income or profession, and juxtaposition of the unequal is ensured. By and large, this has been achieved. Whether it will destroy the notion of class or simply exacerbate antagonism remains to be seen, but, in this context at least, it is the intention that counts.

Social levelling is perhaps the least of the meanings of 'equality' in Swedish. Literally, the word for it – *jämlikhet* – means even and identical, and out of this there arise strong connotations of self-effacement and regimentation. As a corollary, architects are strongly discouraged, where they are not actually forbidden, from putting individuality into their designs. All Swedes are to be provided with roughly the same form of dwelling: a flat (or terraced house) that is comfortable, but not excessively so, a kind of golden environmental mean. It is permissible to have a slightly better flat, but not a spacious split-level apartment; a little larger standard house, but not an individually conceived home for gracious or eccentric living. There is no option in kind; choice is restricted to degree. The citizen must live as the State prescribes.

This doctrine is upheld by the rulers of the country. Mr Hans Löwbeer, the University Chancellor, although of the upper classes, lives in a modern Stockholm suburb called Farsta, incorporating the principles of equality applied to the environment. 'I live like everybody else,' he says, 'we've got to put equality into living.' Mr Olof Palme, the Prime Minister, lives in a terraced house at Vällingby, another socially engineered Stockholm suburb. Both men appear genuinely to believe in the civic virtues of anonymous and uniform living: at all events it makes sound political sense. The Swede suspects a man who lives differently from others; conformity among his leaders is a necessity for his support.

Anonymous architecture ought to be the logical consequence of anonymous living. This is not only the case in Sweden, it might be objected. But what distinguishes the Swedish situation is that anonymity is deliberate official policy, and that, since the State alone determines the form of architecture, there is no competition and no relief. It is as if, in England, all new building were in the hands of the Greater London Council or the Ministry of Works; or, in America, in the control of the Department of Housing and Urban Development.

The significance of individual buildings has been abolished in Sweden. It is the relationship between them alone that counts. Of course, any architect with a feeling for artistic unity will try to relate his work to its neighbours. But in Sweden, the principle has been invoked as a conscious aid to anonymity. It has been employed to eradicate vestigial traces of character so that buildings become the visual expression of a collective society. Each town looks very like the other, and there is something oddly disembowelled about all buildings erected since the 1940s. This is not, of course, an inescapable consequence of modern architecture. There was a time, during the first four decades of this century, when the Swedes, although admittedly under Finnish and German influence, designed buildings of some character. And, looking across the Gulf of Bothnia, to Finland, the cradle of contemporary architecture, one sees building after building of tremendous personality. But in Finland the architect is still trying to cultivate architectural beauty in a modern idiom. Consequently, there are buildings in Helsinki with all the distinctive vigour of a Renaissance palace in Italy. To see the work of Alvar Aalto is to succumb to sheer architectural vitality.

But in Sweden, anonymity has become part of the creed of the architect. Professor T. Ahrbohm, a leading Swedish architect and a high civil servant, has this to say: 'I sympathize with anonymous architecture, and disapprove of buildings that are monuments to their designers. Housing is not an expression of an architect's personality, but an instrument of society. Nor is it functional, in the sense of being built with a certain function in view, because it has to take care of changing functions. It has to promote change.'

If the Swedish architectural profession displays classic symptoms of *gleichschaltung*, it is natural to inquire who is directing it? The immediate, and, to a certain extent, the superficial, answer is, the administrative organs of the State. It is only to be expected that in so regulated a country as Sweden, architecture would be subject to control. There is a central government office, the Directorate of Building, that, by establishing norms and making recommendations that have the force of law, can influence design. Furthermore, there is direct control in legal compulsion for all designs to be approved by local authorities, not only for town planning, but for pure architectural values as well. That is to say, a building not only has to fulfil official requirements as to placement and general compatibility with the surroundings, but its shape and plan must be approved by a municipal architect, before building permission is granted. In this way, experiments are prevented. All architecture in Sweden is approved architecture.

But this is only a framework of external control. It would be much more satisfactory if architects could be persuaded to design in the way that their ideological superiors require. And this, in fact, is what the Swedes have accomplished. The plans submitted for approval have kept abreast of developments; rejections remain few. It is as if some authority had not only changed specifications, but had induced changes in the minds of architects as well. Once the new architectural ideology had been conceived in the ruling establishment of State and party, it was soon disseminated. Within a short while, the leadership of the Swedish Architectural Association, the governing body of the profession, had passed into radical hands, so that there was administrative compatibility with official direction.

More profoundly, indoctrination in the new purpose of architecture, i.e. to change society according to ideological guidance, poured out in the professional journals, via the mass media, through official propaganda and, above all, in education. Schools of architecture swung over to the new line within a year or two. The nature of the architectural profession rapidly changed. Among the older architects there remained a vestige of aesthetic ambition, the occasional shadow of a building artist. The type of architect qualifying at the end of the 1960s, however, was not an artist, but a sociologist, whose declared aim was, not to produce beautiful buildings, but to change society.

Some of this is attributable to the new educational system. School-leavers have shown growing ambitions in social engineering, the category in which Swedish architecture now almost wholly belongs. It is worth noting that while the new attitude is naturally freshest and most undiluted among the architects under thirty, it has also been assimilated by their elders. The Swedes have a commendable propensity for learning from their juniors, and for avoiding the stigma of the reactionary.

The new and younger architects have played the decisive role in the formation of architectural policy. They have the ability, and they dominate the departments of State that control the planning of Sweden. Ignoring private practice, nearly all of them have gone into public service, because they find greater satisfaction in 'serving society' than in working for a private client. They have done so because it gives them greater power.

'The political climate helps us,' to quote Mr Jan Strömdahl, an influential younger architect in the Directorate of National Planning. 'Swedish architecture has been successful in encouraging change because there is a powerful machinery for the centralized control of building. This has forced the pace of development.

'I am afraid of living in a detached house, because it causes isolation, and restricts contact. I am interested in collective living, and want to see it spread. I am going to experiment, by putting up some new quarters, with extended community centres. Not only meeting halls, libraries and dispensaries, but laundries and children's play rooms. By removing amenities from the home, and moving them into communal premises, you can force people to live communally. Then I want to see more communal restaurants, so that people eat together. There is nothing as isolating as the family meal, taken together, within four walls.

'I don't think it will be necessary to force people to live communally. Once they see the advantages of the new kind of life, they will *want* to change. It goes without saying that I am against small houses.'

This is a good and succinct enunciation of that other major aim of architecture: the promotion of community or the advancement of the collective, and the undermining of the individual.

Professor Rexed demonstrates another aspect of this goal by saying that: 'Environment has to be planned so that the

family situation can be corrected. Children have to be socialized at an early age, in order to eradicate the social heritage.'
It is an acknowledged aim of Social Democratic ideologists
(and others) in Sweden to break up the traditional family,
because it fosters individuality and because it perpetuates
class distinction and social disability.

With aesthetics dismissed, and his aims settled, the Swedish
architect, therefore, has only economics and technology to
occupy him. Even in these matters, his hands are tied. The
requirements with which he is provided are rigorously detailed. Given the human capacity of the structure, its size
follows automatically. The volume of air, and the area of
floor for each occupant have been scientifically determined;
the height of the ceiling follows as a matter of course. These
are minima; in the interests of economy, they are treated as
specifications. The number of storeys follows from the size
of the building plot. The architect, under these conditions, is
little more than an interpreter of tables and rules; his work
could be done by a computer.

Again, this development is noticeable (and lamented)
elsewhere, but in Sweden it has gone further and been universally accepted. The Swedish architect finds his last field of
discretion in economics. His task has been virtually reduced
to that of selecting the cheapest method of production
for a given purpose. He, too, has become a cog (usually
a willing one) in the social machine, an agent of political
forces.

Since the 1950s, the Swedish architects have been much in
demand. It is not only that they have been required to build,
but that they have had to rebuild as well. The centres of the
main cities, and especially Stockholm, have been pulled down
in a frenzy and swiftly replaced by a new and shiny core.
Economically, this was unnecessary. Many of the old buildings, given reasonable maintenance, could have lasted for
another half century. Slums, they most definitely were not.

In Stockholm, the excised quarters were those in which businessmen, small shops, tradesmen and newspapers were concentrated; in short, the living heart of a city. Many houses of historical and architectural worth fell to the bulldozer. Neither sentiment nor tradition was allowed to stand in the way.

All cities have to be renewed, but the process is usually gradual, so that the inhabitants have time to adjust to change. If one compares Stockholm with the other Scandinavian capitals, its uniqueness becomes apparent. Copenhagen, also expanding and modernized, has carefully preserved its old centre. Helsinki offers an even better standard of comparison. If Copenhagen has a splendid core to preserve with Danish Renaissance and Rococo buildings, the Finnish capital has very little. There, jerry-built acres of singularly little charm wait for merciful extinction. Yet the Finnish town planners are careful not to remove a whole street at once, let alone entire quarters, as the Swedes do. Rather, they replace scattered buildings, so that the renewal of a given urban environment will be spread over some years. By so doing, they maintain continuity. People have time to adjust to change, and are spared the discomfort of losing their bearings.

This consideration is entirely absent in Sweden. It may be that, on the contrary, the intention was to disorient the population. It is, after all, an elementary rule of human manipulation that one of the most effective ways of eroding a man's resistance is to destroy his time sense. That this may be accomplished by destroying familiar surroundings and replacing them with something entirely new is testified by elder Stockholmers, who confess to a distressing sense of confusion among the bulldozed remnants of their city. It is not the relatively innocuous sense of being topographically lost that follows upon the disappearance of physical landmarks, but a deeper disorientation, concerning both space and time, that touches personal identity and the frontiers of sanity. When new tenants move from the country into the freshly thrown up suburbs of Stockholm, one of their first actions is to ask about ancient habitation on the site of their glistening flats. Archaeologists at the Historical Museum in Stockholm deal with a constant flood of inquiries. The questioners exude relief upon being told that people have lived before on the ground under their floors, and that it is not quite virgin soil: they seem to find their bearings again after a period of confusion.

These people are mostly young, so that it is not the nostalgia of an older generation. Moreover, they are the product of a school system that is anti-historical, and that is concerned exclusively with the future, so that their background does not encourage them to brood over what has gone before. But in their natural habitat they have time beacons on their doorstep; the Swedish landscape is full of prehistoric relics, like burial mounds and stone circles. Having moved, these new city dwellers find themselves physically uprooted and suspended in time, deprived of the signposts to the past in their previous homes.

It has not infrequently been the practice of innovators to construct brand new surroundings to symbolize the advent of a new order and insist visually that the past has been abolished. The Swedes are following in a respectable tradition known to many civilizations.

The changes in Stockholm are not, as in the case of similar redevelopment in other countries, the result of commercial enterprise and private initiative. They are the product of official planning. Most civilized societies have public checks on private building, to prevent excesses, architectural or otherwise. But in Sweden the municipalities (and ultimately the State) establish the pattern of building. It is the public authorities alone who actively create plans, where elsewhere they are very often confined to the passive function of judging them. Initiative is denied the private developer; insofar as he is allowed to function, he must follow the directions of authority and, in the final analysis, he is merely the instrument of official intentions. Able to expropriate at will, and impose their ideas, the authorities lord it over the environment like children playing with bricks. What happens in the domain of building is, therefore, not so much the consequence of economic forces, as emanations of the official mind. And, as the ideologists concede, architecture and town planning are used in order to realize political intentions and to induce a change of mentality.

Destruction of the centre of Stockholm has had the effect of cutting off the past. It was done with a callousness and ruthlessness that suggests a fear or hatred of what had gone before. When the new plan was adopted in the 1950s it was presented as a symbol of the future. 'Everything before 1932 must be forgotten,' said a city alderman. That, it will be remembered, was the year the Social Democrats came to power, but it has a symbolism beyond simple party politics. The 1930s saw the birth of modern Sweden, and the opening of the Swedish technological age. Irrespective of political creed, this to many Swedes is the era they like to commemorate, and anything else is best consigned to limbo.

Yet, there are some Swedes who prefer mellowed surroundings, even if not up to contemporary standards. But in Stockholm, a socialist alderman in charge of housing says he insists on demolishing all older buildings because he wants everyone to have the same high standard (equality again). A woman threatened by demolition wrote thus to a Stockholm newspaper: 'We who live in these condemned buildings love our scruffy old quarters. And we more than willingly give up modern conveniences in order to live cheaply, centrally, and in a pleasant atmosphere. I think that we who are young and healthy should have the right to GIVE UP material standards and comfort, if we consider it worthwhile.'

The answer to her plea came, indirectly, at a conference of

municipal housing experts. A certain official, who knew what he was talking about, and was a power in the land, explained how 'research' had decided what kitchens, shape of room and lighting installations were best for people, and that these would, willy-nilly, be provided for tenants. 'Do you mean to say,' asked a rare, rebellious delegate, 'that you are going to tell people how to live?' 'Yes,' was the answer. 'That's my job.'

A Stockholm city councillor always refers to old buildings as 'dirty'. Official propaganda and the consensus of the mass media underwrite this view. As new quarters arise, the stock cliché is that it is the 'future rising like a phoenix from the ashes of the past'. Among the public there is a demonstrable regret over the disappearance of familiar landmarks. But this never takes the form of action. Campaigns to save threatened buildings are practically unknown; when they occur, they are weak, ineffectual and confined to a small upper-class minority. The last home of August Strindberg, architecturally and historically worth saving, was demolished with scarcely any opposition. The essential point there, as in many similar cases, is that the public would have liked it saved, but that they swallowed their regrets, because they believed that progress demanded it.

Citizens looking at the bulldozed remains of a building that they have known and liked will not bitterly consider how it might have been saved. They will say that it is the inescapable consequence of change; in the appropriate cliché it is dismissed as the 'demand of the times'. Behind this lies the usual Swedish determinism. It is accepted by the rulers, not only the ruled. A Stockholm alderman puts it in these words: 'Town planning is a long-range question, so that even if we want to save some old houses, we can't. What happens today was decided years ago, and the ideas of that time are only now coming into force. Technical forces are irresistible.'

The centre of Stockholm has been redesigned for the motor car instead of men. It has been conceived for driving through, instead of living in. Of course, this is nothing unique, but what is peculiar to Sweden is that criticism is virtually absent. Many Stockholm inhabitants are willing to concede that the centre of their city has become sterile, charmless and uninhabitable, but this does not bother them: in the words of yet another popular cliché (borrowed, like so many others, from the mass media) the centre 'functions, because at least it allows the traffic to move'.

People accept the reconstruction of their cities as a necessary accompaniment to changes in society. They see no reason to preserve the old, as they see no reason to resist the advances of a new ideology. Their environment has predisposed them to change. 'Politicians,' in the measured words of a Stockholm alderman, 'undoubtedly want to influence people through town planning.' And if Swedish architecture is the mirror of their minds, they seek to impose uniformity and regimentation.

There is no dash, no individuality, nor even the unabashed vulgarity of an exuberant commercialism in modern Swedish architecture. It produces a sense of submission and restraint. Like all 'political' architecture, it is a monument to the party that has built it. If there are ideological thoughts behind the rebuilding, they have been notably successful. The environmental mill has ground away yet more of the desire to oppose.

13. The Mass Media as Agents of Conformity

To judge solely by its mass media, Sweden appears to be run by a tolerant dictatorship. Press, radio and TV show a remarkable similarity, as if guided by some Ministry of Propaganda. Criticism of the government there may be, but it is almost exclusively confined to administrative trivialities, and covered by the formula: 'First you decide on your goals, and then you discuss the means. There is no other discussion.' Almost never is there questioning of political fundamentals, or critical examination of the institutions of the State. All the media seem to be of one mind, advocating the same consensus, professing the same slogans, always, it seems, following the convolution of some party line. They give the impression of existing, not to question authority, but to avoid disturbing the public peace of mind; not to criticize, but to indoctrinate with a certain point of view.

If radio and TV hawk official viewpoints, that is understandable, since they are a State monopoly. The press, however, is privately owned, mostly non-socialist, its liberty guaranteed by law. Some occult powers, no doubt, have been invoked to steer editorial minds. To this, we return later.

That the ether is the prerogative of the State, need not necessarily (outside a dictatorship) mean that it is the mouthpiece of the government. It was the case in Gaullist France, but the BBC, when it ruled alone, before ITV and (the threat of) commercial radio, displayed an honourable independence. The Swedish system can be compared with neither. Radio and TV are nominally independent, although

State-supervised; they reject all accusations of being a government organ. But they display a bias and propagate views which the government would like the population to absorb.

As in so many other things, Swedish broadcasting, on superficial inspection, appears to resemble its counterparts in Western countries, but on closer examination turns out to be something rather different. The first distinction lies in its position in the organization of the State. In almost all Western democracies radio and TV are administered by departments of *communications*, which suggests a passive medium, but in Sweden (as in many dictatorships) they are the concern of the Ministry of *Education*, implying an instrument of guidance. Since, under the Social Democrats, education has become a means of tailoring minds and changing society, the ether, quite reasonably, may be expected to share those aims.

In Western countries, to make another comparison, the purpose of radio and TV is, theoretically at least, to *inform* people; in Sweden, the official function is to *form* opinion. This is no quibbling over a prefix; the Swedish authorities are acutely aware of the difference between the two concepts. In opting for the one, they have had a deliberate purpose in view. It is interesting, indeed, to note that, in the official jargon, broadcasting is always 'an opinion-forming medium'.

The power of broadcasting in Sweden is somewhat greater than in Western countries because the bulk of the population, being intellectually backward, and only just emerging from isolation, is more than usually susceptible to indoctrinating forces. 'Swedes,' to quote Mr Örjan Wallquist, head of the Swedish TV's second channel, 'are intellectually primitive and underdeveloped. And TV works in this way: it creates emotions and intellectual life, and therefore it *creates* opinions. It is an opinion-*making* medium.'

Mr Wallquist is a socialist, and belongs to the intellectual leadership of the Labour movement. 'TV is a *very* powerful medium,' he says. 'TV sets are more concentrated in Sweden than in other countries. *Aktuellt* (a news programme), for example, has an audience of fifty per cent of the population.

'TV is a very powerful indoctrinating medium, and one has to be extremely careful in using it.

'TV would never attack the Prime Minister and government, because the average Swede identifies himself with the State and with the corporations that exercise political influence. So TV feels part of the State.'

An official admits that broadcasting is a medium of indoctrination. It has two aims, he says: to persuade the Swedes that they live in the best of all possible worlds, and to condition them to the ideology of the sitting government.

To induce a nation to believe that it enjoys the happiest lot on earth is an elementary device to secure compliance with a government and forestall criticism. In reporting from abroad, the Swedish radio and TV are concerned, not so much to show how other people live, but to illuminate the superiority of things Swedish. They concentrate on the defects of foreign countries, drawing comparisons to the advantage of Sweden. The viewer is invited to see how badly off people are everywhere else and to consider how fortunate he is. Press and periodicals take the same line. It is not only that the Swede is told that he has the highest standard of living, and the best social security, but that he really is superior in all things, most particularly in politics and culture. An article on child care in France, published by a women's magazine, seemed to have no other purpose but that of serving up a homily on how much better Swedes looked after their children. Even travel writing often contains disparaging remarks, in order specifically to draw a moral in praise of Sweden, usually concerned with poverty abroad and prosperity at home.

Most nations entertain a high opinion of themselves but, unless their rulers nurse ulterior motives, official media of communication do not normally insist, as a matter of policy, on advertising domestic superiority. Still less do they pursue this aim by denigrating foreign institutions. The Russians, to quote an obvious example, notoriously do so. If the Swedes act likewise, it is for a similar reason: to generate contentment among the population. Like the average Russian, the average Swede therefore has a biased view of the world outside as something inferior and undesirable, that has been formed by his mass media.

In the indoctrination of the public with government policies, Swedish radio and TV has been of the greatest value. The tenor of programmes follows ministerial thinking with great accuracy. From 1968, when the government adopted an anti-American policy (mainly, but not entirely, over Vietnam), the ether followed suit. Radio and TV became almost laughably biased, colouring news reports, and broadcasting material (some emanating from Cuba) that could only be classified as unmitigated propaganda. Producers were told that no programme on the United States would be considered unless it was unfavourable. Even allowing for general feeling against American policy at that time (not, of course, confined to Sweden), the Swedes became notoriously militant in their attitudes. A popular anti-Americanism grew with the propaganda on the air. Then, in 1970, while Sweden was negotiating with the Common Market, it was a thinly veiled secret that the government was less than keen on full membership and wanted public opinion to be suitably primed. Radio and especially TV conducted a virulent and persistent campaign against the EEC until the official Swedish rejection of full membership in March 1971.

As the party has extended its grip on the State, so has broadcasting become an instrument of party propaganda. Towards the end of the 1960s, it took about three months for party trends to be incorporated into radio and TV programmes. Usually, this would happen before they had been officially adopted as party policy. The purpose, as in education, is to prepare the ground. When the new ideas finally appear on a political manifesto, the public has accepted or at least grown used to them, and the party appears to be professing self-evident truths.

In September 1969, the Social Democrats at their party congress adopted a platform of egalitarianism, in which equality of the sexes was given a leading role. For months beforehand, radio and TV imprinted the necessary concepts on the public consciousness. 'Equality' became a universal catchword on the air. Equality of the sexes (and its logical corollary, women's liberation) was propagated as received dogma.

Equality, although it is a perfectly unexceptional sentiment, had nevertheless become associated uniquely with the Labour movement. In every sense of the word, it had turned into party propaganda. It was incorporated into children's broadcasts, so that those in the most impressionable age, between three and seven, were brain-washed. Even Christmas programmes were turned into pretexts for propagating the slogan of equality.

Similarly, radio and TV, when the government required it, fed anti-American attitudes into children's programmes. A series about Red Indians, aimed at five- to seven-year-olds, for example, was so slanted as to be a grotesque attack on the United States. Obviously, the treatment of the American Indians is not entirely a credit to the white settlers, but neither is its exploitation, as in the Swedish case, to damn American society as a whole, reasonable or justifiable. A Stockholm newspaper published a number of children's letters which suggested that this kind of propaganda was proving efficacious. 'I think,' wrote a six-year-old, 'that all Americans are swine.'

Also in the name of equality, the party had launched a campaign against finance and industry. Radio and TV did so as well. All this (at least in the beginning) was exclusively the property of the Social Democrats. It was partisan propaganda, not government rescript, and certainly not yet the law of the land. What was ultimately advance campaigning for the 1970 General Elections was presented as accepted truth, to be hammered securely home.

Intermittent campaigns apart, the Swedish radio and TV constantly accept the evaluations of the Labour movement. In the vital field of industrial relations, the trade-union viewpoint dominates, and the employers are presented disadvantageously. It is virtually impossible for anybody opposing the government to get a hearing. Broadcasting has been turned into a servant of the party and the State.

It is not inherent in its condition. Until the 1950s, the Swedish radio and TV was reasonably impartial, with the aim of being a disinterested public service comparable to the BBC. The change came with the appointment in 1962 of Mr Olof Palme, later Prime Minister, as Minister of Communications. Mr Palme had studied in the United States and, ahead of his countrymen, he assimilated and applied the work of the American communicators. He grasped the powers of TV. In Sweden, they were formidable. When the little screen first swept into the homes of Sweden, during the 1960s, it also constituted the arrival of the outside world. It broke, for the first time in history, the isolation of the Swedish population. Many Swedes saw a foreigner for the first time on TV. The population were dragged out of the early nineteenth century and brought face to face with the mid-twentieth century. 'Intellectually primitive and undeveloped,' to quote Mr Wallquist, the Swede was terribly vulnerable to the new medium. Mr Palme understood this. He turned it into a political weapon and, when he was made Minister of Education, he took broadcasting with him. He had distilled the wisdom of the American commercial persuaders and applied it to a monopoly of the State. Instead of the 'countervailing forces' of private business, there was the untrammelled prerogative of the central government. The indoctrinating privileges thus conferred on the party were formidable.

Harnessing the ether necessitated a political take-over. The Swedish radio is nominally an independent corporation and, until the Social Democrats turned their attention seriously to the control of mass communications, it was directed by men whose consensus was of the centre. Its construction, however, is such that the government, at least if Social Democrat, can assume control. It is a corporation of corporations. Its board of governors is drawn from the main political parties and corporate organizations. The employers, trade unions and cooperative societies are represented. This means that the Labour movement has a majority, and the government can get its way. Furthermore, certain vital committees are in the gift of the government. Until the 1960s, however, these had been appointed in a non-partisan manner. Mr Palme, however, made them political, and dominated by Social Democrats. A particularly important committee thus reconstituted was that concerned with the selection of programmes and staff. Socialist nominees were appointed to most senior administration and production posts. The bias of the staff, indeed, moved somewhat to the left of the official party Social Democratic position, but this was consistent with the views of party strategists. They required a shift of public opinion several points leftwards of their immediate aims, so as to enjoy political leeway.

Between 1965 and 1968, the Social Democrats profited from the Vietnam war by supporting the protest movement and thereby engaging the sympathy of youth. At that time, the issue was at its emotional zenith and, correctly handled, politically valuable. Where Western governments fought the trend, the rulers of Sweden made an ally out of it. Cabinet ministers, including Mr Palme, made demagogic orations against Washington and in praise of Hanoi. Radio and TV gave generous coverage to every demonstration, often out of all proportion to its size. They conferred respectability on the Swedish Viet Cong sympathizers, several tens of thousands strong. Teenagers, and in their early twenties, they became an accepted part of the landscape, with the long hair, the buttons, badges and hippie-like dress, familiar everywhere. They did, however, display a notable curiosity. The mass media did not, as elsewhere, call them FNL *sympathizers,* but FNL *members,* so that news reports gave the impression that a branch of the Vietnam war had opened in Sweden. It was an example of the Swede's craving for the action and significance denied him by his neutrality.

All this was to the government's advantage. Youth had an outlet for its energy, and the party was on its side. Radio and TV continued to play up the demonstrations and protest meetings. By the end of 1969, however, the protest movement had lost glamour and political respectability. It was taken over by Maoists inimical to the government. Radio and TV stopped its coverage, although demonstrations continued as extensively as before. One of the largest meetings of its kind was held on 20 December 1970 before the American embassy in Stockholm in honour of the foundation of the Viet Cong, but it was scarcely mentioned on the air. This change kept pace with a shift of government attitudes. While the media were withdrawing their support, Mr Palme was turning on his erstwhile allies.

The party is most concerned over maintaining control of TV, and takes care to anticipate future developments. When the first cassette TV was about to enter Sweden, the government stepped in to acquire what was virtually a monopoly of production and distribution. Private companies, although theoretically free to act as they wished, were forced behind the scenes either to abandon their plans or to accept State partnership and supervision.

Few Western governments are as perturbed as that of Sweden over the possibility of direct TV transmissions from satellites to private receivers. Politicians are quite openly concerned at the prospect of foreign programmes reaching their citizens for, when that comes, the State will no longer have a monopoly of its own ether. Consequently, the Swedes are trying to have future satellite broadcasting banned internationally. Under present conditions, however, the Swedish government retains its control on the air. In many ways, it is only making assurance doubly sure. Without political supervision, the party would still get its way because the communicators are on its side.

The Swedish communicators act as a corporate body, collectively following the trend of the moment. They are conformist to a fault, wanting only to promote the consensus. It is tradition reinforced by education. Party ideologists say that the new educational system has conditioned the rising generation to think as they want it to. Indoctrination in the schools has been in progress since the 1950s; the products now dominate the media. Their seniors have absorbed the necessary attitudes through other channels. Anxious only to expound what their colleagues believe, the Swedish communicators need no compulsion to toe the party line. In their mental world, departure from the accepted norm is a kind of treachery. It is part of conditioning to group thinking, which makes personal divergence a sin, and acceptance of the collective opinion a cardinal virtue. They have an urge to think as everybody else does. In consequence, they have developed a kind of inhibition, what the Russians call the 'inner censor', that tailors the expression of their thoughts to prevailing views. Since they act corporatively, by conditioned reflex as it were, it is relatively easy to harness them to a particular ideology. It suffices to convert a select few at the top of the hierarchy, the rest following obediently.

From this it follows that the press also supports the policies of the State, and that the question of ownership is largely academic. In fact, most daily newspapers belong to the opposition;* almost all are owned by a political party. The independent journal run on commercial lines is a rarity and, of so institutional a nature, it is scarcely surprising that the Swedish press shows so little vigour. The tendencies of the communicators working for the State-run broadcasting system are no different from those of their colleagues on the privately owned press. This *gleichschaltung* is further aided by the existence of schools of journalism. It has increasingly become the practice of Swedish newspapers to recruit their journalists from those institutions. But, in the manner of the Swedish educational system, schools of journalism have followed the indoctrination of the party and State. They have moved consistently to the left, and turned out graduates with uniform opinions. These may be broadly described as radical Social Democrats, with possibly a tinge of Maoism. The actual direction is, of course, irrelevant; the point is that there is a direction at all. Like their colleagues in architecture and the social sciences, these journalists regard themselves as social engineers, with the ambition of changing society, and indoctrinating their fellow-men.

Yet the government appears not quite content with the communicators' sanction in its natural form. An influential school of thought within the Social Democratic party wants the press removed from private ownership and brought under public control. One outcome was a law, passed in 1971, ostensibly to subsidize the press and guard its independence, but in practice a threat to its freedom. Struggling newspapers are to receive subsidies financed by a tax on advertisements in the successful ones, to be paid by the papers. The effect is to transfer money from opposition to government journals, since in Sweden (as elsewhere) non-Socialist organs are

---

* About seventy per cent of Swedish daily newspapers (covering seventy per cent of the circulation) belong to the opposition parties, or support them. The rest belong to the Labour movement. There is one Communist newspaper.

usually more successful than Socialist ones. A State committee decides who pays and who receives. In the long term, many profitable newspapers will become unprofitable and depend on State subsidies for survival. The effect on editorial independence is unlikely to be pleasant. In the end, opposition will probably be subdued.

But this may be superfluous caution. Today, newspapers are as biased as TV and radio, giving the same peculiar view of the world, designed to bolster the Swede's self-esteem. In a Swedish newspaper, it is difficult to separate news, facts, the reporters' views and editorial opinion. The idea of reserving news columns for facts, and putting comment in the leading articles, is alien. Swedish journalists believe, on the whole, that facts are subsidiary, and possibly mutable; that, in the interests of objective truth, their opinions must colour their reporting. Like their colleagues on the air, they see their function as the *formation* of public opinion.

'News,' says Dr Olof Lagercrantz, the editor of the Stockholm *Dagens Nyheter*, one of the two national daily newspapers in Sweden, 'must be used to change society and influence people. If it is objective, and designed only to inform, then it is conservative. Now in a small country like Sweden, a newspaper of *Dagens Nyheter*'s size* has tremendous power. Single-handed, we can change public opinion.'

There is more than a little substance in this claim. The Swedes are particularly susceptible to the influence of the mass media. Their newspapers are designed to tell them what to think. The man in the street hesitates to express a view of his own, but needs an opinion provided by an expert. He wants to be sure that what he says will correspond with what those around him are saying. Again, it is the pursuit of consensus. It is a sardonic joke occasionally heard that a man 'will not

---

* Its circulation is 600,000, the largest in Sweden. Its sole competitor, *Svenska Dagbladet*, sells about 200,000. The total Swedish population is slightly under 8,000,000.

know what to think today until he has read the newspapers'.

'A small country,' to quote Dr Lagercrantz again, 'cannot afford to have individuals getting up and taking a stand on their own. There has to be a group. And, of course, since Swedes react in groups, they are easily influenced.' He is no Social Democrat, but a somewhat leftish liberal; *Dagens Nyheter* supports the Liberal party. His view of opinions on his right is that 'it is impossible to hold a conservative point of view in a society that is continuously changing'.

This is a rare articulation of a dominant viewpoint. It expresses the tyranny of what Ibsen once called 'the compact majority'. It is an effective method of destroying opposition. The dissident cannot be taken seriously, because the view of the majority excludes by definition the possibility of a conflicting view. 'In Sweden,' a Swedish professor once observed, 'there is room for only one idea at a time.'

The demand for a supply of approved views may be seen in a particular feature of the Swedish press. Most newspapers and magazines run columns by well-known intellectuals in which they do not offer comment so much as provide ready-made opinions. There are perhaps fifty or sixty and, at a given moment, they all profess the same views, altering them as women do their hemline to the dictates of the fashion designers. They are not, as explained before, centrally direc-ted; they are simply acting like a herd. There is a range of tolerated opinions, and a narrow one it is: woe betide him who departs from it.

That tolerance is independent of party affiliation: the consensus evolves within the communicators' establishment which, in its turn, functions as one of the corporate bodies deciding the conduct of the State. During the latter part of the 1960s, the consensus was social change, technological pro-gress, radical attitudes and equality. The communicators all agreed that society was changing, and that it ought to do so rapidly. To be acceptable, it was absolutely necessary to adopt the label 'radical'. And equality, in the sense of an egalitarian society, and of levelling out all conceivable differences, was the war-cry, of both the party and the communicators. All laudable aims, but to avoid excesses some opposition might be thought desirable. It did not exist, for the reasons adduced above. Dissenting communicators could literally be counted on the fingers of one hand, virtually outcasts from society. Both left and right were represented. Mr Jan Myrdal, a Maoist and son of Professor Gunnar Myrdal, was one of them; another a Catholic and a conservative, Dr Leif Carlsson. Dr Carlsson writes in the Swedish conservative press. This is how he describes his position: 'I am a Conservative. Therefore I am an outsider. That is because there is no opposition in Sweden. Everybody from left to right pays lip service to the fundamental tenets of Social Democracy, because that is the government, and that, therefore, is the consensus of the time.

'So, even though I work on a nominally Conservative newspaper, I can't write what I think. Everybody believes in equality now – of course, but Heaven help me if I try to take the opposite view. There's no chance that direct attack would get into print, so I have to camouflage my thoughts.

'The only way I can publish unpopular thoughts is to bury them. But if, in some book review, I mention in disguise that perhaps there is something to be said for class as a prescriptive right, rather than a meritocracy; or that tradition ought not to be dismissed out of hand, then the Conservative party will tell my editor to see that I keep my mouth shut.

'Take another example. The only permissible way to discuss sex roles in Sweden is to dig out a new example of discrimination and propose its abolition. You may not, say, put in a plea for preserving differences and the mystique of women.'

Conformity is accepted as a virtue. The average Swede would, indeed, be surprised to have it brought to his attention, because it seems the natural way to act. Yet, concern there is; on rare occasions it is brought to light. The following exchange took place in the correspondence columns of *Svenska Dagbladet,* the conservative national daily newspaper:

'I was on holiday,' ran a letter to the editor, apparently written by an older reader, 'and was for once able to listen to a youth programme on the radio, where a representative for the morning, afternoon and weekly press talked about their correspondence columns. The editor of a weekly magazine said that she never printed letters *against* aid to the under-developed countries . . . It seems as if discussion is banned, and permission only granted for expression of certain points of view approved by politicians. Is it true that certain questions, for example those decided by politicians above our heads, are taboo in *Svenska Dagbladet*'s correspondence column?'

'Of course, the question of technical aid may be discussed in our correspondence columns,' ran the editorial reply subjoined to the letter. 'Recognition of our responsibility for problems outside our own borders is, however, so general that it can be the explanation that letters to the editor criticizing technical aid are so rare. *But, of course, those who want to discuss the formation and direction of technical aid are welcome to write to us. Other letters will swiftly be returned to their senders.*'

The communicators' sanction upholds the consensus of the governing establishment, and the median of popular unanimity. This assumes that technological advancement is the sole path to happiness, and the Gross National Product the only measure of national success.★ It also assumes that the good of the collective at all times must take precedence over the good of the individual. It prescribes that the fundamentals of

★ This also is a potent weapon in the campaign to prove that the Swedes live in the best of all possible worlds. Constantly in the mass media, statistics are served up (expressed *per capita*) to prove that Sweden is the best or runner-up in this or that sphere of production. Those unfamiliar with local conditions might assume that it is a symptom of some collective neurosis.

Swedish society must never be questioned or discussed. This convention gives the Swedish press (and broadcasting) a curious triviality. It lacks the vigour and questioning of the best of the Anglo-Saxon press. Taboos are correspondingly far more developed in Sweden; they are comprehensive to the point of weirdness in a country where the freedom of speech obtains. They encompass everything upon which the system rests, and the consensus is the first of them: and that covers everything else. There is a taboo on discussing the encroachment of the State on personal liberty: society has the interests of the citizen at heart and, therefore, conflict and criticism are impossible. The Saltsjöbaden agreement and the foundation of labour relations are taboo. So too is the power of the trade unions. So also is questioning of any change. It has been propounded that Swedish society is now in a state of flux, and that all change is necessarily for the good. It is not permissible to cast doubt on any particular reform, because that implies the rejection of change for its own sake.* And upon neutrality lies the strictest taboo of all.

By interaction between State and communicators the press, as well as government broadcasting, may be used in order to prepare the public for government ideas. Such was the case, for example, of compulsory pre-school training. The leading opinion-makers accepted and propagated it. Opposition was not permitted to appear in print. The government's principal aim of bringing children into the collective at an early age was presented as if it had been universally accepted.

The result is described by Mrs Camilla Odhnoff, Minister

* Another aspect of the power of the consensus is that opinion-makers, of most political persuasions, are afraid of being branded as 'reactionary' when the sanction is that of 'progressive'. Nobody will risk being so condemned. For that reason, although there are numbers of 'reactionary' Swedes, there are hardly any public expressions of 'reactionary' opinions. There is nothing, theoretically, to stop the concenus being on the right some time in the future, as it has been in the past.

of Family Affairs: 'At first, there was some resistance to the idea of pre-school training, but when people had been correctly informed they dropped their antagonism. Our campaign had reduced resistance, and pre-school training is now seen to be a good thing.'

The assumption here is that, provided a full explanation is given, the correct deduction will necessarily be drawn. There is only one 'objective' truth to fit given data. This attitude serves to outlaw opposition. Rejection of the approved viewpoint becomes, not valid criticism to be judged on its merits, but error. The critic becomes a heretic, and is thereby neutralized.

A newspaper will rarely take issue on a matter of principle. Even if it is nominally an opposition mouthpiece, it will accept the policies of the government, quibbling over the best means of carrying them out. This simply reflects the behaviour of politicians. A formula commonly invoked by opposition representatives is that, 'We are all agreed that such and such is desirable, but is this quite the way to carry it out?'

As in the Diet, so in the mass media, there is a settled air of triviality. Debate is confined to the minutiae of administration and social welfare. All doubt is absent, and a splendid complacency reigns. There is none of the self-searching and questioning of fundamentals that so noticeably plagues the West.

At the ceremony in Stockholm where the Russian author, Alexander Solzhenitsyn, was awarded the Nobel Prize, a Swedish scientist, Professor Arne Tiselius, gave a speech on what he termed 'pollution of the intellect'. He complained that 'truth was no longer fashionable', and that 'words no longer mean what they used to mean. They have been manipulated in order to indoctrinate people, and give power to the already powerful mass media.' Professor Tiselius's remarks were almost completely ignored by press, radio and TV. Yet, a former Nobel prize-winner, he is a celebrity in Sweden, and the other speeches at the ceremony were reported to their full platitudinous extent. And his words clearly are apposite, not least at home. It was a small, but significant example of bias in Swedish reporting.

With the help, if not the leadership, of the mass media, the Swedish language has been debased and manipulated so that, as in Orwell's Newspeak, the ability to express unapproved thoughts has been eroded.

When sexual equality was promulgated, and it was decided that a woman's place was not at home but out at work, there was a rapid change in the language. The customary Swedish for housewife is *husmor*, which is honourable; it was replaced by the neologism *hemmafru*, literally 'the-wife-who-stays-at-home', which is derogatory. Within a few months, the mass media were able to kill the old and substitute the new term. By the end of 1969, it was almost impossible in everyday conversation to mention the state of housewife without appearing to condemn or to sneer. Swedish had been changed under the eyes and ears of the Swedes. *Husmor* had been discredited; the only way out was to use *hemmafru* ironically.

Connected with this semantic shift, there was a change in feeling. Women who, a year or so before, had been satisfied, and possibly proud, to stay at home, began to feel the pressure to go out to work. The substitution of one word for the other had been accompanied by insistent propaganda in the mass media, so that it was as if a resolute conditioning campaign had been carried out. Very few were able to recognize the indoctrination in the linguistic manipulation; in the real sense of the word, the population had been brain-washed.

Opposition has never been a respectable concept in Swedish, and the words associated with it have therefore almost exclusively had pejorative undertones. Nevertheless, they existed, and ideas in that field could be expressed. Now it is extremely difficult, because the vehicle for doing so has been severely damaged.

The language has been so manipulated that it has become virtually impossible to express opposition, particularly in the case of the State and the collective. As explained before, the word 'collective' can only have a favourable meaning. 'Individual' has a faintly derogatory ring. This applies to all words in those spheres. 'Eccentric' is only an insult. 'Dissidence' is not a nice concept. Conversely, words like 'the State', 'Society', 'the Administration', 'Bureaucracy', all have only favourable connotations. This means that it is practically impossible adequately to express opposition of the individual to the State: the State is good, and there is no simple way of putting the antithesis. A corollary is that society is better than the individual; that the individual exists to serve society: all this lies in the words themselves. Unless one of the rare Swedish dissidents is extremely sure of his audience, he will not be certain that what he is saying will have the meaning he intends. If he thinks he is praising the individual against the collective, he will probably find that his listeners get the impression that he is committing lese-majesty against the State and therefore being offensive.

Another example. In English, the word 'uniform' is almost always derogatory. In Swedish, on the contrary, it is one of the most prized descriptions. It is a branch of the idea of the consensus. This means, obviously, that a Swede has difficulty in expressing the idea that uniformity is bad; he is forced to say that it is good because there are no words to the contrary. If he feels strongly enough about it, he can say that 'uniformity' leads to 'monotony', but there he is on thin ice, because he is involved in a value judgement, and the retort will be that if you must give it a name 'harmony is the better one'.

Since politics in Sweden have for so long been a matter of economics alone, it is not surprising that political terms have become economically loaded. Such has been the fate of the word 'democracy'. That term, so richly distorted in the machinery of human misunderstanding, may signify more or less what you want it to. Etymologically it can, with a little goodwill, be made to embrace the wildest of contradictions. In its literal sense of rule by the people, it can be persuaded to signify both parliamentary government and dictatorship of the proletariat. Given the premises of Westminster, the White House and the Kremlin, the word can cover almost opposite circumstances. It depends what you understand by 'people' and 'rule'. But at least in these three cases the word 'democracy' has two constant elements; it is a political term, and it is a symbol of virtue. But in Sweden only the last remains.

We are all democrats and some, of course, are more democratic than others. In Sweden, the word 'democracy', has turned into a fundamentally economic term. It means more prosperity, more security, and more social welfare. It could conceivably denote a state of tyranny, provided certain material advantages subsist. It means economic egalitarianism alone. When the government displays authoritarian tendencies and ignores the Diet, it is not considered undemocratic, but a pause in the rise of living standards is thought to be so.

'Liberal', which used to be a term of praise, has now become a thing of disrepute. First in the party, and then among the communicators, it was used as an antithesis to 'socialist'. It has been extended to mean the absence of welfare and security on the Swedish model; it means competition, cruelty and capitalist wickedness. 'Conservative' is in an even worse condition: it has become an unword, so that conservatives are ashamed of owning up to it, even among themselves. The political vocabulary of Sweden has been so manipulated that only the terminology of the Social Democrats exists. This means that even those who do not agree with their politics are nevertheless forced to speak their language. As a result, it is not only difficult to articulate deviationist thoughts, but it not infrequently happens that a man will say the opposite of what he means. 'Liberal' means 'reactionary', and the words of dissent are being successively removed from the language.

There is no resistance to linguistic conjuring of this nature, because there is no opposition among the communicators. The percipience of a man like Professor Tiselius is rare; the temerity of expressing it in public, rarer still. Whether the abuse of language has been deliberately exploited in the interests of mass conditioning, or whether it simply emerges unconsciously as the product of a particular intellectual bent is a moot point. The effect is the same, and either way it serves the purposes of the Swedish rulers equally well. It demonstrates the advantages of having the communicators on the side of authority. Thought control becomes a distinct possibility, and opposition can be disarmed gently and naturally.

14. Culture in the Political Armoury

'The most important Manhattan Projects of the future,' says Huxley, 'will be vast, government sponsored enquiries into what the politicians will call the ''problem of happiness'' – in other words, the problem of making people love their servitude.'* The Swedes have carried out their 'Manhattan Project', and found culture to be one of the answers. Its purpose may not be defined in precisely Huxley's terms, but the spirit is the same. 'The purpose of culture,' in the words of a Swedish bureaucrat, 'is to give a meaning to life in a technological society.'

Culture, in the definition of the Oxford English Dictionary, is 'the training and refinement of mind, tastes and manners . . . the intellectual side of civilization'. In its true sense, it is a part of life, taken for granted like eating, drinking and walking. In Sweden, it is a device employed by the State, Marxist fashion, as an agent for political ends.

Sweden is a good laboratory for experiments of this nature. Possessing no modern culture of his own, the Swede has a virgin mind open to foreign imports and external imposition. Cultural impact is greater than in more highly developed countries, and its effects may be more easily guided and assessed. The historical peculiarities of Sweden have isolated her from the intellectual life of Europe. Modern culture was an alien import and an upper-class privilege. The sole indigenous culture belonged to the peasants. Apart from a small aristocratic coterie, few Swedes had acquired a

* Introduction to *Brave New World*.

European education or contact with contemporary civilization. In the nineteenth century, as communications began to improve, there came the first infusion of Western culture. But it turned out to be a flirtation only and, after a few decades, Sweden once more turned her back on the world, to relapse into her customary twilight of spiritual isolation. Strindberg was the grand product of the lucid interval.

Strindberg is one of the major European dramatists of the nineteenth century. He was a pioneer of the impressionist drama and a precursor of the theatre of the absurd. His influence on later dramatists (Eugene O'Neill for example) was profound. He was one of the first to bring the war of the sexes (in its naked, pathological form, that is) into the theatre. But, in his work, he was not really Swedish. He was a writer who happened to be born in Sweden. His inspiration was German, and he seemed almost a German playwright. It was only after he had been recognized in Germany that he was accepted by his countrymen. But it was almost as an alien. To this day, Swedes are not really at home with him. They may respect his ideas, and express pride that he was of their nationality, but they do not regard him as one of themselves. It is almost as if they had been taught to admire him, but that he was far above their heads. The trouble is that Strindberg is a representative of 'high' culture, and the Swedes are really at home only with 'low' culture.

There has ever in Sweden existed an acute consciousness of the difference between the 'high', or imported, and 'low', or indigenous, culture. Without (as in Western Europe and England) an enlightened middle class to bridge the gap, the 'high' culture could not be naturalized, nor a national tradition established. The lower classes looked with suspicion on the intellectual property of their betters and they, in turn, regarded the unpolished art forms of their subordinates with contempt. Sweden, like Imperial Russia, but unlike the countries of Western Europe, was a society of two cultures.

The political changes of the Swedish nineteenth century were in all but name a peasants' revolt. The peasants took over the country, imposing their culture and their values. They brought with them an invincible prejudice against 'high' culture as the despicable amusement of the old ruling classes, and Sweden was intellectually severed from Western Europe and the outside world.

Not until the communications revolution, in its successive waves of cinema, radio and TV, overtook Sweden was this isolation finally threatened. That development did not culminate until the 1950s, when psychological barriers were undermined and, for the first time in history, the Swedes were exposed to a massive cultural invasion that ignored all social barriers. But by then the Swedish rulers had grasped the power of culture, and had the theory and the means to exploit it for their own purposes.

The State has poured money unstintingly into culture, as it has subsidized all institutions that promote the smooth running of society. However, it is not done as the encouragement of some unself-conscious spiritual part of everyday life, but as the provision of a material possession. It is as if some government office were stockpiling a newly discovered commodity. Indeed, the terminology of Swedish cultural politics is a hybrid of Marxism and the Stock Exchange. It proposes to offer not artists and the arts, but 'cultural workers' producing a 'culture supply' for 'cultural consumers'.

Culture to the Swedish Social Democrats is yet another political instrument. 'Marxism,' in the words of Mr Olof Palme, 'makes it possible to see art not only as a product of society, but also as a weapon in the class war, as an *instrument for changing society*. . . So far I will go in confessing a Marxist attitude to life and art.'[*]

Like radio and TV, culture is considered an opinion-forming

[*] From a speech delivered to the (British) Labour party conference in 1969.

device and, like them, is the concern of the Ministry of Education.* In that ministry a reliable party ideologist serves as under-secretary for culture. During the 1960s, the incumbent was Mr Roland Pålsson, one of the authors of modern Swedish cultural policy. He defines government aims in this way:† 'Culture, besides giving a meaning to life in a modern society, must strengthen the collective. We reject individualism: the individual has no meaning except as the member of a group.

'Then, we use culture to show that the State cares for all. Some of our opponents see the State as their enemy, but the government wants to prove that the State is the friend of everybody. And I think we have succeeded. We believe that a mass quality culture can be spread to fifty per cent of the people, and we want the government to be the bearer of culture. Even if a lot of people aren't interested in culture, anyway, they see what we're doing for it. And that appeals to the population.'

The control and distribution of culture is remarkably centralized in Sweden: the State provides most of it, and is seen to do so. In music, the State is sole impresario, and private concert agencies are illegal. A single public organization has an official monopoly. All symphony orchestras are either municipal or State, and all concerts in the provinces are organized by a specialized State agency concerned with the spread of culture. By law, the budgets of all public building must include a proportion for artistic decoration. Schools, underground stations, town halls, all must have their quota of original work.

* It is interesting to observe that education, broadcasting and culture, the three faces of intellectual guidance, have been gathered under the same and avowedly ideological roof. It is as if it were desirable to maintain efficient centralized direction of the principal ways of guiding thought and feeling. Cf. the 'Ministry of Emotional Engineering' in *Brave New World*.

† From a private conversation.

In this way, artists owe most of their bread and butter, and most decorative art owes its existence, to the public authorities. The State also supports writers with grants and allowances. Such patronage is received as a kind of social welfare and, with the catalyst of relevant political indoctrination, has the effect of reinforcing a sense of obligation to society. It also magnifies a feeling of gratitude towards the party, which, in turn, strengthens ideological bonds with 'cultural workers'.

In 1970, the State took the first experimental step in using artists and writers for agitprop. A number of authors and film producers were commissioned to turn out works that would, to quote their brief, 'create a public opinion for the underdeveloped countries'. The government then required greater popular enthusiasm in order to justify plans for greater technical aid.

Perhaps the most interesting developments have occurred in the drama, which, of all the arts, has possibly the greatest potential as an instrument of indoctrination and emotional guidance. The centre of the Swedish stage is the Royal Dramatic Theatre in Stockholm, a State institution, and the Swedish National Theatre. Since being built in the 1880s it has had a fairly staid career, although distinguished by the world premieres of some Eugene O'Neill plays, and, in the 1960s, by the presence of Ingmar Bergman as artistic director. His successor, an actor called Erland Josephson, was the first ideological appointment. A Social Democrat, Mr Josephson was given the post in order to carry out party policy.

'The purpose of the theatre,' he says,★ 'is to expand emotional life. A country must have a rich emotional life. Without this, politicians *cannot* bring about changes, or appeal to the public. You see, our people are emotionally and culturally undeveloped. The arts, and particularly the theatre, are being used to accelerate and bring about a maturing of emotional life.

★ From a private conversation.

'Without a proper emotional life among the people, politicians cannot work on their audience. They can only appeal to the grosser, natural feelings like hate, envy and greed. This is too narrow a spectrum, and the theatre has to broaden it. Otherwise, politicians would find it hard to work. The theatre has to prepare the ground. There's an example in English history, if you like. Take Churchill's war speeches; a lot of their appeal depends on associations with poetry and drama, like Henry V's address at Agincourt. Without Shakespeare, Churchill couldn't have had his effect.

'But it is not enough to produce a general cultural climate. Political undercurrents have to be encouraged. Society is changing, and the theatre must follow. But it must not only follow. It must help to move society in the direction it is taking.'

The repertoire of the Royal Dramatic Theatre has been restricted to left-wing plays and, where the classics are concerned, to those dramas which can be interpreted in a socialist manner. Only those plays that promote the Social Democratic ideas of community and egalitarianism are produced. Brecht became a favourite. Younger Swedish dramatists were commissioned to write plays promoting the Social Democratic ideals of community and equality. The drama, says Josephson, must promote the intentions of the government. While it is difficult to give an accurate definition of the kind of plays that he allows, it is easy to describe those that he does not. Nothing he says, that contradicts the changes in Swedish society is permitted to appear.

'Education,' he says, 'is turning out people who have learned how to fit into society. So that means I won't allow any plays that glorify the individual. That excludes most of the romantic dramatists, like Schiller. And it definitely cuts out most of Ibsen. *Brand* and *Peer Gynt* are two Ibsen plays I definitely do not want to see performed.

'But that doesn't mean I have dismissed the classics. I think those critics who are against the classics are hysterical [referring to local writers who consider all older drama as reactionary and inimical to the proper trends of the day]. The classics have such a broad spectrum, you can make of them what you want.

'*Coriolanus,* for example, can be interpreted in a radical way. Brecht has done so. And we put it on, in the same manner, as an attack on bourgeois values.

'What I would say is that any classic that can only be given one interpretation, which doesn't fit our radical ideology, would not be performed. That's why I disapprove of *Brand* and *Peer Gynt*. And, of course, the same holds for all plays, new or old. Henri de Montherlant, for example, is a dramatist I would definitely not allow. Ideologically he is not suitable.

'And among the Scandinavian classics, I would not do Holberg. His morality is doubtful. He's aristocratic, and we've got to be democratic.'

Holberg, a seventeenth-century Dane, was the first Scandinavian playwright. A northern Molière, his repertoire mainly comprises satirical comedies, aimed at hypocrisy, affectation and social climbing. He aimed his wit frequently at the lower orders of society, and he clearly believed that a man must know his place. Josephson is right: Holberg is no democrat. On the other hand, he is very funny, and the greatest of the Scandinavian dramatists after Ibsen and Strindberg.

The implacable rivalry of the great pair of nineteenth-century Scandinavian masters is echoed by Josephson. Even if Ibsen is Norwegian and Strindberg Swedish, Strindberg is favoured not on nationalistic grounds, but because he is progressive; he professed socialism at one period of his life, and he is included in the Social Democratic canon. Ibsen, on the other hand, is considered too conservative and his plays, being inpermissible paeons to individuality, are not deemed to be 'oriented towards society'.

In short, the Swedish National Theatre steers its repertoire in an ideological manner. Although it has no legal powers to do so, it guides the direction of the Swedish stage. The trend promulgated by the top of the hierarchy is instinctively and rapidly adopted by the subordinate levels. The provincial theatre, run by the municipalities, has followed suit. Furthermore, touring companies sent out by the Royal Dramatic Theatre, and a central State ensemble, naturally subscribe to the principles enunciated by Mr Josephson. In this way, drama in Sweden has broadly conformed to the wishes of the party. The existence of a commercial theatre is clearly an obstacle to complete official domination. And, indeed, the State has plans to take over what remains of it in Sweden. By 1970, most had been destroyed by various devices.

Since the late nineteenth century there have been privately owned theatres in Gothenburg and Stockholm. By the 1960s, all had been removed from Gothenburg through financial pressures originating in punitive taxation. By 1970, four of the eight in Stockholm had been destroyed by redevelopment. The new city plan permitted no replacement; on the other hand, it prescribed substitution by municipal theatres in a new House of Culture.

If the authorities had deliberately set out to eradicate the commercial stage, they could scarcely have chosen a better way. To ban it would be politically impossible; demolition was accepted by the public as an act of God. Town planning, in the Swedish mind, is an inexorable natural force. If it happens to involve the disappearance of certain theatres, then so much the worse – or better – for the drama.

'I am,' says Mr Josephson, 'against the commercial theatre, because it has to live by its profits. The theatre must be non-profit-making. I want the commercial theatre to close, and let the State take over. The whole thing's academic anyway, because I think you'll find that all private theatres will disappear within ten years. Most of them are scheduled for demolition anyway,* and so the whole question has been settled for us by the town planners.†

'Society will take over the stage. [The Royal Dramatic Theatre] must prepare for the situation. We are planning for the day when the State will have a virtual monopoly of the theatre, and a supply of staff will have to be provided. To prepare for tomorrow's stage, forty-five new actors are being turned out each year from the schools of drama, together with the necessary producers and technicians.'

If the Swedish theatre is guided by the party, that is perfectly understandable, since, like broadcasting, it is under State direction. Yet, in the world of publishing, although mostly in private hands, there appears to be a censorship that imposes roughly the same ideas. But it is not the result of external pressure since by law the printed word is free; it is the consequence of voluntary restraint.

There is in Swedish publishing, as in newspapers, a noticeable and consistent bias. Clearly, the publisher, as a type, possesses highly personal tastes and, in most free countries, his list will display characteristic leanings. But partiality will vary with the firm and prejudice counter prejudice, so that there is breadth and balance over the book market. But, in Sweden, the selectivity of one publisher is the selectivity of all, and, at a given time, all books follow a particular trend. This is present to a degree far greater than the normal shifts of literary tastes.

The steering of book production within a small country of a minor language, such as is the case of Sweden, is especially obvious and easy. Publishers are relatively few, so that quasi-monopolistic situations may obtain. Indigenous authors cannot by themselves satisfy local demand, so that translations

* 1970. Three of the four remaining private theatres were in fact threatened.

† Another example of acknowledging the use of economic means to political ends. Cf. conversation about removal of Catholic Church (in same redevelopment area as theatres).

of foreign works must fill the gap: in current affairs, they usually predominate. Bias in their selection becomes fairly evident. That it need not *necessarily* exist may be seen, to take a few examples, from Denmark, Norway, Finland and Holland. Why should it then be so in Sweden?

Most publishers concede that there is a bias, usually explaining it as the reflection of consensus among the reading public and writers. But it is not the whole answer.

'I admit to certain inhibitions,' says a leading publisher, 'I want to keep within the trend, and I am afraid to go against it. This is partly because it is sound business sense, and partly because I feel that the outsider's opinion is not valid, but only that of the majority or the consensus.'

He cited, in illustration of this last consideration, a sociological investigation of Israeli soldiers after the Six Day War. The dialogue was uninhibited, and the soldiers were quoted as saying things like, 'We love shooting Arabs', or 'Six million Jews died during the last war; it's either them or us'. But the publisher's firm considered that the book 'would hurt the Jewish cause', since Swedes would be revolted at frank talk of this nature. Now, at the time, the general consensus was in favour of Israel, so that nothing injurious was to be published. None of the other major Swedish publishers accepted the book either, for the same reason.

Cuba is another subject in which selectivity is exercised. It happened to be a favourite of the Swedish intellectual establishment, and a considerable number of books on the subject were issued by various publishers. They were all pro-Castro, and mostly polemical. No censorious works were permitted to appear. René Dumonte's *Cuba, est-il Socialiste?*, normally considered one of the standard works in the field, was not translated into Swedish because it was considered too critical.

Publishers do not dare to oppose the trend in their lists. 'We have to keep within certain limits,' as one put it, 'because if we deviate too far from the general direction of society, we would get a bad name.' Malcolm Muggeridge, to take perhaps an extreme example, has not been translated, although it is allowed that on his merits he ought to be. All three of the major publishing firms refuse to touch him. Bonniers, the largest, excuse themselves on the grounds that 'Muggeridge has said some terrible things about Sweden'. Another publisher begs off because 'he is not only a reactionary, but a religious reactionary'.

That puts him out of court completely. It was accepted among Swedish intellectuals at that time (the end of the 1960s), that atheism was the only permissible viewpoint, and that no sentient person could seriously discuss religion. Ergo, religion was not to be discussed. For that reason, books on religion were considered unsaleable, and virtually all withheld from publication. As a result, Teilhard de Chardin was unobtainable in Swedish. Works of philosophy suffered a like fate. An oversimplified materialism was then in vogue, and nothing that smacked of metaphysics was considered admissible.

The Swedish paperback market at the end of the 1960s was dominated by the new left and radical extremists. In non-fiction, there was a uniform anti-American and anti-Western trend. It was as if some unseen hand was directing the selection of books in order to indoctrinate the public and create a biased view of the world. It must be realized that it was not the selectivity as such that was new, but its nature. Since the last war, the Swedes have become the most thoroughly Americanized of nations in Europe or Scandinavia. At first, this took the form of mimicking the standard clichés of Americana, in publishing as well as in other fields. But later, with racial troubles and Vietnam, the Swedish intellectuals turned in a body against what they termed the 'official' America, accepting instead the militant American left-wing critics only. To judge by publishers' lists, the only contemporary

American writers are Stokely Carmichael, Eldridge Cleaver and Noam Chomsky.

A disproportionate number of books are published suggesting the disintegration of the West, and the advantages of a Marxist way of life. The trend implies that the Swedes, provided they continued on a leftwards path, will evade some impending *Götterdämmerung* and (like broadcasting and the press) suggest that they therefore live in the best of all possible worlds.

A thoroughly unbalanced view of things is therefore conveyed through translations: a superficial comparison with the books available in English, French and German indicates publishing bias. As far as Swedish authors are concerned, the trend is the same, but the background is rather different.

Original Swedish works published during the latter part of the 1960s showed a virtually identical trend. Fiction and non-fiction were all radical, all advanced socialist thought of one form or another, and they all accepted the doctrine that Swedish society was moving left and that it was the task of literature to help that change. It was as if the party cultural policy had been carried out, to order. This process did not depend on editorial selection. Virtually every manuscript submitted for consideration followed the trend, at most offering minor variations on the consensus. Dissidence, opposition, the desire to stand against the tide, was almost completely lacking. It was not a new phenomenon.

At any given moment, virtually all Swedish writing follows a particular direction, often defined within extraordinarily narrow limits. A leading publisher agrees that the position is summed up in the phrase, already quoted, that 'first you agree on your goals and then you discuss the means'. He goes on to say that, 'We think controversy over principles is useless. It doesn't get you anywhere. It's not constructive. You can only be constructive if you all agree on where you're going. Otherwise, it's just sniping at one another.' Another publisher admits, 'There *is* a consensus, and the natural instinct is to follow it. But I for one am impressed by the rapidity with which it changes. That means our society is dynamic.' He then added the rider that, 'Of course, it doesn't make for great originality. The trouble is everybody's so predictable. If I go to a new play, however radical, I know exactly how it's going to end. I can anticipate every line. I could almost write it myself. For that reason, I love the London theatre. I go over whenever I can. You see, even if a play's reactionary, at least it's unexpected.'

After the Social Democrats had launched their 'equality' campaign for the 1969 elections, equality soon became the dominating theme of the arts. It was as if it were a message to be relayed by various media. 'As soon as something is declared to be not in agreement with equality,' to quote a provincial newspaper editor, 'the argument is over; the matter is settled.' 'I would not,' said the editor of *BLM*, a respectable literary magazine, 'publish anything that questioned the assumptions of equality in all its meanings.'

The concept of uniformity in the arts is normally a nightmare joke. In Sweden, it is the accepted state of affairs. Partly, it is due to the conformist tradition, and an innate acceptance of hierarchical structure. Where masters lead, the others implicitly follow. But also the schools have been turning out people with a collective mentality. The younger intellectuals are the product of a system that has conditioned them to a uniform way of thinking and a dependence on the group.

Consequently artists act, not as individuals, but as limbs of some centrally directed body. What is so politically significant is that they are part of the establishment. That means that they are on the side of the government, which distinguishes Sweden from most other countries.

In the West, the intellectual and the artist are generally against authority on principle; in the Communist world, they will frequently revolt as far as the system permits them. In both cases there is a distaste for official supervision. But in Sweden the intellectuals voluntarily support the State, and that gives the State a singular advantage, because it means that the communicators are on its side.

This does not mean that they slavishly repeat the party line. But, in a general sense, they tend the way the government wants to go. In film-making, the field in which the Swedes have been most famous and successful, scripts are sometimes aimed against the government, but always from the left. And that suits the government very well. Although there are private film producers and distributors in Sweden, the industry has, since the 1960s, been guided by a State organization, the Swedish Film Institute. It has subsidized indigenous production, and discovered most of the younger directors, like Bo Widerberg, who have begun to make their name abroad.

As in all other fields of art and culture, the purpose of the Film Institute is to change society. 'But it is useless to try and do so by manipulating the content of films,' to quote the former director of the Institute, Mr Harry Schein. 'Look at Russia: their films are so dull that nobody goes to see them. The important thing is to *change*. It is velocity, not direction, that matters. When a body is in motion, it is easy to deflect; whereas when it is stationary, it has to be given momentum. So I want films to induce change by association. By making the public used to change, and predisposed to it, we can execute our political aims more easily.'

Swedish drama, literature and films are broadly left, and convey ideas that help the party. The necessity of social change is the usual content of their message, and the virtue of equality too. Business executives are often the subject of attack, but never the trade unions. Sexuality is frequently invoked, but in a political, rather than an emotional sense, with two aims in view. The first, by casting doubt on old morality, and preaching new attitudes, contributes to a sense of change and the breaking up of established society. Its other, and perhaps more cogent function, is to give release to political frustrations by offering a vision of liberation through sex. Its appeal is to the young, and it acts as a kind of euphoric sex-freedom drug. We will return to this in the next chapter.

Although these aims (particularly that concerning sexuality) are included in the spoken and unspoken party programme, a great deal of creativity is rather far to the left, and certainly beyond the Social Democratic orbit. This is no disadvantage to the party. It wants the country to move to the left, and extreme trends in the cultural field simply move the centre of gravity a little more in the required direction. With a handful of exceptions, the whole creative and intellectual establishment is on the left. There are almost no intellectuals of the (comparative) right. For this reason, there is no debate in Sweden. Instead, there is competition in putting the same viewpoint, and castigation of those who do not achieve the accepted degree of fervour. The lack of articulate conservative voices, and the resulting uniformity of opinion, makes for a degree of monotony that occasionally distresses the communicators themselves. A publisher says, 'Sometimes I wish that I got the occasional right-wing manuscript, so that I could have some contrast. But I just don't get any.'

The mistrust of the individual takes some odd, if illuminating forms. During the lifetime of Dag Hammarskjöld, the late UN secretary general, he was assumed at home to be a normal Swede, with normal opinions, and was tolerantly regarded. But when his poems, on their posthumous appearance, showed him to have been a mystic, he was reviled by the Swedish intellectuals. He had professed religious feelings, which betrayed the then current acceptance of materialistic and atheistic values. No reputable Swedish intellectual defended him.

It has been accepted that any artist or communicator must necessarily be a socialist and, whenever a person of that description is presented in the mass media, he is fitted into the pattern. For example, when Ingmar Bergman, the film director, was interviewed in *Expressen*, a Stockholm evening newspaper, the interviewer worked in the statement, 'You are a Socialist, Ingmar Bergman', although it was out of context. Bergman agreed, in a perfunctory manner, as if it were part of a liturgy. Again, when the public relations officer of the Royal Dramatic Theatre in Stockholm (a rather handsome young woman) was being presented to the readers of a lady's magazine in a decidedly non-political manner, the writer felt constrained to say that, 'her husband is bourgeois, and she lives in a bourgeois environment . . . but her colleagues in the theatre belong to the extreme left and, if she voted, it would probably be somewhere in between'. Neither *Expressen* nor the lady's magazine is left wing, and the profession of socialism need not be taken at its face value. It is simply a code to show the world that there is no deviation. If originality occurs, it must do so under a mask of uniformity. 'Ours is a difficult society to live in,' says Kjell Grede, a rising young film director, 'that's the problem that obsesses me.' Yet he accepts the consensus. 'If you are different,' says a Catholic historian (a terrible outsider in a Swedish context), 'life can be unbearable.'

The pressure to conform, while probably of little hardship to most Swedes, may be of considerable strain to those of talent or individuality. This appears to bear some relation to the peculiar form that suicide takes in Sweden. Suicide in Sweden is high, although not quite the highest in the world ★

★ In fact, Sweden is fourth according to the World Health Organization statistics for 1969. The incidence of suicide for the leading nations was then as follows (per 100,000 inhabitants): West Berlin 40.0; Czechoslovakia, 23.9; Austria, 21.9; Sweden and Finland 21.6 each. Great Britain with 9.4 and the United States with 10.8 were well down the list.

The interest, however, lies not in *how many* do away with themselves, but *who*.

Among the Swedes, it is often gifted and individual people who seek their quietus. An extraordinary number of intellectuals, particularly writers, have taken their own lives. A selection of those who have done so include Stig Dagerman, a playwright of the 1940s; two recent women poets, Karin Boye and Eva Neander; Birger Sjöberg and Hjalmar Gullberg, well-known poets of this century; a dramatist of the 1920s called Hjalmar Bergman; and a novelist of the 1880s, Victoria Benedictsson. This is quite a respectable proportion of Swedish literary figures over the past century. It is as if something like a third of the leading poets, novelists and playwrights in England and America had committed suicide.

The lives and works of these writers suggest that they were overwhelmed by a fearful *Angst* that arose out of a sense of being different. When Peer Gynt, the ultimate eccentric, is asked what he is, he answers proudly that it is

'The world behind my brow.
That makes me what I am
and no one else.'

But Ibsen, being Norwegian, came from a recognizably Western society in which an individual could not only exist, but glory in being different from his fellows. By contrast, in a short story by Hjalmar Söderberg, a well-known *fin-de-siècle* Swedish writer, a character who finds that he cannot be the same as the people around him attempts suicide *because of the difference*. The eccentric and the outsider in a Western country can live his own life, reasonably happy in being sufficient unto himself, because the recognition of individuality within his culture allows him a significance on his own. But in Sweden a man, being a collective creature, has no existence outside the group. To discover that he is different is to find himself deprived of all sense of identity (where it can well be enhanced by the same circumstance in other societies) and to lose his justification as a living creature. Quite simply, he ceases to exist.

There is another side to the matter. To be different in Sweden is to be burdened with a sense of guilt and to be the worst of failures. And it has been established by at least one psycho-analyst★ that suicide in Sweden is almost exclusively due to failing to fulfil rigid expectations, with excessive self-hate accompanying failure. And a man does not only have to bear his own reproaches, he also has to cope with a society that, rejecting the individual and the outsider, insists on explaining him away. Often this takes the form of a coldly passionate jealousy. It is a collective emotion, as well as a personal one, and it is turned on anyone who diverges from the norm. It is most frequently expressed by constant denigration, and treatment of a person as if he does not really exist. This may not necessarily lead to suicide, but can easily cause mental illness. It is well illustrated in the comparison between Ibsen and Strindberg. Ibsen, having quarrelled with his society, became angry, but Strindberg went through fits of insanity. It was, in the view of one authority,† a mechanism of self-defence: 'the play within the play . . . he had to go mad to keep his sanity.' The fate of genius in Sweden has been particularly hard.

What is lacking in Swedish society is not the *appreciation* of the outsider (which is not noticeably prominent in most other countries) but recognition of his existence. By and large, in Western countries, he may be disliked, but at least his presence is acknowledged, and his right to a place in the sun is allowed. But in Sweden the outsider is denied the right to exist. Either he must be brought, willy-nilly, into society, or he must be explained away. Often this is done in psychiatric

★ Dr Herbert Hendin, of Columbia University, who spent four years in Scandinavia investigating suicide. He published his work in *Suicide and Scandinavia* (New York, 1964).

† Mr Alf Sjöberg, a well-known Swedish theatrical producer, with a deep knowledge of Strindberg.

terms, so that a dissident may be talked into believing that he is mentally ill.

Whatever the merits of such action, at least it is most convenient to a society that believes in absolute conformity. It is a potent weapon in the enforcement of community, and, by a form of militant consensus, it achieves the type of regimentation which, at first sight, would appear to demand the apparatus of dictatorial control.

Artists and writers are not normally the most disciplined or easily organized of people. But in Sweden they have entered with no external compulsion into the corporate life of their country, and voluntarily belong to their various trade unions. Membership is virtually complete; it is the intellectual closed shop by consent. Most of these unions are affiliated to central organizations, so that intellectuals have been brought into the Labour Market structure. The government wants it this way. Official aid to the arts is generally channelled through the intellectual unions; and the artist is expected to belong.

Despite all these forces harnessing Swedish culture to their ends, the party appears to seek more substantial methods of guidance. It disapproves of commercial publishing. As mentioned before, it is establishing a State monopoly in university and school books. In general publishing, it is the intention to establish a measure of official influence. A State publishing house for children's literature has been proposed. Furthermore, the State financially aids various cooperative publishing enterprises, which more or less advance party policies.

Culture, then, has been exploited by the Swedish government for ideological ends. It is an aid to the creation of the new man for the new society. Officially culture is good, because it makes life bearable; therefore, say the people, as long as it is provided, existence must be all right. There is, near Stockholm, a hospital so thoroughly computerized and mechanized that even some of the staff felt qualms about its dehumanization. So, too, did the designers, and they put sculptures in the entrance, explicitly to provide an air of humanity. It is a neat symbol of culture in Sweden; the anodyne of the masses.

15. The Sexual Branch of Social Engineering

Sexual morality is, very broadly, a matter of convention. Changes are the product of social forces, doubtless reacting in some obscure manner to the *zeitgeist*. In the Western democracies today, morals are generally considered a private matter, whatever the dictates of custom. As a matter of historical fact, there may be legal curbs to behaviour, but these are gradually being removed. The State is abdicating from its time honoured rôle of public censor. Politicians may deplore contemporary ways, but they lack the power to correct them. The government, in general, has ceased to guide the relations between the sexes.

It can be argued that this is a transient phenomenon, the epilogue of a liberal nineteenth century which imposed limits on the State and debarred it from caring (however worthy the intention) for every detail of the citizen's life. Total solicitude may be inescapable in the future. Certainly it is already to be found in the secular theocracies of the Communist world, where authority assumes the care of the whole man. The same situation reigns in the Welfare State perfected. Thus it is that Sweden must be classified, together with the Soviet Union, among those societies where, in distinction to the countries of the West, the State is concerned with the control of morality.

On the face of it, this may seem improbable. The Soviet Union is animated by a puritan ethic, and the authorities do their best to suppress improper conduct. Sweden, on the other hand, has pursued sexual emancipation with indefatigable tenacity. But licence is not necessarily a spontaneous thing, and it may be just as politically motivated as constraint.

In most countries, legal restraints in the sexual field have been lifted reluctantly by governments who, finding that old rescripts no longer command public respect, submit to change with more or less good grace. But the Swedish rulers have taken the initiative in removing such impediments. They have been active leaders of the moral revolution instead of a passive rearguard. They have sponsored and directed the new permissiveness. The reasons are ideological. 'The State,' in the words of Mr Ingvar Carlsson, Minister of Education, 'is concerned with morality from a desire to change society.'*

'As political and economic freedom diminishes,' says Huxley,† 'sexual freedom tends compensatingly to increase. And the dictator (unless he needs cannon fodder and families with which to colonize empty or conquered territories) will do well to encourage that freedom. In conjunction with the freedom to daydream under the influence of dope, the movies and the radio, it will help to reconcile his subjects to the servitude which is their fate.'

'Freedom' in Swedish is a word that appears to be taboo. It does not exist in the political vocabulary, and it is rarely mentioned in everyday language, in spite of the advancing regimentation of the country. There is one exception, however, and that is in sexual matters. In the same way that 'security' is the creed of politics, so is 'liberty' that of sex.

The word 'freedom' is almost entirely confined to the sexual field in Sweden. In every other department of life it has been replaced by the vocabulary of the collective and of restraint. Jargon like 'interests of the community', 'oriented towards society', 'social responsibility', 'socially well adjusted', and 'inculcation of the correct social attitudes' constantly bombards the public.

* From a private conversation.
† Preface to *Brave New World* (1948 edition).

But in sexual terminology, the words connected with liberty well up like a semantic tidal wave. It is as if there were some deep urge for freedom, repressed elsewhere, and allowed to surface only in this one circumscribed sphere of existence. Indeed, the word 'freedom' in Swedish has come to mean almost exclusively sexual freedom, product perhaps of an unadmitted realization that it is absent, or unwanted, elsewhere.

Through sex instruction at school for the young, and incessant propaganda in the mass media for the older generations, most of Sweden has been taught to believe that freedom has been achieved through sex. Because he is sexually emancipated, the Swede believes that he is a free man, and he judges liberty entirely in sexual terms. He compares his own country with others in that way. When popular journalists write from abroad, they generally pay some attention to sexual customs, not in order to titillate the readers, but to prove that there is more liberty in Sweden.

One of the curiosities of Swedish reporting from the Anglo-Saxon world is an undercurrent of denigration of its political institutions. The tendency is to demonstrate that, despite what Swedes have in the past been taught about political liberty, it is in actual fact illusory. Coupled to this is the suggestion that in sexual matters the Anglo-Saxons are repressed ('double morality' is the usual cliché) where the Swedes are emancipated, and therefore that Sweden has the only true freedom. A writer well known in Sweden, Mr Artur Lundquist, once paid a visit to Australia, a goal of Swedish emigration, and on his return published a series of articles in the Stockholm press. Deliberately or not, he set out to denigrate Australia, as if to discourage future emigrants. He could not avoid mentioning its qualities as a pioneer country, which might be supposed to appeal to the kind of person considering a move, but he attacked it through the agency of sexuality. By showing that the Australians in that field were more repressed than the Swedes, he implied that Sweden had more freedom on the whole.

The Swedish government has taken what it is pleased to call 'the sexual revolution' under its wing. Children are impressed at school that sexual emancipation is their birthright, and this is done in such a way as to suggest that the State is offering them their liberty from old-fashioned restrictions. The aims of the politicians appear to be political, saying in so many words to adolescents that the party has given them their liberty, and that in gratitude they might repay with their votes.

The sexual profligacy of the Swede – 'Swedish sin', in the cant phrase – is by now one of the better established legends of the north. In reality, there is little to choose between the behaviour of the Danes, the Finns, the Norwegians and the Swedes. They all take a mundane view of the sexual act, regarding it with a certain pagan insouciance, and more or less ignoring the Judaeo-Christian morality of the West. This may be explained by the fact that the Church in Scandinavia never penetrated deeply enough to supplant heathen custom so that, throughout the Christian centuries, the old Norse hedonism survived among the people. If anything, it is the Norwegians who have best preserved the ancient attitudes, and who consequently treat the sexual issue in the most natural manner.

But the difference between Scandinavia and continental Europe is one of degree only. The sexual morals of the countries of the industrial West show little difference and if, for example, the English have acquired a reputation for inhibition and repression, that is dissolving with ostentatious rapidity. It is doubtful whether there is any difference between the sexual activity of the younger English and the younger Swedes today, except that the former may be more romantic. The distinguishing mark of the Swede is that *his* behaviour is a matter of official direction.

Morals are best attacked in the classroom and, since 1956, sexual education has been compulsory in all Swedish schools. It starts at the age of twelve, and comprises both the physiology of reproduction and the mechanics of the sexual act. But it is not to be supposed that Swedish schools have been turned into temples of a fertility cult. It is the Pill, or rather contraception in all its forms, that is the kernel of instruction.

Contraception is taught so young that children understand the distinction between sexuality and reproduction at a very early age. When they arrive at what is dispassionately described to them as their 'sexual debut', they will have consequently gained the impression that coitus is sufficient unto itself, to be judiciously cultivated without the risk of undesired consequences. This is the desired effect. Swedish sex education is not the mere abolition of technical ignorance, but a link in the mechanism of changing society. The tenor of instruction is that morality is irrelevant, and that attitudes learned at home are to be discarded. 'We have a clear duty to support the young generation,' writes Mrs Birgitta Linnér, a prominent sex educationist, 'with the knowledge they need so desperately.' To put it another way, the State has sided with youth against its elders. It is one of the few occasions in history in which established authorities (as distinct from revolutionaries) have done so. It is an original, and as far as can be judged successful, attempt to win over the young through their gonads.

On the face of it, sexual education in Sweden stems from a pluralistic attitude to society. Teachers are required to adopt a neutral pose, and to explain different moral codes without prejudice so that children may choose. But the effect is that an amoral view prevails, and what finally emerges is a physiological conception of sex as a bodily function, to be practised in the interests of good health, like eating, drinking, keeping one's bowels open and a reasonable amount of sport. Indeed, Swedish attitudes to sex may be compared to the classical

English public school cultivation of games, but without the character-building adjunct.

'We have no ethical standards in education, and no rules for sexual behaviour,' in the words of Dr Gösta Rodhe, the head of the department of sexual education in the Directorate of Schools. It will be recalled that, as the central authority of a monolithic organization, it dictates the activities of all schools in the country. Dr Rodhe may be described as the executive officer of government sexual policy.

'We don't care at what age children start going to bed with each other,' continues Dr Rodhe, 'as long as they are prepared. We don't tell them that they've got to wait until such and such an age to start their sex life. Statistics tell us that the average age is about sixteen, so that is the age when teachers have been circularized to start instruction in birth control. But if they know that children in their school are more advanced, then they have to adjust their syllabus. The new school is not terrified of thirteen-year-olds starting sexual intercourse; what we are worried about is if they are not prepared. So some teachers will explain birth control methods to twelve- and thirteen-year-olds.

'We do not approve of the view that coitus is the highest expression of human love; or a kind of consummation. Its importance has to be reduced.'

'But does a child require no rules at all?'

'No. You can't make special rules for sexual behaviour, because sexual behaviour can't be isolated from life: the one affects the other. Rules mean repression. And the repression of sexuality leads to aggression. Conversely, by introducing sexual freedom, we remove aggressions. In America, they do the opposite. They allow aggression but prohibit sexuality.'

'But isn't there some evidence that sexual discipline encourages creative work? I mean, using Freudian terminology, you would talk about the sublimation of sexual urges.'

'Oh yes, I know that repressed sexuality can lead to creative activity. But the dividing line between this and aggression is indistinct.'

'There is a staggering amount of talk and dissection of sex in Sweden. I don't know of any other country where the sheer volume of discussion is so great. Don't you think that this destroys feeling?'

'Perhaps. But we don't want children starting their sex in a cloud of emotion. Emotion has got to be removed from sex. What we want is that children talk it over, and come together *rationally*.'

'Yes, I understand that. Leaving aside what might be called educational and philosophical talk, there remains a great deal of public debate. Again, I don't know of any other country in which there is so much. It's almost as if there's nothing else to discuss.'

'Yes, you're quite right. You see, since there's a lack of tension in Swedish politics, younger people have got to find release and excitement in sexual tension instead.'

'Would you say, then, that sexual restraint was related to political tension? After all, despotisms sometimes have puritanical ideas. Russia, for example.'

'Oh, but you've taken a very bad example there. There is a pretty widespread resort to drink and sex in Russia as a release from political tyranny.'

'Which, on your own showing, suggests a similarity between Russia and Sweden.'

'Yes, there is. But with one important difference. In Russia, political activities are prohibited by despotism, whereas in Sweden there is no excitement in politics, by common consent.'

Dr Rodhe's views are those of the ruling establishment. They are also those of the dominant faction of a public controversy. Sexuality has, in Sweden, become an issue of politics. On the permissive side are ranged the forces of progress. That comprises the left wing; Social Democrats and beyond, liberals and the radically minded of other parties. Opposing them are the forces of reaction, which means principally the Church and the die-hard conservatives. A polarization of this type is naturally profitable to the politicians on the side of permissiveness. It is only to be expected that, in an environment where sexual licence has become the norm, there is political gain in upholding that licence. Conversely, there is only obloquy to be obtained from denying it.

By a not uncommon process, licence has become precept and Swedish sexual policies have not so much brought emancipation as replaced one convention by another. If the old morality entailed repression, the new permissiveness has led to compulsive sexuality. There is, among Swedish school-children a pressure to have sexual intercourse, whether they want it or not. Even if a boy and a girl might prefer a platonic relationship, they will nevertheless usually force themselves into a sexual one. It is the custom of their society, and the hidden fear is that, without immediate coitus, normality cannot exist. Similarly, in *Brave New World,* a small schoolboy is considered for observation because he runs away from a girl who wants to start one of the customary sexual games.

The educational theories of Huxley's fantasy laid down that every child had to have constant sexual intercourse in order to be well adjusted. Feelings were outlawed: only the physical act counted. One of the instructional manuals issued to Swedish schoolchildren at the end of the 1960s, *Togetherness*, had this to say about sexuality: 'Every human being has a sexual urge, or let us call it appetite, that has to be satisfied . . . the need to eat is common to all human beings. It is the same with sexual needs.

'All people, however, do not manage to live together with a partner in a regular sexual relationship. Inability to find a partner, divorce, age, etc., can put obstacles in the way. Nevertheless, the sexual urge can be strong, and it may have to be relieved somehow, for example by masturbation with or without the reading of pornography.' This is a sexual primer for young teenagers approaching their first intercourse.

If Swedish schools do not exactly 'have steel and rubber benches conveniently scattered through the gardens',* at least the educational authorities imply that adolescent copulation is officially approved as a sport for the well-adjusted. But this attitude is not confined to education and growing up. The benefits of sexual emancipation have been extended to the whole population. This may sound trite and commonplace, the obvious comment being that they could have taken the necessary steps themselves. But in sex, as in all things, the State wants to be in control. It wishes to appear as the bringer of good, and the leader for others to follow.

Where abstinence is preached, there is rebellion in the bed. But in Sweden, since sex is officially sanctioned, to indulge is to cooperate with authority. It would be too much to suppose that the State has altered habits by a ukase or two, for clearly the efflorescence of sexuality is a diversified and widespread phenomenon. But the Swedish rulers have been very careful not to oppose the trend, from a deep and well-grounded fear of appearing to be a killjoy antagonist of youth. In this, they have distinguished themselves from most other governments, East or West, which have attempted to impose restraint, or grudgingly accepted changes, with a predictable hostility of the young as the consequence.

'I think that young people in the United States feel very much the same as young Swedes,' says Mr Ingvar Carlsson, the Minister of Education. 'But the United States authorities are slow in following up developments. In Sweden we are quicker.'

If the party wants to change society it has preferred not to be seen working too hard at it but, through suitable kneading of public opinion by other agents, to give the impression of answering a need rather than enforcing an idea.

* *Brave New World.*

The corporate State facilitates this, with a specialist organization to cover each necessary field. Thus, in politics, there is the ABF; in sex and morals there is the RFSU, *Riksförbundet för Sexuell Upplysning* – the National Association for Sexual Education.

The RFSU is a corporate organization closely related to the Labour movement. It has three functions: the dissemination of erotic technique, the encouragement of birth control and the change of morality. Since the 1940s, the party has accepted the desirability of birth control, but has been politically unable to encourage it too openly because of certain popular resistance, notably among the puritanical working classes and country dwellers who provided the backbone of their votes. The RFSU carried out the necessary propaganda, and was given State grants to do so.

Almost single-handed, the RFSU has made Sweden contraceptive-conscious, and propagated a progressive, rational attitude to sex. Through clinics and shops it has made contraceptives cheap, and brought birth control to the masses. Its most important work has been in sexual ideology.

The RFSU has advanced a mechanical view of sex as a necessary physiological function. It was what the radical party ideologists wanted to implant among the public and, without the RFSU spadework, they would have been hard put to do so.

Compulsory sex education in the schools had been a government desire from the early 1940s, but it could not be imposed until a hostile public opinion had been parried. The RFSU campaigned tenaciously and eventually, in 1956, the measure could be carried through as an answer to a need. Much of it took the form of RFSU demands. The organization is small, with about 5,000 members, but by the number of their approaches they gave the impression of a popular demand. In this way, the government was able to minimize political controversy on the subject.

The RFSU has done a great deal to eradicate the sexual obscurantism that once belonged to Sweden. A few examples of how far they have succeeded may not be out of place. New departures in contraceptive equipment are advertised on the streets, but excite less attention than a new beer. A garage will sport a well-designed poster showing two cats cuddling. 'For you who make love,' says the caption, 'a neat kit; condoms and hygienic antiseptic cleaning tissues. Remember your hygiene.' A reputable travel agency includes in a brochure for young people this advice to girls: 'Don't forget contraceptives. It's all very well to have your fun on holiday, but you'll have to pay the bill later, with a pregnancy during the dreary winter if you don't look after yourself. It's a good idea to take condoms as well. Foreign boys often don't have them, and it shows good taste to be able to offer one. Even if you're on the Pill, it's sensible to insist on your partner taking precautions to prevent diseases.* And if you use some other form of birth control, it's an extra margin of safety.'

The RFSU has promoted a view of sex as the escape valve of society. 'Our aim,' says an RFSU official, 'is to encourage liberation through sex.' In no other field would that be said. The aims, as adumbrated before, are all the other way, towards regulation and submission to the collective.

The Pill has been thoroughly impressed on the Swedish consciousness and officially endorsed. The authorities, alone in Europe, perhaps alone in the world, have brought about the true sexual revolution. This is not the propagation of birth control, but popular understanding that the sexual act is no longer identical with procreation.

The law has closely followed sexual custom. Previously

* Gonorrhoea has shown a catastrophic increase, coinciding with the advance of the Pill and the change of morals. It is hard to say which is the leading cause. The age at which it is concentrated has sunk continually, having been observed in 1970 among eleven- and twelve-year-olds. This is not specifically Swedish, but confirms experience elsewhere.

Swedish, like most Western, jurisprudence was informed by Christian ethics. Marriage was assumed to be permanent and divorce a regrettable aberration. Professor Alvar Nelson, a government legal expert, says that 'our aim is to remove all traces of Church morality from legislation'. Already (1970) adultery has been removed as what is termed an 'extraordinary cause'. In Sweden, divorce has long been virtually by consent, with a separation of one year necessary before the decree was granted. In the case of proven adultery, however, the delay was waived. This no longer holds, with the implication that faithfulness is no longer considered a part of marriage.

The new legislation, coming into force during the 1970s, is devoid of moral superstructure. Marriage will be a contract, to be made or cancelled by the signatories at will, through a simple act of registration. In the case of weddings, a civil or religious ceremony is an optional extra.

But the state of marriage is virtually superfluous, except where a woman wants her husband's name. Cohabitation is legally equivalent as far as housing and taxation are concerned. Illegitimate children have the same right of inheritance as those born in wedlock: biological parentage is the only kind now recognized in law. There remains only the question of what to do with unwanted children. Abortion is liberal in Sweden, praised as the ultimate guarantee of sexual emancipation. When the photographer Lennart Nilsson published his celebrated film and book★ on the birth of a baby, he was bitterly attacked by Swedish medical critics for 'anti-abortion propaganda', although his intention had merely been to depict what he considered a miracle of nature.

While most of Swedish society is littered with taboo, sex has been absolutely cleansed of it. In this one field, the authorities have been extremely anxious, as they officially proclaim, to remove all guilt feelings. As social and economic

★ Published in Britain as *The Everyday Miracle* and in the US as *A Child is Born*.

regimentation has progressed, so has sexual liberation, and the propaganda around it. The Swede is extraordinarily proud of this one freedom, seeing in it a proof of his own superiority in all fields.

But it is not permissiveness; it is licensed release. The State, anxious to control the citizen absolutely, has taken sexuality in hand as well. Even in the fundamental human act, the welfare mentality has intruded, and the Swedes, while encouraged to release their political frustrations through the reproductive procedure, are yet admonished to do so decently, hygienically and properly. The citizen must feel that the State cares for him, even in what should be the last resort of privacy.

16. Brave New Swedish World

Even allowing for the relief offered them in the form of sex, the Swedes are faced with residual, but by no means negligible strains. They are well-adjusted to their situation. They have accepted a degree of control as yet alien to most Western countries. They have submitted to their rulers in return for security. They have made a virtue of the conformity that is necessary for the proper running of their society. Mutiny is not consciously a part of their nature. And yet they are not entirely content. Welfare produces its own frustrations; regimentation breeds irritation and resentment which cannot, as the Swedes have discovered, be entirely suppressed, with all the self-discipline and goodwill in the world. Safety valves are a necessity.

The sexual safety valve is a release from the grosser tensions. But it, too, has its limitations. Although its net effect is probably on the credit side, it has contributed to the strains it is required to relieve. The physical emphasis put upon it has enveloped the population in a permanent cloud of *depressio post coitus*. By eradicating ritual and taboo, excitement has been dissipated, and the function of sex as a surrogate for political tension therefore handicapped.

In spite of themselves, the Swedes from time to time betray a yearning for something beyond the mechanics of sex. Maudlin cries for feeling appear in the correspondence columns of newspapers and in articles in women's magazines. Writers, moved sometimes by a powerful urge to touch on sentiment, are prevented by a yet more powerful inner censor. This situation recalls yet another scene from *Brave New*

World. The Savage has been reciting *Romeo and Juliet* to Helmholtz Watson, the Emotional Engineer, who interrupts with gales of laughter, and says: ' "I know quite well that one needs ridiculous, mad situations like that; one can't write really well, about anything else. Why was that old fellow such a marvellous propaganda technician? Because he had so many insane, excoriating things to get excited about. You've got to be hurt and upset; otherwise you can't think of the really good, penetrating, X-rayish phrases. But fathers and mothers." He shook his head. "You can't expect me to keep a straight face about fathers and mothers. And who's going to get excited about a boy having a girl or not having her? . . . No . . . it won't do. We need some other kind of madness and violence. But what? What? Where can one find it? . . . I don't know . . . I don't know." '

Licence to copulate has led to a sexual obsession pervading the whole of Swedish life. It has brought in its train a certain amount of mental illness. This is a subject on which the authorities are silent, and the organizers of sexual instruction prone to concealment. Nevertheless, it seems to have been established that much of expanding neuroses among school-children and students is to be attributed to failure in the sexual rat race. Nervous breakdowns on this account are not uncommon.

Beyond sex there are drugs. In juvenile addiction, Sweden is ahead of Western Europe, and beginning to approach the United States.* Boredom would seem to be the usual motivation; boredom generated by a conformist and sterile society and, worst of all, by sexual *ennui*. The government

* A government commission of inquiry in 1969 came to the conclusion that about four per cent of all Swedish schoolchildren had tried drugs, while one per cent were regular users. Cannabis and amphetamines predominated. In Stockholm, eighteen per cent of the pupils in the senior classes of the basic school (14–15 years) had taken drugs. About ten per cent were regular users, and four per cent were on hard drugs, chiefly heroin and LSD.

disapproves of existing stimulants, from alcohol upwards, because of the deleterious side-effects, and the resultant damage to the national economy. Research has therefore been commissioned to find some chemical which will produce the same kind of euphoric feelings as known stimulants but without the undesired consequences. When this is discovered, it will probably be sold freely, and all other drugs suppressed. Quoting Huxley again, 'We require . . . a substitute for alcohol and the other narcotics, something at once less harmful and more pleasure-giving than gin or heroin.' Soma, no less; it is just around the corner in Sweden.

Perhaps the worst of Swedish frustrations lies in the lack of political commitment and muzzled criticism at home. Neutrality has also exacted a price. It has produced a kind of moral castration, so that collectively the Swedes may feel an urge to act, but lack the power to do so. These disabilities may be self-inflicted, but are none the less galling. They are compensated by a specialized use of conscience.

Conscience in the normal sense, as the spiritual guardian of the conscience holder in his personal actions, is scarcely acknowledged among the Swedes. It has come to mean conscience to the world. It is not an individual, but a collective concept. It means condemnation of other countries and other people for undesirable actions. In the way that it has been applied, it is directed to remote corners of the world, from which no immediate danger may be anticipated. It is always on the side of the angels. A selection of post-war targets includes France for Algeria, the United States for Vietnam, Britain for Rhodesia and White America for the Negroes. The feelings are passionately expressed, and deeply felt, although the distinction between righteous and self-righteous indignation may not always be apparent.

Now this conscience is exclusively an exercise in mass emotion. It is always directed against one target at a time, chosen by the intellectual and ruling establishments, and communicated to the whole population by the corporative organizations. An unshakeable unanimity is observed. At a given time, prime minister and street sweeper will display the common touch, venting their disapproval on the same recipient.

Swedish conscience is, in fact, catharsis through ritual hate. It is akin to the 'two minute hate' of *Nineteen Eighty-Four*. Indeed, during the Vietnam war, the popular Swedish dislike of President Johnson had something of the grotesque fury against Goldstein in Orwell's novel. 'I feel so *emancipated*,' a Swedish housewife once said in a newspaper interview after a particularly violent demonstration before the American embassy in Stockholm.

Of course, kindred phenomena have occurred elsewhere, but the distinction of Sweden lies in the fact that the rulers have exploited them, and the whole population has been involved. It is the controlled use of mob hysteria.

Before the Second World War, foreign travel was a rarity among the Swedes, but it has been brought to the average man in Sweden, as in other affluent societies, by prosperity and by cheap air transport. But Swedish travel displays certain peculiarities. It is of the packaged and guided tour type to a far greater extent than in any Western country. Even more than the Germans, the Swedes insist on travelling in groups; and they are exceptional in not only using, but also regarding travel as a release from social tensions. Most people on holiday abroad are in search of change. The greater the strain at home, as a rule, the greater the reaction abroad. Excepting the Danes, who have Continental manners, Scandinavians are repressed in the field of drinking, so that they cut loose abroad. But even among them, the Swedes are distinguished for their pertinacity.

Most Swedish holiday traffic goes to Majorca, the Canary Islands and certain resorts on the Italian Adriatic coast. There, in what are usually extensions of the Swedish environment in holiday camp form, the Swedes find relief in companionable orgies of sex and alcohol. Once abroad, the Swede allows the criticism to come to the surface that his inner censor represses at home. 'There are so many rules in Sweden' and 'It's wonderful to get away from the Swedish snooping complex' are two of the common clichés uttered in such circumstances. Usually, the same people at home uncomplainingly accept everything about their society, and it would rarely occur to them to say things of that nature.

On the whole, tourists of most nationalities, whatever their condition, display a rudimentary curiosity about where they are going. For that reason, travel advertising, whatever the country, features the destination. In Sweden, however, it usually concentrates on the point of departure. Where, in other countries, the customer is assumed to be going *towards* something interesting, in Sweden his first concern is believed to be *getting away* from an unpleasant situation. Publicity, as often as not, dismisses the identity of the goal, concentrating on escaping from the Swedish situation. 'Miserable', 'grey', 'dreary' are terms constantly recurring in descriptions of the environment that putative tourists are invited to relinquish for a spell. The tenor of the appeal is that it doesn't matter where one goes, as long as one gets away from Sweden.

The government looks upon this, if not approvingly, at least with tolerance and understanding. Swedish foreign travel has been one of the heaviest burdens on a large and worrying balance-of-payments deficit that began to obtrude itself in the 1960s. But currency restrictions were never considered. By blocking a safety valve, they would have entailed political and psychological repercussions too serious to be considered. It is an everyday occurrence for distressed customers to enter, or agitated voices to telephone, travel agencies, demanding a trip anywhere, as long as it gets them away immediately, or next week-end by the latest. This is not confined to a particular social class. Foreign travel has been made so accessible that a fortnight abroad costs about a fortnight's pay for a shopgirl or a factory worker. A typist is just as likely to make her escape as a senior bureaucrat. Rules are such, in both private and public employment, that it is usually possible to take annual holidays at odd times, or to have unpaid leave of absence. Moreover, taxes are so punitive that it is customary to accept compensatory leave instead of payment for overtime.

Sex, culture, country cottages and holidays abroad may act as outlets for the worst of pressures, so that the political sublimation of personal aggressions has been largely forestalled. But there remain two irreducible aberrations: crime and alcohol.

Belief in the perfectibility of man has taken some hard knocks in Sweden. The fulfilment of total welfare has not improved the bad Swede; it has simply persuaded him to learn new ways of being naughty – precisely as in other affluent countries. Despite the Swedish practice of excusing misbehaviour as a product of environment alone, there is no social injustice to speak of. Slums do not exist, and it requires some ingenuity to escape a comfortable existence. Nevertheless violence has risen, juvenile delinquency is the highest in Western Europe, and the crimes of avarice, notably embezzlement and cheque frauds have become a scourge.*

Drinking has always been a burden to the Swedes. Through the ages, they have done so immoderately, so that the present

---

* Between 1950 and 1966, the number of crimes reported to the police rose from 161,778 to 410,904, an increase of over 250 per cent. The figures correspond to 23 and 52.6 per 1,000 inhabitants. In the same period crimes of violence rose from 12,665 to 26,862 or 1.8 to 3.4 per 1,000 inhabitants. Bank robberies, which in 1950 were virtually unknown, have become common. In Stockholm, a city of about 800,000 inhabitants, they take place at the rate of about one per week. In 1968 there were 32,085 cases of juvenile delinquency, mainly petty theft and assault. Cheque frauds have been gaining popularity among teenagers.

endemic abuse cannot exclusively be visited on political and social strains. Drunkenness is a national plague, in all classes. This again must seriously question another time-honoured theory, that alcoholic abuse is a consequence of poverty. Although the Swede is so affluent, he drinks to get drunk with the same single-minded devotion that his poor and underprivileged ancestors did in the eighteenth and nineteenth centuries. In fact, the ritual inebriation that so distinguishes Swedish society is by origin an upper-class custom. But in all ages, drinking has been, as so many Swedish writers have demonstrated, a means of evading a repressive society. It has been the only way of escaping from formal manners, self-discipline and social restraint.

Since Swedish society has maintained those characteristics, drinking may be said not to be a trouble, but the oldest safety valve of them all. Although the State, under pressure from a strong temperance lobby, gives the impression of wanting to stop drinking, yet it does not give it any priority. Official concern is concentrated on the disarming of political opposition, so that *ordinary* crime is of less importance.

'What you ought to do,' says Mustapha Mond in *Brave New World*, 'is on the whole so pleasant, so many of the natural impulses are allowed free play, that there really aren't any temptations to resist.' That, more or less, is the condition of the Swede. Not all the ingenuity of the Swedish rulers would have been of any use without the submission of the populace. And that has been willingly given. Little persuasion was necessary. The Swedes have had to adapt themselves sometimes to the point of discomfort. But, since it has been in exchange for economic and technological benefits, the price has been considered worthwhile.

The Swede has accepted a patterned and organized existence, because in return he has been given comfort and security. He wants nothing else; he sees nothing beyond his Welfare State. 'Given the choice between Welfare and

Liberty,' says the editor of a liberal newspaper, 'I would choose welfare every time.'

The price of contentment in Sweden is absolute conformity. Personal desires must be tailored to the desires of the group. Mostly this is forthcoming. Where it is not, society imposes uniformity. Methods are civilized, rational and humane, but still remorseless. Difference in the Swedish world has always been something undesirable, half sin, half disease. In the modern Welfare State, its eradication has become an obsession, because its continued existence is a flaw in the system. The skeletons in the Swedish cupboard are, indeed, concerned with outsiders: the Lapps and the gipsies. Both are under pressure, but not because of racial bigotry alone.

The Lapps are the aboriginals of Scandinavia. A nomad people of the tundra, they are of different racial extraction to the Swedes. They speak a language which is completely alien to Swedish, and which belongs to the Finno-Ugrian group, related to Finnish and certain Siberian dialects. There are 10,000 in Sweden, mostly in the wild northern part of the country. They live by the reindeer, which they follow between mountains and lowlands with the seasons. They have little in common with the Swedes, or with any Europeans for that matter. They had their own customs and their own way of life, which they wanted to keep. But as the Swedes extended their Welfare State, they insisted on including the Lapps as well. Gradually, the Lapps have been pressed into a Swedish pattern of life, sometimes settled, like the Svappavaara peasant-miners, in subtopias in the wilderness. What they wanted was their old life in mountain cottage and under canvas. What they got was the ordered existence of the Swede.

At least the Lapps, although considered by the man in the street, and treated by the authorities, as second-class citizens,*

---

* The treatment of the Swedish Lapps compares unfavourably in many ways with that of the American Indians. At least the New World

have submitted, and tried to become Swedes. 'We are not a warlike people,' in the words of one of their leaders, 'and we don't fight. Our culture is primitive, and I suppose we have to give in to the stronger one.' For this reason, the Lapps incur no great dislike: they are not outsiders. Bigotry, therefore, is reserved for the gipsies.

There are only a few thousand gipsies in Sweden, but they have been unable to assimilate. Partly, this is their own desire, partly the result of popular prejudice. The reason is immaterial: the result is that they remain outsiders. And that, to the Swede, is unforgivable. That they are dark and racially different is of subsidiary importance; that they are outside society and do not act precisely like the Swedes is the crux of the matter. The gipsies are genuinely and explicitly hated for not belonging and for not conforming. Attitudes towards them are similar to those displayed towards the Africans in South Africa, although on moral, rather than racial grounds. Among the Swedes themselves, this same kind of hate is poured on the non-conformist. But he is a rare bird, indeed. There are a few among the intellectuals, but they are isolated and of no account.

Whether the Swede is happy in his Utopia is a moot point. At least he is acquiescent, and he has his compensations. He would certainly not want to change his condition. He is burdened with certain imperfections which are, however, reasonably counterbalanced. Thus, as he himself admits, lack of contact with his fellow-men is a plague. It is a very ancient

---

settlers openly stole, cheated and conquered. But the Swedes in the sixteenth century promised the Lapps possession of their land 'for eternity', in the words of a royal charter. Nevertheless, the Swedes dispossessed the Lapps, and, when iron was discovered in northern Lappland, paid no compensation. Later on, money was made available in modest amounts, but administered by Swedish authorities at their discretion alone, as charity. The United States government is now paying mineral royalties to the surviving Indians: the Swedes have yet to make comparable amends.

complaint. It leads to the paradox that, while the Swede is immersed in the collective, and looks upon community and solidarity as the most desirable of attributes, he is locked up in himself, isolated from other human beings. While he is at ease with an organization, he is most uncomfortable when faced with an individual. As a result, the Swede dislikes serving other men, but is quite at home serving a machine. Consequently he has by nature found it easy to adjust to his technological society.

Of personal charity there is very little. Swedish doctors are notoriously callous and unfeeling, with no human sympathy; they tend to treat their patients as inanimate, pathological specimens. This is an accepted part of Swedish life, and occasionally elder members of the medical profession are moved to protest. But the Welfare State mitigates some of the unpleasantness; without its rules and regulations, the evidence suggests that the Swedes would largely decline to help each other.

To the outsider, Sweden is a spiritual desert, but that seems to have no ill effect on the Swede. His contentment depends entirely on material possessions. He lives as a consumer, and, allowing his tastes to be directed rather more easily and more specifically than other Western nations, he is invaluable raw material for the economy.

On May Day, the Swedish Socialists parade reverently with tasselled banners, like a secular Corpus Christi procession. Religious feelings, where they have not been expunged, have been transferred to politics. Mouthing the slogans, and singing the songs of a struggle long past, the Swede on that day makes obeisance to a proletarian myth, while his chief concern is to find a parking place for his motor car.

Politically, the Swedes have all the trappings of constitutional democracy, but they do not have democracy in their heart. They are perfectly content to leave the running of the country to the bureaucrats, provided the façade is correctly dressed.

And so, modern Sweden has fulfilled Huxley's specifications for the new totalitarianism. A centralized administration rules people who love their servitude, so that technology may be efficiently exploited. Mentality has been guided to follow change and avoid conflict. It has all been achieved with means known to the West. Nothing that the Swedes have done is, in itself, original; their originality lies in the application.

Personality has been suppressed, the collective worshipped at the expense of the individual. Given the European ethos, this might be expected to arouse rebellion. But not among the Swedes. They love their servitude.

The Swedish experience suggests that the choice before us is between technological perfection and personal liberty. The Swedes have chosen perfection. But it would be wrong to suppose that only they would do so. It is wrong to be deceived by their historical peculiarities. Much of what they have done is different only in degree from what has happened in the West. Others can be similarly moulded, if with somewhat more trouble. The Swedes have demonstrated how present techniques can be applied in ideal conditions. Sweden is a control experiment on an isolated and sterilized subject.

Pioneers in the new totalitarianism, the Swedes are a warning of what probably lies in store for the rest of us, unless we take care to resist control and centralization, and unless we remember that politics are not to be delegated, but are the concern of the individual. The new totalitarians, dealing in persuasion and manipulation, must be more efficient than the old, who depended upon force. And it is straining optimism to the limit to suppose that other men will necessarily choose freedom simply because, unlike the Swedes, they are still taught to admire it. 'Liberty,' says Don Juan in *Man and Superman*, 'will not be Catholic enough: Men will die for human perfection, to which they will sacrifice their liberty gladly.'

Index